The Easter Story
Jesus Helps Us Follow Him
Peter Serves

Pre-K & K, Spring
Teacher Guide

Loveland, Colorado

www.HandsOnBible.com

Group

Hands-On Bible Curriculum™, Pre-K & K, Spring
Copyright © 1995 and 1997 Group Publishing, Inc.

2001 edition

Visit our Web site: **www.grouppublishing.com**

Credits
Contributing Authors: Melissa C. Downey, Liz Shockey, and Debbie Trafton O'Neal
Editors: Susan L. Lingo and Jody Brolsma
Senior Editor: Lois Keffer
Chief Creative Officer: Joani Schultz
Copy Editors: Pamela Shoup and Debbie Gowensmith
Art Directors: Lisa Chandler and Kari K. Monson
Cover Art Directors: Debbie Collins and DeWain Stoll
Designers: Lisa Chandler and Jean Bruns
Cover Designer: DeWain Stoll
Computer Graphic Artist: Randy Kady
Cover Photographer: Bohm-Marrazzo
Illustrators: Judy Love, Joan Holub, Megan Jeffrey, Bonnie Matthews, and Jan Knudson
Audio Producer: Steve Saavedra
Production Manager: Dodie Tipton

ISBN 0-7644-0231-5
10 9 8 7 6 5 4 3 2 1   03 02 01
Printed in the United States of America.

Contents

Which Age Level of Group's® Toddlers Through 6-Year-Olds Hands-On Bible Curriculum™ Is Right for Your Class?

Maximize your teaching success by choosing the curriculum that's best suited to the needs of the children you teach. With preschoolers, a few months can make a big difference in what works in the classroom and what doesn't! This overview shows how Group's® **Hands-On Bible Curriculum™ for Toddlers Through 6-Year-Olds** carefully tracks with developmental guidelines.

Toddlers & 2s

- colorful, three-dimensional Interactive StoryBoards™ with sensory items for children to touch, taste, and smell
- supervised play centers
- emphasis on large motor skills
- simple rhymes and finger plays
- repetition and encouragement
- simple questions and responses

Preschool, 3s & 4s

- an exciting variety of Bible-story tools, including Learning Mats™, *Bible Big Books™*, Jumbo Bible Puzzles™, and Fold-Out Learning Mats™
- guided options in "Let's Get Started" and "For Extra Time"
- side-by-side play
- age-appropriate craft ideas that don't require cutting
- simple interaction using pair-shares and assembly lines

Pre-K & K, 5s & 6s

- Bible stories with more depth based on Learning Mats™, *Bible Big Books™*, Jumbo Bible Puzzles™, and Fold-Out Learning Mats™
- more individual choices and independent learning activities
- thought-provoking questions
- more challenging craft activities
- more frequent use of interactive learning

Of course, *every* age level of **Hands-On Bible Curriculum for Toddlers Through 6-Year-Olds** includes

- exciting, easy-to-prepare lessons
- a CD of lively songs that teach
- photocopiable take-home papers to help parents reinforce Bible truths at home
- a solid biblical point in language young children can understand
- memorable five-senses learning carefully tied to the Bible truth
- big, bright, exciting Bible art
- interaction with a puppet friend who learns from the children
- options that allow you to customize each lesson for your class

Choose the age level that most closely matches your students' needs, then teach with confidence, knowing that you're providing the optimum learning environment for the little ones God has entrusted to your care.

How to Use This Book

Welcome to Hands-On Bible Curriculum™

There's nothing more rewarding than helping young children know, love, and follow Jesus Christ. But getting the message across to preschoolers can be a challenge! Five- and six-year-olds aren't ready to absorb abstract theological concepts, but they can certainly understand that Jesus loves and cares for them.

Hands-On Bible Curriculum™ for Pre-K & K presents simple Bible truths in a fresh, interactive setting that capitalizes on children's need to experience life with all their senses. With *Group's Bible Big Books*™, *Group's Jumbo Bible Puzzles*™, and *Group's Learning Mats*™, you'll help children discover Bible lessons in creative, active ways that will capture their attention and will keep them coming back for more.

Each Hands-On Bible Curriculum lesson for Pre-K & K is based on an important Bible story. Each lesson Point distills the Bible story into a simple, memorable Bible truth that five- and six-year-olds can understand and experience.

Active Learning: What I Do, I Learn

Group's Hands-On Bible Curriculum uses a unique approach to Christian education called active learning. In each session, children participate in a variety of fun and memorable learning experiences that help them understand one important Point.

Research shows that kids remember about 90 percent of what they *do* but less than 10 percent of what they *hear.* The five- and six-year-olds in your class learn best by doing, smelling, tasting, feeling, hearing, and seeing. They need to be actively involved in lively experiences that bring home the lesson's Point.

With active learning, the teacher becomes a guide, pointing the way for the learner to discover Bible truths through hands-on experiences. Instead of filling little minds with facts, you'll participate alongside your students in the joy of discovery, then will carefully summarize each Bible truth.

Don't be alarmed if your classroom seems a little noisier with active learning! Educators will tell you that children process new information best by interacting with one another. Having quiet and controlled students doesn't necessarily mean that your class is a success. A better clue might be seeing happy, involved, excited children moving around the classroom and discovering Bible truths with all their senses.

To succeed with active learning, you'll need an attention-getting signal. An attention-getting signal, such as flashing the lights or raising your hand, will let children know it's time to stop what they're doing and look at you. You'll find instructions for a signal in the "Setting the Stage" section of each lesson. Each week, remind the children of your signal and practice it together. Soon, regaining their attention will become a familiar classroom ritual.

Interactive Learning: Together We Learn Better

From their earliest years, children learn from interacting with people around them. Bolstered by the encouragement of parents and friends, they try, then fail, then try again until they learn to walk, talk, run, write—the list goes on and on. Because children truly want to learn, they keep seeking help from those around them until they master a concept or skill.

Children don't learn in isolation. Interactive learning comes naturally to young children. So why not put its benefits to work in the church?

In Hands-On Bible Curriculum, children work together to discover and explore Bible truths. The interactive Bible lessons also help children learn kindness, patience, and cooperation. As they assume unique roles and participate in group-learning activities, children discover firsthand that church is a place where everyone can belong and where no one is left out.

Use the following guidelines to help make interactive learning work for your class:

● **Establish guidelines for acceptable behavior.** Invite the children to help you create classroom rules. Here are some rules that work well with five- and six-year-olds: Use quiet voices, stay at your workplace, work together, help each other, and say nice words to others. Children will enjoy reminding each other to follow rules they've helped create.

● **Use paired instruction.** Pair up children with similar abilities during activities. When you ask a question, have children ask that question of their partners.

● **Assign specific tasks to individuals working in groups.** When children work in groups of more than two, each child should be assigned a unique and important task. To help children remember their tasks, consider using colored necklaces, headbands, or badges.

● **Discuss each activity with the children.** Ask children to tell you what they did—and what they liked and didn't like about it. Invite them to share their learning discoveries with you and with other groups. Praise groups that seemed to work together well, and soon other groups will follow their example.

Learning Is an Exciting Adventure!

Let the Holy Spirit be your guide as you teach this quarter of Hands-On Bible Curriculum. With active and interactive learning, your students will enter a whole new world of Bible discovery. They'll be fascinated with *Group's Bible Big Book, rubber stamps,* and other learning materials in the Learning Lab®.

Sound exciting? Walk through a lesson and discover how Hands-On Bible Curriculum for Pre-K & K will work for you.

The Point

● **The Point contains the one important Bible truth children will learn in each lesson.** Each Point is carefully worded in simple language that five- and six-year-olds can easily understand and remember. Each activity reinforces

The Point. You can find The Point by looking for the pointing-pencil icon that accompanies The Point each time it occurs in the text.

● **Be sure to repeat The Point as it's written each time it appears.** You may feel you're being redundant, but you're actually helping children remember an important Bible truth. Studies show that people need to hear new information up to seventy-five times to learn it. Repetition is a good thing—especially for five- and six-year-olds. So remember to repeat The Point as you sum up each activity.

The Bible Basis

● **The Bible Basis gives you background information you'll need to teach the lesson.** The first paragraph provides details and background for the lesson's Bible story. Read the Bible story ahead of time to familiarize yourself with key details. The second paragraph tells how the story and Point relate to five- and six-year-olds. Use the developmental information in this paragraph to help you anticipate children's responses.

This Lesson at a Glance

● **The Lesson at a Glance chart gives you a quick overview of the lesson and lists supplies you'll need for each activity.** Most of the supplies are items you already have readily available in your home or classroom. Simplify your preparation by choosing which Let's Get Started and For Extra Time activities you'll use. Then gather only the supplies you'll need for those activities and for the main body of the lesson.

● **Take time to familiarize yourself with the Learning Lab items.** Read the *Bible Big Book,* unfold the *Learning Mat,* listen to the *CD,* and stamp with the *rubber stamps.* Pray for your five- and six-year-olds as you have fun preparing.

Welcome Time

● **Your class begins each week with a time to greet children and welcome them to class.** Five- and six-year-olds love familiar adults, so use your welcoming presence to affirm each child. You can help strengthen developing friendships by encouraging children to welcome each other as well.

● **When you meet the children in your class for the first time, call them by name.** Introduce yourself to parents, and let them know you're glad to be teaching their children. Help children make name tags using the patterns provided in Lesson 1. Consider laminating the name tags after the first week so they'll last the entire quarter. Fasten the name tags to children's clothing using tape or safety pins. Children will enjoy wearing name tags they've made themselves, and you'll find yourself referring to the name tags often when you can't quite remember all the children's names.

● **Model Christ's love to your students by bending down to their level when you listen or speak to them.** Be sure to make eye contact, hold a hand, pat a shoulder, and say each child's name sometime during the class. Take a few moments to find out how each child is feeling before leading children into your first lesson activity.

Let's Get Started

● **Let's Get Started involves children right away in meaningful activities related to the lesson.** Each lesson provides you with several optional activities for children to do as they arrive. You can choose to do one or more of them. These activities prepare children for the lesson they'll be learning and provide them with opportunities for positive social interaction.

● **Set up appropriate areas in your classroom to accommodate each activity.** Let's Get Started activities range from fine-motor manipulatives to dramatic play with dress-up clothing and props to arts and crafts. Allow plenty of space in each activity area for children to move freely.

Five- and six-year-olds use dramatic play to try on roles and process what they know and feel about relationships and the world around them. Set out small dishes and cups, a small table, and typical toy kitchen appliances. If your budget is limited, ask a parent to make play furniture out of wood, or use sturdy cardboard boxes. Dolls, blankets, and a doll bed are important elements in an early-childhood classroom.

Provide dress-up clothing that represents male and female roles as well as items that reflect the children's culture. You can also gather bathrobes and towels to use as Bible-time costumes. Avoid adult pants or other clothing that might cause children to trip and fall. If your church doesn't have a collection of dress-up clothes, consider asking parents or church members to donate old clothes, hats, and purses or briefcases. Dress-up clothes can also be purchased inexpensively at secondhand stores.

If you use tables, make sure they're child-sized. Forcing children to work at adult-sized tables can cause spills, messes, and even accidents. If your church doesn't have child-sized furniture or if you're meeting in a nontraditional space, set up art or manipulative activities on the floor. Trays, shallow boxes, or dish pans can be used to hold the items needed for the lesson. Use masking tape to mark off the area, and cover the floor with newspaper or a plastic tablecloth.

● **Make Let's Get Started work for your class!** Depending on the number of children and adult helpers you have, set up one, two, or all of the activities. Station an adult at each activity area, and run several activities simultaneously, or lead all the children in one activity at a time. If you want to move quickly into the Bible-Story Time, pick one Let's Get Started activity. If you often have latecomers, plan to use more activities.

● **Always discuss each Let's Get Started activity with the children.** Let's Get Started activities allow children to explore The Point independently in a more casual setting. Talking with children about these activities helps them make an important faith connection. For example, five- and six-year-olds may love playing at a nature table, but they won't connect it with a loving, creator God without your help. Circulate among the areas to guide activities and to direct children's conversation toward the lesson. As you have the opportunity, repeat The Point.

● **Vary the activities you use.** Remember that children learn in different ways. The more senses you can involve, the more children will learn. By including a variety of Let's Get Started activities each quarter, you'll be able to reach children of all learning styles and developmental abilities.

Pick-Up Song

● **Sing the Pick-Up Song when you're ready to move on to the Bible-Story Time.** Singing helps young children make a smooth transition to the next activity. Your Pick-Up Song is "We Will Pick Up," sung to the tune of "London Bridge." Shortly before you start singing, tell children that it's almost time to clean up. If you're uncomfortable with singing, use the *CD* or ask a volunteer to help you. At first, children will just listen to the song, but they'll quickly catch on and sing along. Soon, cleaning up the room will become a familiar ritual that children actually enjoy!

Bible-Story Time

● **Introduce and review the attention-getting signal.** Attention-getting signals help you stay in control. Use the signal described in the lessons to let children know it's time to stop what they're doing and look at you.

● **Use "Setting the Stage" to formally introduce The Point and set up the Bible-story action.** To wrap up Let's Get Started activities, have children tell you what they did, and formally connect their experiences to The Point. Then complete the "Setting the Stage" activity to lead children from The Point to the Bible story. Even though The Point is tied to the Bible story, most five- and six-year-olds won't make the connection. The summary statement at the end of the activity will help you provide children with a clear transition.

● **Use "Bible Song and Prayer Time" to teach children to love and respect God's Word.** Choose a special Bible to use for this section of the lesson each week. For example, you could use a big black Bible, a red Bible, or a Bible with gold leaf pages. These special characteristics will make Bible time memorable for the children. Even though you'll be using *Group's Bible Big Book, Learning Mat,* or *Jumbo Bible Puzzle* to tell the Bible story, be sure to tell children that the story comes from the Bible, God's Word. The Bible Song provided in the lesson and on the *CD* will prepare children to focus on the Bible story.

● **Tell the Bible story with enthusiasm.** Read the Bible story, and practice telling it before class. If you'll be using the *CD* to tell the story, listen to it ahead of time. Think about voice changes, gestures and motions, and eye contact. Refer to the Teacher Tips in the Teacher Guide to help you.

Use questions in the Teacher Guide to draw children into discussions and to help them focus on the Bible story. Invite children to help you tell the Bible story if they already know it. Listen to children's questions and responses, but don't let them steer you too far away from the story.

To refocus children when they become distracted, use a child's name and ask a direct question. You might ask, "Cody, how do you think Joseph was feeling when his brothers threw him in the pit?"

● **Move on to "Do the Bible Story" quickly.** Most five- and six-year-olds have a five- to ten-minute attention span. After they've been sitting for "Hear the Bible Story," they'll be ready to get up and move around. The "Do the Bible Story" section lets them jump up and wear out the wiggles without wiggling away from the lesson!

Practicing The Point

● **Practicing The Point lets children practice and teach what they've learned.** In this section, children interact with a puppet friend about The Point. You can use Pockets the Kangaroo, available from Group Publishing, or any puppet of your choice. You can even make your own kangaroo puppet. Pockets is energetic and friendly. She truly wants to understand The Point but often needs to have it explained a few times before she gets it right.

You'll be amazed to discover how much your children have learned as they share the lesson with Pockets. Even children who are shy around adults will open up to Pockets. After several weeks, children will begin to expect Pockets' regular visits and will be eager to set her straight.

For a change of pace, try one of the following ideas for bringing Pockets into other parts of the lesson.

● Have Pockets greet children as they arrive.
● Have children tell the Bible story to Pockets.
● Have Pockets participate in games or other activities.
● Have Pockets ask questions to draw out shy children.
● Have Pockets give the attention-getting signal.
● Have Pockets encourage disruptive children to quiet down.
● Use Pockets to snuggle or hug children.

You can purchase Pockets in your local Christian bookstore or directly from Group Publishing by calling 1-800-447-1070.

Closing

● **The Closing activity gives you an opportunity to repeat The Point once more and to wrap up the class session.** As you complete the Closing activity, encourage children to say The Point with you. Encourage them to share The Point with their families when they go home.

For Extra Time

● **If you have a long class period or simply want to add variety to your lessons, try one of the For Extra Time activities.** For Extra Time activities include learning games, crafts, and snacks related to the lesson as well as suggestions to enhance each lesson's story picture. Most of these ideas could also be used in the Let's Get Started section of the lesson. Each For Extra Time activity lists the supplies you'll need.

Today I Learned . . .

● **The photocopiable "Today I Learned . . . " handout helps parents and children interact about the lesson.** Each handout includes a verse to learn, family activity ideas, a story picture, and an "Ask Me . . . " section with questions for parents to ask their children about the lesson. Encourage parents to use the handout to help them reinforce what their children are learning at church.

Understanding Your Five- and Six-Year-Olds

Physical Development

- Are developing fine-motor skills.
- Can use scissors and can color within the lines.
- Are developing hand-eye coordination; can copy patterns, handle paste or glue, and tie shoes.

Emotional Development

- Are proud of their accomplishments.
- Have their feelings hurt easily.
- Are beginning to gain self-confidence.

Social Development

- Are learning to share and cooperate.
- Can understand and follow rules.
- Enjoy extensive dramatic play.
- Are eager to please teachers and parents.

Mental Development

- Can listen to and create stories.
- Can distinguish between real and pretend.
- Need simple directions—understand one step at a time.

Spiritual Development

- Understand that God made them.
- Trust that God loves them.
- Are beginning to develop sense of conscience.

Dear Parent,

I'm so glad to be your child's teacher this quarter. With our Hands-On Bible Curriculum™, your child will look at the Bible in a whole new way.

For the next thirteen weeks, five- and six-year-olds will trust God to help them learn more about Jesus and how we can follow him. Using active- and interactive-learning methods and exciting storytelling tools such as *Group's Bible Big Books*™ and *Group's Learning Mat*™, we'll help children discover, understand, and apply God's Word.

Our Hands-On Bible Curriculum welcomes you to play an important part in what your child learns. **Each week when you pick up your child, you'll receive a "Today I Learned . . ." handout.** "Today I Learned . . ." tells you what we did in class and provides you with questions and activities to help you reinforce your child's Bible lesson at home.

Let me encourage you to use the "Today I Learned . . ." handout regularly; it's a great tool for reinforcing Bible truths and for promoting positive, healthy communication in your family.

Sincerely,

The Easter Story

It's easy to identify with the joys and struggles of Jesus' disciples as they accompanied Jesus during his last days on earth. The disciples followed their teacher to the Upper Room, where Jesus taught them about servanthood; to Gethsemane, where Jesus taught them the power of faith and prayer; to the cross, where he willingly died for the sins of the world; to the tomb, where he triumphed over death; and to the seashore, where he demonstrated his love. And though we read of these events centuries after the fact, we can still experience firsthand the joy of forgiveness and redemption that Jesus freely offers to all.

The five- and six-year-olds in your class are aware of Easter's joy—but that joy may be focused in the wrong direction. Easter bunnies, Easter eggs, and Easter baskets are fun, but too often they mask the true meaning and fullness of the Easter celebration. Children may be surprised to find out that Good Friday wasn't so "good" at all and that in the midst of Easter joy, there's also solemn sadness. This module will help your kindergartners learn more about Easter and why it's an important celebration of Jesus' sacrifice and ultimate victory.

Five Lessons on the Easter Story

	Page	Point	Bible Basis
Lesson 1 **Servant's Heart**	19	Jesus is our Lord.	John 13:1-15
Lesson 2 **Jesus Prays**	33	Jesus is our Lord.	Mark 14:27-50
Lesson 3 **It's Hard to Follow**	45	Jesus is our Lord.	Mark 14:53-72; 15:21-41
Lesson 4 **Celebrate Jesus**	59	Jesus is our Lord.	John 20:1-9
Lesson 5 **I'm Forgiven!**	71	Jesus is our Lord.	John 21:4-17

Time Stretchers

A Super Sign!

One of the joys of Easter is to proclaim and celebrate that Jesus is risen and that he is our Lord. A fun and different way to help children tell others that Jesus is our Lord is to teach them to sign the words. Not only will you give the children a unique way to express themselves, but you'll also teach them that the good news is for *everyone* and can be expressed in many ways.

Practice signing the words in the margin during each lesson.

Jesus

What Do I Hear?

Play a variation of I Spy in which children take turns making sounds and guessing what part that sound plays in the Easter story. For example, a "cock-a-doodle-doo" sound would represent the rooster's crowing and Peter's denial of Jesus. Use the following suggestions for other sound effects:

- chewing and eating sounds (the Last Supper with Jesus and the disciples),
- "splash, splash" (the water as Jesus washes his disciples' feet),
- marching feet (soldiers coming to arrest Jesus),
- crying (people mourning Jesus' death), or
- laughing (happy disciples because Jesus is risen).

IS

Feed My Lambs

Lord (God)

Young children will enjoy singing this action song to the tune of "Ten Little Indians." Choose one group of children to quickly stand up and sit down on words beginning with the letter L and another group to stand and sit on words beginning with the letter F. This song is not on the *CD*.

Sing

If you love me, feed my lambs.
If you love me, feed my lambs.
If you love me, feed my lambs.
That's what Jesus says.

I love Jesus, yes, I do.
I'll feed his lambs and love
   them, too,
Because my Jesus asked me to.
I love him, don't you?

Remembering God's Word

Each four- or five-week module focuses on a key Bible verse. The key verse for this module is "And every tongue confess that Jesus Christ is Lord" (Philippians 2:11a).

This module's key verse will teach children that Jesus is our Lord and that we want to tell everyone about him. Have fun using these ideas any time during the lessons about Jesus' death and resurrection.

Circle Step

Tape one paper plate for each child to the floor in a circle. Draw a simple Bible on two of the plates. On each of the other plates, draw a simple outline of one of the following: an apple, a church, a flower, and the world.

Read Philippians 2:11a from an easy-to-understand translation of the Bible. Ask:

● **What does it mean to confess something?** (To tell that you did it; to say something; to tell someone.)

● **Why is it important to tell people that Jesus Christ is Lord?** (Because he's so awesome; because he loves us so much; so they can know him too.)

Say: **Let's practice telling about Jesus with a fun game!**

Play music from a CD of your choice as children walk from plate to plate. Stop the music, and have the children standing on the pictures of the Bible repeat the key verse. Then use the *cross stamp* from the Learning Lab to stamp their hands. Then have the other children tell what pictures they're standing on and how those pictures tell us that Jesus is Lord. For example, the apple shows that Jesus is Lord because God gives us food and cares for us. The world shows that he's Lord because God made the world and is in control of everything. The flower represents that Jesus is Lord because God created all of nature and makes things grow. And the church shows that Jesus is Lord because it is his house of faith based upon God's love.

Continue playing until everyone's had a chance to say the verse and receive a stamp. Vary the game by having the children hop, walk backward, or jump on both feet from one plate to the next.

Note:
If the ink pad is dry, moisten it with three to five drops of water.

Confession Session

Let your children really get on the "soapbox" to tell others the good news about Jesus! Explain that when we "confess" something, we admit it or tell the truth. Tell children they'll get a chance to tell or confess who Jesus is to the whole class. Provide a cardboard box large enough for a child to stand in. Let children take turns standing in the box and repeating Philippians 2:11a. For extra fun, use a tape recorder with a microphone to let children repeat the verse on tape. Then play back the recordings and clap and cheer after each one.

Story Enhancements

Make Bible stories come alive in your classroom by bringing in Bible costumes, by setting out sensory items that fit with the stories, or by creating exciting bulletin boards. When children learn with their five senses as well as with their hearts and minds, lessons come alive and children remember them. Each week, bring in one or more of the following items to help motivate and involve children in the Bible lessons they'll be learning. The following ideas will help get you started.

He's Alive Bulletin Board

Decorate a bulletin board that children can interact with each week during the module. Before class, put up a blue sky and green rolling hills for the background. At one edge of the bulletin board, make a cave for Jesus' tomb from a brown paper lunch sack. Place the sack on its side so the opening faces the center of the bulletin board or wall. Refer to the following section for the pieces you'll add each lesson.

Lesson 1

● Bring a variety of sandals to class for the children to model. Explain that people wore sandals in Jesus' time and that their feet became dusty and dirty and had to be washed before going into someone's house. Ask the children how sandals are different from the shoes they're wearing.

● Bring in bread and grapes for the children to enjoy. Tell them that today they'll hear a Bible story about how Jesus ate a meal which included bread and the juice from grapes.

● For the bulletin board, let children draw pictures of the twelve disciples and Jesus. Place the pictures in the center of the bulletin board.

Lesson 2

● Create a quiet garden in one corner of the room. Set up a table, and drape a large sheet or blanket over the table to make a private area. Sprinkle pretty silk flowers around and under the table on the floor. Explain to the children that this is a quiet place to talk to God. Tell them that Jesus especially liked to pray to God in a beautiful, quiet garden. Let each child spend ten or fifteen seconds inside the quiet garden. Encourage them to tell God, "I love you" or "Thank you."

● Bring green and black pitted olives for the children to taste and touch. Tell the children that olives were an important food in Jesus' time that grew in special gardens. Explain that the garden Jesus prayed in was called Gethsemane, and Gethsemane means "oil press." Have the children feel the oily olive skins, and explain that olives are pressed to make oil that's used in cooking.

● For the bulletin board, make three brown paper crosses, and have children tape them to one of the hills in your picture.

Lesson 3

● Cut eight or nine footprints from construction paper. Set the footprints on the floor in an unusual pattern. Have the children follow the footsteps; then re-arrange them into a new pattern for children to follow. Talk about how difficult it sometimes is to follow someone exactly, and tell children that we want to follow Jesus the best we can.

● Bring in a small bottle for the children to touch and hold. Explain that long ago, people sometimes kept their tears in bottles. Ask children to think of how many tears it would take to fill a bottle. Tell children they'll hear a Bible story about a time when many people cried because their best friend died.

● For the bulletin board, have a child place the picture of Jesus in the lunch sack and fold it closed.

Lesson 4

● Bring in a wilted or dead flower. Pass the flower and ask children if the flower can come alive again. Explain that we can't make a dead flower live. Tell children they'll hear a wonderful Bible story of how Jesus died but rose from the dead and is alive today.

● Bring in a butterfly or a picture of a butterfly. Give children time to talk about any butterfly adventures they wish to share. Explain that a caterpillar is given new life as a butterfly and that Jesus rose from the dead and went back to heaven.

● Bring in candy gummy caterpillars (worms) for the children to eat. Talk about the fact that a caterpillar stays in a cocoon before it turns into a butterfly. Explain that a cocoon is like the tomb that Jesus was placed in. When a butterfly emerges from the cocoon, it reminds us of Jesus' coming to life again!

● For the bulletin board, remove the picture of Jesus from the lunch sack before class, and hide it in the room. Reseal the sack. Let children open the sack and peek inside. Ask them where they think Jesus could be. Explain that Jesus' followers didn't know where he was, either. Have children hunt for the picture of Jesus. When it's found, tape it to the bulletin board.

Lesson 5

● Bring in fishing props such as a fish net, fishing poles with no hooks, hip boots, or a tackle box. Let the children hold the items and talk about fishing trips they have taken. Encourage children to tell what kinds of fish they caught. Explain that fishing was important in Jesus' time and that they'll hear a story about a sad fisherman who was forgiven by Jesus.

● Bring in fish-shaped crackers or candies. Explain that many people in Jesus' time ate fish for breakfast, lunch, and dinner. Tell children they'll hear a story about some fishermen who shared breakfast with a very special guest!

Servant's Heart

The Bible Basis

John 13:1-15. Jesus washes the feet of his disciples to teach them how to be servants.

In biblical times it was common for disciples to serve their teachers, just as Joshua served Moses and Elisha served Elijah. What a powerful turn of events when Jesus assumed the lowliest role of a servant by washing his disciples' feet! After removing his outer clothing, God's Son knelt before each disciple and washed and dried his dusty feet. In that dramatic role, Jesus taught an incredible lesson about the importance of being a servant.

Most five- and six-year-olds are eager helpers. When given the opportunity, they're more than willing to help adults and other children in a variety of ways, such as clearing the dinner table, picking up classroom projects, folding laundry, or washing the dog. It's important for kindergartners to realize that even though Jesus was God's Son, he willingly accepted the role of a servant. Use this lesson to help children learn the joy in serving others.

Another verse used in this lesson is Matthew 25:40.

Getting The Point

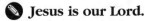 **Jesus is our Lord.**

It's important to say The Point just as it's written in each activity. Repeating The Point again and again will help the children remember it and apply it to their lives.

Children will
- discover that Jesus is our Lord,
- understand that Jesus showed his love and care for others by serving them,
- teach Pockets that serving others can be fun, and
- experience ways they can serve others.

 The Point

This Lesson at a Glance

Before the lesson, collect the necessary items for the activities you plan to use. Refer to the Classroom Supplies and Learning Lab Supplies columns to determine what you'll need. Remember to make photocopies of the "Today I Learned..." handout (p. 32) to send home with your children.

Section	Minutes	What Children Will Do	Classroom Supplies	Learning Lab Supplies
Welcome Time	up to 5	**Welcome!**—Receive name tags and be greeted by the teacher.	"Cross Name Tags" handouts (p. 30), markers, pins or tape	
Let's Get Started Direct children to one or more of the Let's Get Started activities until everyone arrives.	up to 10	**Option 1: Lemonade Stand**—Make and serve cool lemonade to each other.	Plastic pitcher, presweetened lemonade mix, water, spoon, small paper cups, measuring cup	
	up to 10	**Option 2: The Wonder Wash**—Help each other wash their hands with soap and water.	Wash tub, water, bar of soap, towels, plastic tablecloth	
	up to 10	**Option 3: Smile 'n' Serve Cafe**—Prepare a pretend meal to serve each other.	Paper plates and cups, magazines, box, plastic tableware, place mats, napkins, scissors, tape	
Pick-Up Song	up to 5	**We Will Pick Up**—Sing a song as they pick up toys and gather for Bible-Story Time.	CD player	CD: "We Will Pick Up" (track 2)
Bible-Story Time	up to 5	**Setting the Stage**—Use charades to act out different ways to serve others.	"Serving Charades" handout (p. 31), scissors, box	
	up to 5	**Bible Song and Prayer Time**—Sing a song, bring out the Bible, and pray together.	Bible, construction paper, scissors, basket or box, CD player	CD: "God's Book" (track 3), cross stamp and ink pad
	up to 10	**Hear the Bible Story**—Learn from John 13:1-15 about a special way Jesus served his disciples.	Bible and water, wash tub, plastic tablecloth, and towels from Option 2	Bible Big Book: Peter Tells the Easter Story
	up to 10	**Do the Bible Story**—Play an exciting game of serving others.	Bible	Cross stamp and ink pad
Practicing The Point	up to 5	**Chalk Talk**—Teach Pockets that serving others makes everyone feel good.	Pockets the Kangaroo, chalk dust, towel	
Closing	up to 5	**Finger-Fold Prayer**—Identify ways to serve, then say a prayer.		
For Extra Time		For extra-time ideas and supplies, see page 29.		

Jesus is our Lord.

Welcome Time

Welcome! (up to 5 minutes)

- Bend down and make eye contact with children as they arrive.
- Greet each child individually with an enthusiastic smile.
- Thank each child for coming to class today.
- Say: **Today we're going to learn that  Jesus is our Lord.**
- Give each child a photocopy of a cross name tag from page 30. Help children write their names on their name tags and pin or tape them to their clothing. You may want to cover the name tags with clear adhesive paper so they'll last the entire quarter.
- Direct children to the Let's Get Started activities you've set up.

● The Point

Let's Get Started

Set up one or more of the following activities for children to do as they arrive. After you greet each child, invite him or her to choose an activity.

Circulate among the children to offer help as needed and to direct children's conversation toward today's lesson. Ask questions such as "How does it feel when someone does something for you?" and "Who's a person you've helped or served?"

☐ Option 1: Lemonade Stand (up to 10 minutes)

Before class, use the directions on a package of presweetened lemonade to measure the correct amount of cold water into a plastic pitcher. Do not stir in the lemonade mix.

On a small table in one corner of the room, set out a spoon, small paper cups, the lemonade mix, and the pitcher of water. Let children take turns pouring lemonade mix into the pitcher until the package is empty and then take turns stirring the lemonade. Remind the children that ● Jesus is our Lord and that he wants us to serve other people at all times.

Let children take turns serving one another. Have children fill small paper cups halfway. Request that all "customers" enjoy their lemonade at the lemonade stand—not anywhere else in the room. Supply a wastebasket so children may serve by keeping the lemonade stand clean.

● The Point

✔ For extra excitement, use a sheet of poster board to create a sign for the lemonade stand such as "Friendly Service Lemonade." Tape the sign to a large box, and set the box beside the stand.

☐ Option 2: The Wonder Wash (up to 10 minutes)

Spread a plastic tablecloth on the floor in one corner of the room. Fill a wash tub halfway with warm water, and set the tub in the center of the tablecloth. Place a bar of soap in the water. Set a few terry cloth towels or paper towels beside the wash tub. Allow children to work with partners and take turns washing and drying each other's hands. As the children "clean up," mention that they'll hear a Bible story about a special way that Jesus served his friends. Remind children that Jesus is our Lord and that Jesus is also our friend.

● **The Point**

OPTION 3: Smile 'n' Serve Cafe (up to 10 minutes)

Place the following items in a box beside a table: place mats, paper plates and cups, plastic tableware, napkins, and magazines. Let children take turns being a Waiter, a Chef, or a Customer. The Waiter may seat the Customers and set the table with place mats, tableware, cups, and napkins. Let Customers order a meal. Have the Chef cut out pictures of food from the magazines and tape the pictures on paper plates for the Waiter to serve. Encourage children to exchange roles often. Sit down as a Customer, and make comments such as "My! What friendly service at this cafe" or "You have such a nice smile; you must enjoy serving people." Tell the children that they'll hear a Bible story about one way Jesus served his friends. Remind them that ●Jesus is our Lord and wants us to be good servants.

● **The Point**

After everyone has arrived and you're ready to move on to the Bible-Story Time, encourage the children to finish what they're doing and get ready to clean up.

Pick-Up Song

We Will Pick Up (up to 5 minutes)

Lead children in singing "We Will Pick Up" (track 2) with the *CD* to the tune of "London Bridge." Encourage children to sing along as they help clean up the room.

You'll be using this song each week to alert children to start picking up. At first they may need a little encouragement. But after a few weeks, picking up and singing along will become a familiar routine.

If you want to include the names of all the children in your class, sing the song without the *CD*, and repeat the naming section. If you choose to use the *CD*, vary the names you use each week.

Sing

We will pick up all our toys,
All our toys, all our toys.
We will pick up all our toys
And put them all away.

I see (name) picking up,
Picking up, picking up.
I see (name) picking up
And putting toys away.

(Repeat)

Bible-Story Time

Setting the Stage (up to 5 minutes)

Tell the children you'll clap your hands to get their attention. Explain that when you clap, the children are to stop what they're doing, raise their hands, and focus on you. Practice this signal a few times. Encourage children to respond quickly so you'll have time for all the fun activities you've planned.

Before class, photocopy the "Serving Charades" handout on page 31. Cut the cards apart, and place them in the basket or box from the "Bible Song and Prayer Time" activity.

Pretend you're an usher, and help each child find a special place to sit on the floor. Act as though you're seating them for a formal movie or play. When all the children are seated, ask:

● **What did I just do for each of you?** (Helped us sit down; found us a place to sit.)

Say: **I helped you find a special place to sit for our Bible story. I wanted to do something nice for you and to help you.** Ask:

● **When's a time someone served you?** (At a restaurant; when I was sick; at a party; at school.)

● **Do you like having someone serve you? Why or why not?** (I like it because then I don't have to do it; I don't like it because I want to serve others instead.)

Hold up the basket or box containing the charades cards. Say: **There are many ways to serve others. Let's play a game called Serving Charades. Draw a card, and act out what the picture shows. The rest of us will guess how you're serving.** Let each child have a turn acting out a charades card. If you have more children in your class than cards, repeat some of the cards or let children create their own serving charades to act out. When everyone's had a turn, ask:

● **Why do you think it's good to serve others?** (Because we can help them; maybe someday we'll need help; because Jesus wants us to serve others; it shows we like the people we serve.)

Say: **Serving others is a good way to show our love. Today we're going to hear a Bible story about a special time when Jesus served his disciples. And we'll also learn that ● Jesus is our Lord.**

● The Point

Bible Song and Prayer Time (up to 5 minutes)

Before class, make surprise cards for this activity by cutting construction paper into two-by-six-inch slips. Prepare a surprise card for each child plus a few extras for visitors. Fold the cards in half, then stamp the *cross stamp* inside one of the surprise cards. Mark John 13:1-15 in the Bible you'll be using.

Have children sit in a circle. Say: **Each week when we come to our circle for our Bible story, I'll choose someone to be the Bible person. The Bible person will bring me the Bible marked with our Bible story for that week. Before I choose today's Bible person, let's learn our Bible song. As we sing, I'll pass out surprise cards. Don't look inside your surprise card until the song is over.**

Lead children in singing "God's Book" (track 3) with the *CD* to the tune of "Old MacDonald Had a Farm." As you sing, pass out the folded surprise cards.

If you want to include the names of all the children in your class, sing the song without the *CD*, and repeat the naming section. If you choose to use the *CD*, vary the names you use each week.

Sing

Now it's time to read God's Book	**Now it's time to read God's Book**
And hear a Bible story.	**And hear a Bible story.**
It's fun to be here with my	**It's fun to be here with my**
friends	**friends**
And hear a Bible story.	**And hear a Bible story.**
(Name)'s here.	**(Name)'s here.**
(Name)'s here.	**(Name)'s here.**
Here is (name).	**Here is (name).**
Here is (name).	**Here is (name).**
Now it's time to read God's Book	**Now it's time to read God's Book**
And hear a Bible story.	**And hear a Bible story.**

After the song, say: **You may look inside your surprise cards. The person who has the cross stamped inside his or her card will be our Bible person for today.**

Identify the Bible person, then have the rest of the children clap for him or her. Ask the Bible person to bring you the Bible. Help the Bible person open the Bible to the marked place and show children where your story comes from. Then have the Bible person sit down.

Say: (Name) **was our special Bible person today. Each week, we'll have only one special Bible person, but each one of you is a special part of our class! Today we're all learning that ⬤Jesus is our Lord.**

⬤ **The Point**

Let's say a special prayer now and ask God to help us remember that Jesus wants us to serve others. I'll pass around this basket. When the basket comes to you, put your surprise card in it and say, "God, please help me serve other people."

Pass around the basket or box. After you've collected everyone's surprise card, set the basket aside, and pick up the Bible. Lead children in this prayer: **God, thank you for the Bible and for all the stories in it. Teach us today that ⬤Jesus is our Lord. In Jesus' name we pray, amen.**

⬤ **The Point**

✔ Choose a Bible to use for this section of the lesson each week. A children's Bible or an easy-to-understand translation, such as the New International Version, works best. Some of the children in your class may be reading. If children can understand the words in the Bible, they'll have more interest in reading it—and they'll learn more from it.

Hear the Bible Story (up to 10 minutes)

Bring out the *Bible Big Book: Peter Tells the Easter Story*. Spread the plastic tablecloth from Option 2 in the center of the floor, and set the wash tub on the tablecloth. Be sure the tub is filled halfway with warm water. Place the towels beside you. Ask:

● **What do you think this water is for?** (Washing hands; cleaning up.)

Say: **In our Bible story today, you'll find out what the water is for. So listen carefully. In Jesus' time, people didn't wear socks and shoes like they do today. They wore sandals or went barefoot. Their feet got very dusty and dirty!** Ask:

● **How would you feel visiting someone if your feet were all dirty?** (I'd feel embarrassed; I wouldn't care.)

Say: **You'd want visitors to your house to feel comfortable and clean. So in Bible times, servants washed the feet of guests who came to visit. Today we'll hear how Jesus was a loving servant to his good friend Peter and to the other disciples. Before we open our** *Bible Big Book,* **stand up with me.** Pause. **Let's see what Jesus and his disciples had been doing. All day they'd been walking in the dusty streets around Jerusalem.** Walk around as you talk, and encourage children to follow your actions. **It was time for supper, and they were tired and hungry.** Rub your stomach. **Jesus had sent Peter and John to prepare a meal earlier in the day, and it was ready. Jesus spoke to Peter, "It's time for the Passover meal. Go into Jerusalem and find a man with a water jug.** Pretend to hold a heavy jug. **Follow him to the house he goes into.** Walk in place. **Say to the man there, 'The Teacher wants to know where the room is where we can eat the feast.' "**

Jesus and the twelve disciples came to the house and walked up the steps. Pretend to climb stairs. **They went into a room called the Upper Room. Jesus was sad because he knew this would be his last supper on earth. Jesus knew that soon he would die to take away our sins. Jesus also knew that one of his disciples didn't love him. But Jesus sat down to eat with all the disciples gathered around.** Sit on the floor.

Hold up the Bible and say: **Our story is found in the book of John in the Bible.** Hold up the *Bible Big Book* and say: **Our** *Bible Big Book* **shows us pictures of our Bible story. Now let's hear the rest of the story. It's written as Peter might have told it. You can help tell today's Bible story. Whenever you hear the word "feet," take off one of your shoes and set it beside you.**

Open the *Bible Big Book* to page 1. From the back cover, read:

Hi. I'm Peter—one of Jesus' disciples and best friends. I want to tell you a story about the last days Jesus was with us on earth. Let me begin with what happened one surprising night at suppertime.

Jesus and the rest of us disciples were in an upstairs room in Jerusalem. We sat on the floor and shared the Passover meal that John and I had prepared earlier in the day. (We didn't know it would be Jesus' last supper before he died—but Jesus knew.)

During supper, Jesus did a surprising thing. He stood and wrapped a towel around his waist. Then he poured water in a bowl and began washing our <u>feet</u>! (Pause while children remove one of their shoes.) **"No, Lord," I cried. "You'll never wash mine!" That was a servant's job, and Jesus is our Lord! I was embarrassed. How could I let Jesus serve me?**

Jesus said, "If I'm your Lord and I wash your <u>feet</u>, (pause while children remove their other shoes) **you should also wash each other's."**

Even though Jesus was our Lord, he loved us and wanted to serve us. And Jesus wanted us to serve other people, too.

It was an amazing meal. But what would happen next?

Close the *Bible Big Book* and ask:

● **How did Jesus serve his disciples?** (He washed their feet.)

● **Was it right for Jesus to wash the disciples' feet instead of them washing Jesus' feet? Explain.** (Yes, Jesus wanted to teach them; no, Jesus was more important.)

Say: **Peter thought Jesus was too important to wash the disciples' feet.** Ask:

● **Can anyone be too important to serve or help others?** (No, everyone can serve and help others.)

 The Point

Say: **Peter knew that** 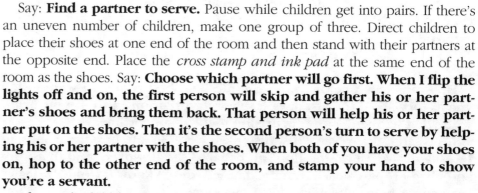 **Jesus is our Lord. But Jesus wanted to show Peter and the disciples that he loved them enough to serve them by washing their feet. Jesus wants us to serve others, too. When we serve and help people, it's a way to spread Jesus' love.**

Say: **I see lots of toes that need shoes! Let's serve each other in a fun game.**

Have the children gather their shoes to use in the next activity.

✔ If some children are reluctant to take off their shoes, reassure them that it's fine to watch and share the fun that way.

✔ A good way to help children understand about being a servant is to offer to wash children's feet or hands. Don't pressure reluctant children to participate. Instead, ask if there's anything else you could do for them, such as help them tie their shoes or carry their craft projects to their cars for them.

Do the Bible Story (up to 10 minutes)

Say: **Find a partner to serve.** Pause while children get into pairs. If there's an uneven number of children, make one group of three. Direct children to place their shoes at one end of the room and then stand with their partners at the opposite end. Place the *cross stamp and ink pad* at the same end of the room as the shoes. Say: **Choose which partner will go first. When I flip the lights off and on, the first person will skip and gather his or her partner's shoes and bring them back. That person will help his or her partner put on the shoes. Then it's the second person's turn to serve by helping his or her partner with the shoes. When both of you have your shoes on, hop to the other end of the room, and stamp your hand to show you're a servant.**

 The Point

After each child has been stamped, gather children in a circle on the floor. Say: **Peter learned that even though** 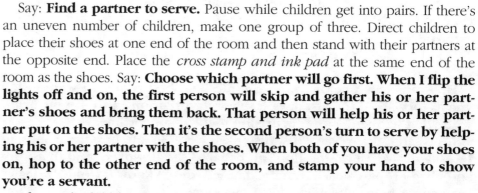 **Jesus is our Lord, he was still willing to serve others. And Jesus wants us to serve others as he served. Listen to what the Bible says about serving others. When we serve others, we're serving Jesus.** Read aloud Matthew 25:40. Say: **It's important to know**

 The Point

that 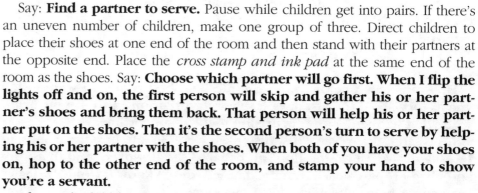 **Jesus is our Lord. It's also important to know that we can serve others and show them Jesus' love. Let's see if Pockets knows how important it is to serve others.**

Practicing The Point

Chalk Talk (up to 5 minutes)

Before class, make a few chalk-dust smudges on Pockets' face. Place the damp towel from the "Hear the Bible Story" activity beside you. Let the children call for Pockets the Kangaroo. Then go through the following puppet script. After you finish the script, put Pockets away and out of sight.

Chalk Talk
PUPPET SCRIPT

Teacher: *(Looking at watch)* I wonder where Pockets is. She's usually here by this time. Can you help me call her? *(Encourage the children to call Pockets' name with you.)* Pockets! Pockets, where are you?

Pockets: *(Out of breath.)* Here I am. Sorry I'm late.

Teacher: You must've been having a good time. What were you up to, Pockets?

Pockets: I was drawing with chalk on the sidewalk. It's really fun, you know.

Teacher: I'm sure it was fun, Pockets. But I see that your face is dirty. We can help you wash your face.

Pockets: I don't need anyone's help. I'm a big kangaroo now, and I can wash my own face.

Teacher: Yes, you're a big kangaroo, but it's nice to be helped, and we'd like to serve you. We've been learning about serving others. Children, can you tell Pockets what Jesus did for his disciples? *(Allow time for children to tell about the Bible story. Lead children in saying, ✏ "Jesus is our Lord.")*

Pockets: Washing the disciples' feet? Icky! But you said, ✏ "Jesus is our Lord." Why would Jesus wash someone's feet?

Teacher: Children, why did Jesus wash his disciples' feet? *(Encourage children to respond with answers such as "Jesus served his disciples" and "Jesus wanted to teach us to serve other people.")*

Pockets: Wow! If Jesus can serve others, I can too. And I can let you serve me! Would you help me wash my face? *(Call on one or two children to use the damp towel to wipe Pockets' face.)* I feel better. Serving makes <u>you</u> feel good, and being helped makes <u>me</u> feel good. Thanks for reminding me that even though ✏ Jesus is our Lord, he was willing to serve others and wants us to serve others, too. Goodbye!

● **The Point**

● **The Point**

● **The Point**

TODAY I LEARNED...

We believe that Christian education extends beyond the classroom into the home. Photocopy the "Today I Learned..." handout (p. 32) for this week, and send it home with your children. Encourage parents to use the handout to plan meaningful family activities to reinforce this week's topic. Follow up the "Today I Learned..." activities next week by asking children what their families did.

Closing

Finger-Fold Prayer (up to 5 minutes)

● **The Point**

Say: ●**Jesus is our Lord, and Jesus wants us to serve others just as he served his disciples when he washed their feet. We can serve others in many ways.** Have children find a friend.

Say: **Hold your hands in front of you so your palms face your partner's palms. When I tell a way to serve others, put the thumbs of both your hands against both your partner's thumbs. When I tell another way to serve, put both your first fingers against both your partner's first fingers. We'll continue until all your fingers and palms are touching your partner's.** Repeat the following rhyme to name ways to serve.

> **When we help,**
> **when we share,**
> **when we love,**
> **when we care, and**
> **when we're in prayer.**

● **The Point**

Say: **Now that our hands are together, let's pray.** Pray: **Dear God, thank you that ●Jesus is our Lord. And please help us serve others in all we do and say. In Jesus' name, amen. When I flip the lights, one of you will tell your partner one way you can serve someone this week. Then it will be your partner's turn to tell one way he or she will serve someone.** When children have told their ideas, say: **I'm so happy that**

● **The Point**

●**Jesus is our Lord and that we can serve others as Jesus serves us.**

For Extra Time

If you have a long class time or want to add additional elements to your lesson, try one of the following activities.

LIVELY LEARNING: Finger-Rhyme Fun

Have children repeat the finger rhyme they learned in the Closing activity to remind them of ways they can serve others as Jesus served. For a variation, encourage children to name ways they can help someone, share with someone, or love and care for someone this week.

When we help,
when we share,
when we love,
when we care, and
when we're in prayer.

Remind the children that ✏ Jesus is our Lord and that we can serve others in many different ways.

MAKE TO TAKE: Dip 'n' Dye Towel

Give each child a section of a heavy paper towel or a coffee filter. Fold the paper towel or coffee filter in half two or three times. Place one teaspoon of water in each of five muffin-tin cups. Add a few drops of different food coloring to each cup. Demonstrate how to dip the edges of the paper towel into the colored water. The colors will "bleed" into the paper towel, making unique designs. As they work, tell children that the towel is to remind them how Jesus served the disciples when he washed and dried their feet at the Last Supper.

TREAT TO EAT: Servant Sandwiches

Let children serve each other by cooperatively preparing delicious finger sandwiches. Have a couple of children cut three slices of bread into four squares using plastic knives. Other children may spread peanut butter on the bread squares. Another group may spread marshmallow creme on the sandwiches. And the last group of children may fold the sandwich squares in half. As the children work, remind them that Jesus served others and wants us to serve others, too.

STORY PICTURE: Jesus Washes His Disciples' Feet

Hand each child a photocopy of the "Today I Learned..." handout from page 32. Set out markers, glue, and two-by-two-inch pieces of fabric or paper towels. Let children glue the fabric pieces in Jesus' hands to dry the disciples' feet. As children work, talk about the ways that Jesus served people and the ways we can serve others.

● The Point

> **Note:**
> Before preparing the snacks, make sure children are not allergic to the ingredients.

Cross Name Tags

Photocopy this page. Have children cut out the name tags, decorate them, and write their names on the crosses.

Jesus is our Lord.

Serving Charades

Photocopy and cut the cards apart. Act out each way to serve.

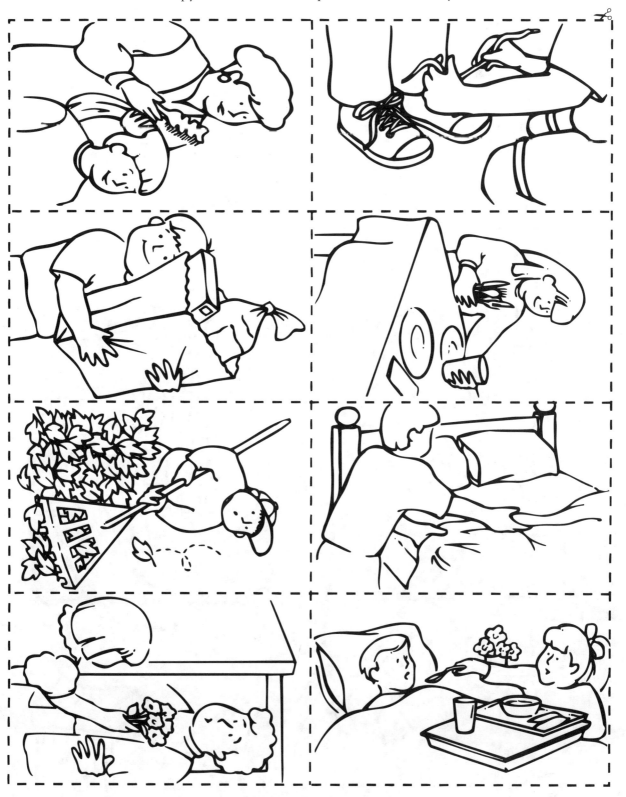

TODAY I LEARNED . . .

The Point ✏ Jesus is our Lord.

Today your child learned that Jesus is our Lord. Children learned how Jesus served his disciples by washing their feet. They talked about the importance of serving others as Jesus served.

Verse to Learn

"And every tongue confess that Jesus Christ is Lord" (Philippians 2:11a).

Ask Me . . .

● Why did Jesus wash his disciples' feet?
● What's one way you can serve others?
● How can we serve each other in our family?

Family Fun

● Have a servant supper one night. Let your child help prepare a simple meal for the family. Before eating, wash and dry one another's hands. Share a family prayer asking God to help each family member look for ways to serve one person every day that week. Finally, let your child serve food to each family member at the table.

● Let your child use fabric paints to decorate a plain hand towel. Use the towel in your kitchen as a reminder to serve as Jesus served.

Jesus Washes His Disciples' Feet (John 13:1-15)

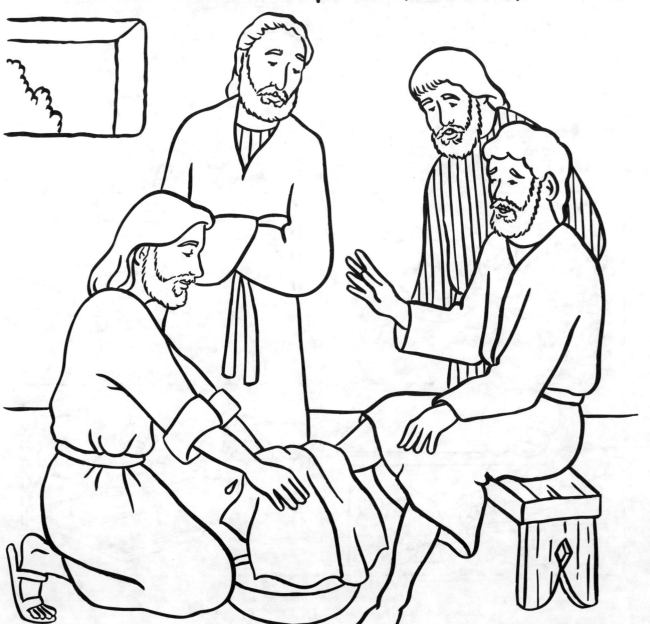

Jesus Prays

The Bible Basis

Mark 14:27-50. Jesus prays in the garden before his arrest.

The night before Jesus' death, he walked with his followers to a small garden of olive trees called Gethsemane. Aptly named, Gethsemane means "oil press." An oil press was used to squeeze precious oil from olives. It was in the "oil press" where Jesus knelt and prayed to his Father while the weight of the world's sins and the events yet to unfold crushed him. He told his disciples, "My soul is overwhelmed with sorrow to the point of death. Stay here and keep watch." But the disciples didn't keep watch—they slept. Jesus prayed alone in the garden and ultimately submitted to making the sacrifice that would bring salvation to the world.

Kindergartners are usually eager to share their feelings. When they're happy, we see it in their faces. When they're excited, we feel it in their energy. But when children are sad or afraid, they may try to hide their feelings. Perhaps it's because "big" boys or girls aren't supposed to feel afraid, or children don't want to appear to be "sissies." It's important for young children to realize that when Jesus faced difficult things, he found strength in prayer. Use this lesson to help children understand that they can turn to God in prayer just as Jesus did.

Another Scripture used in this lesson is Psalm 34:15.

Getting The Point

Jesus is our Lord.

It's important to say The Point just as it's written in each activity. Repeating The Point again and again will help the children remember it and apply it to their lives.

Children will
● understand that Jesus prayed to God,
● help Pockets realize that God hears prayer, and
● know they can talk to God any time and anyplace.

 The Point

This Lesson at a Glance

Before the lesson, collect the necessary items for the activities you plan to use. Refer to the Classroom Supplies and Learning Lab Supplies columns to determine what you'll need. Remember to make photocopies of the "Today I Learned..." handout (p. 44) to send home with your children.

Section	Minutes	What Children Will Do	Classroom Supplies	Learning Lab Supplies
Welcome Time	up to 5	**Welcome!**—Receive name tags and be greeted by the teacher.	"Cross Name Tags" handouts (p. 30), markers, pins or tape	
Let's Get Started Direct children to one or more of the Let's Get Started activities until everyone arrives.	up to 10	**Option 1: In the Garden**—Spend quiet time with God in a beautiful "garden."	Bedsheet, silk or plastic flowers, Bible picture book	
	up to 10	**Option 2: How Does Your Garden Grow?**—Work together to build a garden of flowers from building blocks.	Building blocks, construction paper, tape, scissors	
	up to 10	**Option 3: Prayer-Hands Balloons**—Make unusual balloons to remind them to pray.	Latex gloves, markers, ribbon, scissors, stickers	
Pick-Up Song	up to 5	**We Will Pick Up**—Sing a song as they pick up toys and gather for Bible-Story Time.	CD player	CD: "We Will Pick Up" (track 2)
Bible-Story Time	up to 5	**Setting the Stage**—Send their prayers to heaven and learn that God listens when they talk to him.	Bible, balloon	
	up to 5	**Bible Song and Prayer Time**—Sing a song, bring out the Bible, and pray together.	Bible, construction paper, scissors, basket or box, CD player	CD: "God's Book" (track 3), cross stamp and ink pad
	up to 10	**Hear the Bible Story**—Learn from Mark 14:27-50 how Jesus prayed in the garden of Gethsemane.	Bible, CD player, construction paper, scissors, marker, tape	Bible Big Book: Peter Tells the Easter Story, CD: "Peter Tells the Easter Story, Part I" (track 4)
	up to 10	**Do the Bible Story**—Play an exciting game as Followers or Guards.		
Practicing The Point	up to 5	**Prayer for Pockets**—Help Pockets learn that God wants us to pray to him.	Pockets the Kangaroo, scarf	
Closing	up to 5	**Prayer Song**—Sing a song and pray together.		
For Extra Time		For extra-time ideas and supplies, see page 43.		

Welcome Time

Welcome! (up to 5 minutes)

- Bend down and make eye contact with children as they arrive.
- Greet each child individually with an enthusiastic smile.
- Thank each child for coming to class today.
- As children arrive, ask them about last week's "Today I Learned…" discussion. Use questions such as "How did you serve someone last week?" or "How did you feel when someone helped you last week?"
- Say: **Today we're going to learn that**  **Jesus is our Lord.**
- Hand out the cross name tags children made during Lesson 1 and help them attach the name tags to their clothing. If some of the name tags were damaged or if some of the children weren't in class that week, have them make new name tags using the photocopiable handout on page 30.
- Direct children to the Let's Get Started activities you've set up.

⬤ The Point

Let's Get Started

Set up one or more of the following activities for children to do as they arrive. After you greet each child, invite him or her to choose an activity.

Circulate among the children to offer help as needed and to direct children's conversation toward today's lesson. Ask questions such as "When do you pray?" and "What are some times you're afraid?"

OPTION 1: In the Garden (up to 10 minutes)

Before class, place a table against the wall in one corner of the room. Drape a bedsheet or blanket over the table to make a private area beneath the table. Place a Bible picture book under the table, and scatter silk flowers on the floor around the table. As children arrive, explain that this is a special "garden" where they can be quiet and talk to God.

Spend a few quiet moments in the garden with the children. Make comments such as "Isn't it nice to be quiet and think about God?" and "Gardens are a lovely gift from God." Softly tell children that ⬤ Jesus is our Lord and that Jesus liked gardens, too. Mention that they'll hear a story about a time Jesus prayed in a special garden.

⬤ The Point

> ✔ Add a few cuddly garden critters to make the quiet area more pleasant. Stuffed toy squirrels, birds, ducks, and mice would be fun additions to your garden. Think about providing soft, soothing music on a CD player to add to the peaceful atmosphere.

OPTION 2: How Does Your Garden Grow? (up to 10 minutes)

Set building blocks in a corner of the room, and invite children to create a garden wall from blocks. Then have children add a variety of construction paper flowers, such as giant sunflowers or smaller daisies and tiny buttercups.

As children build and create flowers, ask questions such as "What would grow in your favorite garden?" or "What makes gardens special?"

The Point

Remind children that Jesus is our Lord. Tell children that they'll hear a Bible story about one night when Jesus prayed in a special garden. Explain that whenever Jesus had something hard to do, he prayed for God to help him.

☐ OPTION 3: Prayer-Hands Balloons (up to 10 minutes)

You'll need a latex glove for each child in class. Latex gloves may be purchased inexpensively in drug stores or medical and dental offices. Blow the gloves up like balloons and tie the ends.

Set permanent markers, stickers, scissors, and a roll of ribbon on a table. Hand each child a "balloon," and ask him or her about the balloon's shape. Tell children they'll make prayer-hands balloons to remind them how important it is to talk with God.

Let children decorate the balloons with the markers and stickers. Then help children write, "I pray every day" in the center.

The Point

Tie ribbon streamers to the end of each balloon. As children work, tell them that Jesus is our Lord and that they'll hear a story about a time Jesus prayed.

> ✔ You may wish to wipe each balloon with a damp cloth before this activity. It will help the stickers stay attached more securely.

After everyone has arrived and you're ready to move on to the Bible-Story Time, encourage the children to finish what they're doing and get ready to clean up.

Pick-Up Song

We Will Pick Up (up to 5 minutes)

Lead children in singing "We Will Pick Up" (track 2) with the *CD* to the tune of "London Bridge." Encourage the children to sing along as they help clean up the room.

If you want to include the names of all the children in your class, sing the song without the *CD,* and repeat the naming section. If you choose to use the *CD,* vary the names you use each week.

Sing

We will pick up all our toys,
All our toys, all our toys.
We will pick up all our toys
And put them all away.

I see (name) picking up,
Picking up, picking up.
I see (name) picking up
And putting toys away.

(Repeat)

Jesus is our Lord.

Bible-Story Time

Setting the Stage (up to 5 minutes)

Tell the children you'll clap your hands to get their attention. Explain that when you clap, children are to stop what they're doing, raise their hands, and focus on you. Encourage children to respond quickly so you'll have time for all the fun activities you've planned.

Blow up a balloon, and squeeze the open end with your fingers. Say: **Help me count to three and then we'll let the balloon fly and see where it goes. One, two, three!** Let the balloon sail into the air. Have a child retrieve the balloon when it lands. Ask:

● **What did the balloon do when I let it go?** (It flew up in the air; it sailed around the room.)

● **Did you know where the balloon would land?** (No.)

Say: **Just as the balloon went upward, our prayers go up to God. But better than the balloon, we know where our prayers are going to land—our prayers land in God's heart! God hears every prayer because he loves us and wants us to talk with him.** Ask:

● **When do you talk to God?** (At bedtime; before meals; when I'm scared; when I say my prayers at night.)

● **Can we talk to God any time?** (Yes, God likes it when we pray all the time; no, God's too busy.)

Say: **Let's send up a prayer right now and ask God to help us remember that ● Jesus is our Lord. I'll pass the balloon around the circle. When it comes to you, say, ●"Jesus is our Lord."** Hold the deflated balloon and say: **Dear God, please help us remember that...** Pass the balloon to the first child, and let him or her say The Point. Continue passing the balloon and repeating The Point until the balloon reaches you. Say: **In Jesus' name, amen.**

Blow up the balloon and let it go. Then say: **Our prayers always go right to God. God always hears our prayers. ● Jesus is our Lord, and God heard his prayers, too.** Read aloud Psalm 34:15 from an easy-to-understand Bible translation. **God hears our prayers because he loves us. Let's hear a story about a time Jesus prayed.** Ask a child to retrieve the balloon, then set it aside.

Bible Song and Prayer Time (up to 5 minutes)

Before class, make surprise cards for this activity by cutting construction paper into two-by-six-inch strips. Prepare a surprise card for each child plus a few extras for visitors. Fold the cards in half, then stamp the *cross stamp* inside one of the surprise cards. Place a marker at Mark 14:27-50 in the Bible you'll be using.

Have the children sit in a circle. Say: **Now it's time to choose a Bible person to bring me the Bible marked with today's Bible story. As we sing our Bible song, I'll pass out the surprise cards. Don't look inside your card until the song is over.**

Lead the children in singing "God's Book" (track 3) with the *CD* to the tune of "Old MacDonald Had a Farm." As you sing, pass out the folded surprise

● The Point
● The Point

● The Point

cards. If you want to include the names of all the children in your class, sing the song without the *CD,* and repeat the naming section. If you choose to use the *CD*, vary the names you use each week.

Sing

| Now it's time to read God's Book
And hear a Bible story.
It's fun to be here with my
    friends
And hear a Bible story.

(Name)'s **here.**
(Name)'s **here.**
Here is (name).
Here is (name).
Now it's time to read God's Book
And hear a Bible story. | Now it's time to read God's Book
And hear a Bible story.
It's fun to be here with my
    friends
And hear a Bible story.

(Name)'s **here.**
(Name)'s **here.**
Here is (name).
Here is (name).
Now it's time to read God's Book
And hear a Bible story. |

After the song, say: **You may look inside your surprise cards. The person who has the cross stamped inside his or her card will be our Bible person today.**

Identify the Bible person, then have the rest of the children clap for him or her. Ask the Bible person to bring you the Bible. Help the Bible person open the Bible to the marked place and show the children where your story comes from. Then have the Bible person sit down.

Say: (Name) **was our special Bible person today. Each week we'll have only one special Bible person, but each one of you is a special part of our class! Today we're all learning that ⬤Jesus is our Lord.**

Let's say a special prayer now and ask God to help us learn more about Jesus. I'll pass around this basket. When the basket comes to you, put your surprise card in it and say, "God, help us know that ⬤Jesus is our Lord."

Pass around the basket or box. After you've collected everyone's surprise card, set the basket aside, and pick up the Bible. Lead the children in this prayer: **God, thank you for the Bible and for all the stories in it. Teach us today that ⬤Jesus is our Lord. In Jesus' name we pray, amen.**

⬤ **The Point**

⬤ **The Point**

⬤ **The Point**

> ✔ You'll probably be able to reuse most of the surprise cards. Each week, throw out any torn or crumpled cards, and make enough new ones for each child to have one. Keep a list of who's had the stamped surprise card to ensure that everyone gets a turn to be the Bible person.

Hear the Bible Story (up to 10 minutes)

Before class, cut a sheet of construction paper in half. On one half, write the letter A, and on the other half, write the letter B. Tape the papers at opposite ends of the room.

Bring out the *Bible Big Book: Peter Tells the Easter Story* and the *CD*. Gather children in the center of the floor. Say: **Let's play a game called**

Hop To It to help us review our Bible story from last week. I'll read a question and give you two answers to choose from. If you think it's A, hop to the A paper on the wall. If you think the answer's B, hop to the B paper. Don't hop until I tell you to "hop to it." Ask:

● **Where were Jesus and his disciples? A. Japan, or B. Jerusalem. Hop to it!** Pause while the children hop to the answer of their choice. Then say: **The answer is B. Jerusalem. Good for you. Now return to the center of the room for the next question.**

Continue the game in this way with children returning to the center of the room after each question and answer. Use the following questions and answers to complete the story review.

● **Why did Jesus wash his disciples' feet? A. Because they lost their sandals, or B. Because he was teaching them to serve others? Hop to it!** (B. He was teaching them how to serve.)

● **Who does Jesus want us to serve? A. Just our friends, or B. Everyone. Hop to it!** (B. Jesus wants us to serve everyone.)

● **When we serve others, who else do we serve? A. Jesus, or B. Ourselves. Hop to it!** (A. We're serving Jesus when we serve others.)

Say: **You remembered the story well. Let's clap for each other.** Pause. **Now quietly hop back to the center, and find a place to sit.**

Hold up the Bible and say: **Our story comes from the books of Mark and Luke in the Bible.** Hold up the *Bible Big Book* and say: **Our Big Book shows us pictures of the Bible story. Today Peter will tell us about a time Jesus prayed. Listen for what Jesus said and why he prayed.**

Open the *Bible Big Book* to page 2, and play track 4 on the *CD*. When you reach the end of page 3, turn the CD player off, and close the Big Book. Ask:

● **How did this part of the story make you feel?** (Sad; I feel bad for Jesus; I wonder what will happen next.)

● **Do you think the guards should've arrested Jesus? Explain.** (No, Jesus hadn't done anything wrong; no, Jesus was God's Son.)

● **Why did Peter and the disciples run off when Jesus was arrested?** (They were afraid.)

Say: **Jesus knew that guards were coming to arrest him. We know that ⬤ Jesus is our Lord. But did you also know that Jesus felt the same things we feel? Jesus felt joy and excitement. Sometimes he felt sadness, and sometimes he felt anger just as you and I do. And when he knew he needed strength, Jesus prayed.**

⬤ **The Point**

● **When do you pray?** Pause for children to tell their ideas.

Say: **⬤ Jesus is our Lord. And Jesus knew that when we pray, God hears our prayers and answers them. Next week we'll hear another part of the story. Now let's play a game about being arrested.**

⬤ **The Point**

Do the Bible Story (up to 10 minutes)

Before this activity, set a few chairs in a row at one end of the room to be the "jail."

Divide children into two groups. Designate one group as the Guards, and have them stand in the center of the room. Designate the other group as the Followers, and have them stand around the edge of the room. Point out the jail you made earlier.

Say: **Guards, you'll follow my orders as you march around the room. The Followers will obey the Guards. The Followers may find a partner to walk arm in arm with to show that they're kind and helpful people. Let's begin.**

After a few moments, begin barking the following orders to the Guards. **Guards, arrest any Followers wearing the color yellow. Take them to jail and guard them!** Pause while Followers wearing yellow are led to jail. **Guards, arrest all Followers who have white shoes. Take them to jail!** Pause for Guards to respond. **Guards, go arrest all Followers who have a nose! Put them in jail!** Pause as the rest of the Followers are led to jail. Then ask:

● **How did it feel to be arrested?** (I was angry; it was because everyone has a nose.)

● **What was it like to obey the Guards?** (It was hard; I didn't mind because it was just a game.)

● **Was the game fair? Explain.** (No, we got arrested for nothing; no, the Guards were free.)

The Point

Say: **Guards arrested Jesus even though he hadn't done anything wrong. But Jesus didn't fight or yell or get angry. That's because Jesus is our Lord, and Jesus knew that God had a plan. Part of that plan was for Jesus to die—so he could take away our sins and so we could live in heaven with him. But dying was hard for Jesus even though he knew he would rise from the dead in three days. Isn't it good that Jesus prayed for God's help? Jesus wants us to talk to God when we need help, too.**

Practicing The Point

Prayer for Pockets (up to 5 minutes)

Before class, tie a scarf or bandanna around Pockets' head as if she has a toothache.

Bring out Pockets the Kangaroo, and go through the following script. After you finish the script, put Pockets away and out of sight.

Prayer for Pockets

PUPPET SCRIPT

Pockets: (Holding her jaw and moaning a little) Oooh.

Teacher: Pockets, why do you have a scarf on your jaw? Is something wrong?

Pockets: I have a toothache. Mommy said I ate too much candy and now I need to visit Dr. Hop-Along, the tooth doctor.

Teacher: You mean the dentist?

Pockets: Yes. I don't want to go, but Daddy says it's the only way my tooth will feel better.

(Continued)

Jesus is our Lord.

Teacher: It sounds like going to the dentist is hard for you to do. We heard a story today about how Jesus had something hard to do and what he did to get help. Children, let's tell Pockets about the Bible story and what Jesus did when he needed strength. (*Encourage children to tell Pockets how Jesus prayed to God when he needed strength and that God hears our prayers.*) Even though  Jesus is our Lord, he asked God for strength to do the things he did. Praying really helps us, Pockets. Can we pray for you?

Pockets: I need strength to be brave. I'd like you to pray for me.

Teacher: Let's join hands. (*Have Pockets hold hands with the children.*) Dear God, please help Pockets be brave. Amen.

Pockets: (*Smiling and giving a little hop*) Thanks for teaching me that prayer helps. I <u>do</u> feel better. (*Rubbing her jaw*) And I know my tooth will feel better, too. 'Bye!

● **The Point**

TODAY I LEARNED . . .

We believe that Christian education extends beyond the classroom into the home. Photocopy the "Today I Learned . . ." handout (p. 44) for this week, and send it home with your children. Encourage parents to use the handout to plan meaningful family activities to reinforce this week's topic. Follow up the "Today I Learned . . ." activities next week by asking children what their families did.

Closing

Prayer Song (up to 5 minutes)

Say: ● **Jesus is our Lord, and when he prayed in the garden, he showed us how important it is to talk to God. God helped take Jesus' fears away and make him feel strong. Let's sing a song about praying to God.**

Lead the children in singing "Only You" (without the *CD*) to the tune of "Jesus Loves Me."

● **The Point**

Sing 🎵

I can talk to God and pray
Any time of night or day.
God will help me with my
cares
When I offer him my prayers.
Yes, God, I'll pray.
Yes, God, I'll pray.
Yes, God, I'll pray.
I'll pray to only you.

I can talk to God and pray
Any time of night or day.
God will help me with my
cares
When I offer him my prayers.
Yes, God, I'll pray.
Yes, God, I'll pray.
Yes, God, I'll pray.
I'll pray to only you.

Say: **Jesus knew that his followers would get scared and run away. Jesus turned to God for strength. Get with a friend.** Pause while children find a partner. Say: **Decide which of you will go first. When I clap my hands, the first person will say, "God hears our prayers." Then I'll clap my hands again, and the other person will say, "And God always cares."**

After you've clapped two times, say: **Let's join hands and pray right now.** Pray: **Dear God, thank you for helping us learn that even though 🔵Jesus is our Lord, he still prayed to you for strength. We thank you that Jesus taught us to pray. In Jesus' name, amen.**

🔵 **The Point**

Say: **Today when you talk to God as Jesus did, tell God, "Thank you that 🔵Jesus is our Lord."**

🔵 **The Point**

For Extra Time

If you have a long class time or want to add additional elements to your lesson, try one of the following activities.

LIVELY LEARNING: **Free the Prisoner**

Use the balloon from the "Setting the Stage" activity. Blow up the balloon and tie the end. Place a three-foot piece of masking tape on the center of the floor, and form two groups on either side of the tape. Tell the children that the balloon is a prisoner who was captured by soldiers. Explain that you'll toss the balloon into the air over the center of the tape and that their job is to free the balloon by blowing it across the tape line. (No hands are allowed in this game.) Point out that Jesus was the soldiers' prisoner but that God would soon set him free because ⬤ Jesus is our Lord.

⬤ **The Point**

MAKE TO TAKE: **Prayer Garden**

Let children plant their own prayer "gardens" to remind them how Jesus prayed in Gethsemane the night of his arrest. Cover a table with newspaper. Let each child plant three bean seeds in a paper cup filled halfway with potting soil. Help them use markers to write "Jesus prayed" on their cups. Read the words aloud, and let children repeat them with you.

As children plant their seeds, ask questions such as "Why did Jesus pray?" and "Does God hear us pray? Explain." Remind them that ⬤ Jesus is our Lord and that we can pray as Jesus did.

⬤ **The Point**

TREAT TO EAT: **Garden Snack**

Have the children work cooperatively to make fun garden snacks. You'll need small paper cups, chocolate cookies, a rolling pin, a plastic bag, toothpicks, plastic spoons, and colorful gumdrops. Have the children form four groups: Rollers, Potters, Placers, and Planters. Rollers place chocolate cookies in a plastic bag and take turns crushing the cookies with the rolling pin. Potters pour cookie crumbs into each cup. Placers stick three gumdrop "flowers" on the tip of each toothpick. Planters plant the gumdrop flowers in each garden.

Enjoy the treats with plastic spoons. As children pick gumdrop flowers from their gardens, remind them that Jesus went to a garden to pray and that ⬤ Jesus is our Lord.

STORY PICTURE: **Jesus Prays in the Garden**

If the weather permits, take children on a walk outside to gather items found in a garden, such as leaves, flowers, twigs, and grass. If it's a rainy day, have children cut out construction paper leaves and flowers.

Hand each child a photocopy of the "Today I Learned..." handout from page 44. Provide glue, and allow children to glue the leaves, flowers, twigs, and grass to the picture. As children work, tell them that ⬤ Jesus is our Lord and that he showed us how important it is to pray.

⬤ **The Point**

TODAY I LEARNED...

The Point ✏ Jesus is our Lord.

Today your child learned that Jesus is our Lord. Children learned that Jesus prayed before he was arrested. They talked about how God hears and answers prayer.

Verse to Learn

"And every tongue confess that Jesus Christ is Lord" (Philippians 2:11a).

Ask Me...

● Why did Jesus go to the garden of Gethsemane?
● When are times you can talk to God?
● What are ways our family can pray for each other?

Family Fun

● Make a fun family prayer reminder. Trace the outline of each family member's hand on construction paper. Cut the outlines out, and write each person's name on his or her paper hand. Have your child tape the hands to drinking straws. Place the prayer bouquet in a vase, and set it on the dining table as a centerpiece.

Jesus Prays in the Garden (Mark 14:27-50)

It's Hard to Follow

The Point
  Jesus is our Lord.

The Bible Basis

Mark 14:53-72; 15:21-41. Peter denies Jesus before Jesus' death.

After Jesus' arrest in the garden of Gethsemane, Peter followed the crowd as they took Jesus to the high priest in Jerusalem. In the courtyard Peter waited, filled with curiosity and dread concerning Jesus' fate at the hands of the religious leaders. As the rooster crowed to herald the sad dawning of day, Peter denied he knew Jesus for the third time—and realized he'd fulfilled Jesus' prophecy of the night before. Peter broke down and wept. Peter's betrayal made him feel as though he'd already killed Jesus in his heart, and the worst still lay ahead.

Perhaps the most difficult Bible story to present to young children is that of Jesus' death on the cross. Even kindergartners realize that Jesus' death was unfair and cruel. Help them begin to understand that Jesus willingly chose to follow God's plan—even though obedience meant a cruel death. Because Jesus loves us, he was willing to give his life so that our sins could be pardoned. Use this lesson to help children understand the events of Jesus' death and learn that when we obey God, we can trust him to make things work out for the best.

Getting The Point

Jesus is our Lord.

It's important to say The Point just as it's written in each activity. Repeating The Point again and again will help the children remember it and apply it to their lives.

Children will
- learn that Jesus died as part of God's plan for our forgiveness,
- understand that we can always trust God,
- help Pockets see that following Jesus is sometimes hard, and
- realize that it can be hard to follow God.

  The Point

This Lesson at a Glance

Before the lesson, collect the necessary items for the activities you plan to use. Refer to the Classroom Supplies and Learning Lab Supplies columns to determine what you'll need. Remember to make photocopies of the "Today I Learned..." handout (p. 57) to send home with your children.

Section	Minutes	What Children Will Do	Classroom Supplies	Learning Lab Supplies
Welcome Time	up to 5	**Welcome!**—Receive name tags and be greeted by the teacher.	"Cross Name Tags" handouts (p. 30), markers, pins or tape	
Let's Get Started Direct children to one or more of the Let's Get Started activities until everyone arrives.	up to 10	**Option 1: Mosaic Cross**—Create a colorful cross.	Liquid starch, tissue paper, paintbrushes, poster board, scissors, newspaper, bowl	
	up to 10	**Option 2: Follow Me!**—Play a simple board game and follow directions.	"Follow Me!" game board handouts (p. 56), beans, pennies, paper cup	
	up to 10	**Option 3: I Don't Know You**—Play a guessing game and tell when you know someone's name.		
Pick-Up Song	up to 5	**We Will Pick Up**—Sing a song as they pick up toys and gather for Bible-Story Time.	CD player	CD: "We Will Pick Up" (track 2)
Bible-Story Time	up to 5	**Setting the Stage**—Play a game and learn what "deny" means.	Paper, tape, marker	
	up to 5	**Bible Song and Prayer Time**—Sing a song, bring out the Bible, and pray together.	Bible, construction paper, scissors, basket or box, CD player	CD: "God's Book" (track 3), cross stamp and ink pad
	up to 10	**Hear the Bible Story**—Listen to the story about Peter's denial and Jesus' death from Mark 14:53-72; 15:21-41.	Bible, thorny rose stem, nail, stone, box	*Bible Big Book: Peter Tells the Easter Story*
	up to 10	**Do the Bible Story**—Sing a song and learn why Jesus died.	CD player	CD: "That's Why He Died" (track 5), cross stamp and ink pad
Practicing The Point	up to 5	**Some Friend**—Help Pockets learn about being loyal to her friends.	Pockets the Kangaroo, facial tissue, tape	
Closing	up to 5	**Crisscross**—Proclaim that they know who Jesus is and say a prayer.	Pretzel sticks	
For Extra Time		For extra-time ideas and supplies, see page 55.		

Jesus Is our Lord.

Welcome Time

Welcome! (up to 5 minutes)

- Bend down and make eye contact with children as they arrive.
- Greet each child individually with an enthusiastic smile.
- Thank each child for coming to class today.
- As children arrive, ask them about last week's "Today I Learned..." discussion. Use questions such as "When did you talk to God last week?" and "When was a time your family prayed together?"
- Say: **Today we're going to learn that 🖊 Jesus is our Lord.**
- Hand out the cross name tags children made during Lesson 1, and help them attach the name tags to their clothing. If some of the name tags were damaged or if children weren't in class that week, have them make new name tags using the photocopiable handout on page 30.
- Direct the children to the Let's Get Started activities you've set up.

🖊 **The Point**

Let's Get Started

Set up one or more of the following activities for children to do as they arrive. After you greet each child, invite him or her to choose an activity.

Circulate among children to offer help as needed and to direct children's conversation toward today's lesson. Ask questions such as "Who do you think of when you see a cross?" or "Why is it important to follow directions?"

☐ OPTION 1: Mosaic Cross (up to 10 minutes)

Before class, cut an eight-inch-high poster board cross for each child.

Cover a table with newspaper. Place a bowl of liquid starch and colored tissue paper on the table. Hand each child a poster board cross and a paintbrush. Have the children tear tissue paper into small pieces and then brush the cross with liquid starch. Show children how to lay the small pieces of tissue paper on the cross.

As children work, explain that the symbol of a cross reminds us that 🖊 Jesus is our Lord and that he chose to give his life for us. Tell children that today they'll hear a story about Jesus and why the cross makes us think of him.

🖊 **The Point**

✔ Encourage children to overlap the tissue paper on the cross to create color variations. Tell them to work on one portion of the cross at a time.

☐ OPTION 2: Follow Me! (up to 10 minutes)

Before this activity, photocopy the "Follow Me!" game board handout on page 56. Make one copy for every two children.

Place ten beans in a paper cup. Hand each pair of children a game board and a penny. Each child chooses a bean for a game marker and places his or her bean at START. Explain that the point of the game is to follow the path until they reach HOME. Have children flip the penny. The person who flips "heads" goes first. Take turns flipping the penny and moving the beans. "Heads" moves ahead two spaces, and "tails" moves back one space. Tell children to follow the arrows on the spaces they land. Play until both players reach HOME.

As children play, circulate and make comments such as "You're following the directions well" and "It's not easy to follow when the path takes you where you don't want to go, is it?" Tell children that they'll hear a Bible story about the disciples following Jesus and Jesus following God's plan. Point out that ● Jesus is our Lord and that he wanted to follow God.

● The Point

☐ OPTION 3: I Don't Know You (up to 10 minutes)

Set a chair in one corner of the room facing the wall. Tell children it's the I-don't-know-you chair. Invite a child to sit in the chair facing the wall. Quietly tap a child to stand behind the chair and give clues about his or her identity, such as "I have brown hair" or "I'm a girl." Each time a clue is given, the person in the chair says, "I don't know you." When the child sitting in the chair thinks he or she can identify the mystery person, the child says, "I know you! You're (name of the child)."

● The Point

As children play, remind them that ● Jesus is our Lord and that soon they'll hear a story about how Peter said he didn't know Jesus. Continue playing the game until each person has a chance to sit in the I-don't-know-you chair.

After everyone has arrived and you're ready to move on to the Bible-Story Time, encourage the children to finish what they're doing and get ready to clean up.

Pick-Up Song

We Will Pick Up (up to 5 minutes)

Lead children in singing "We Will Pick Up" (track 2) with the *CD* to the tune of "London Bridge." Encourage the children to sing along as they help clean up the room.

If you want to include the names of all the children in your class, sing the song without the *CD,* and repeat the naming section. If you choose to use the *CD,* vary the names you use each week.

Sing

We will pick up all our toys,
All our toys, all our toys.
We will pick up all our toys
And put them all away.

I see (name) picking up,
Picking up, picking up.
I see (name) picking up
And putting toys away.

(Repeat)

Bible-Story Time

Setting the Stage (up to 5 minutes)

Tell the children you'll clap your hands to get their attention. Explain that when you clap, children are to stop what they're doing, raise their hands, and focus on you. Encourage children to respond quickly so you'll have time for all the fun activities you've planned.

Before class, write the word "yes" on one sheet of paper and the word "no" on another. Tape the papers to opposite walls.

Gather the children in a circle on the floor. Say: **I'm going to read each of you a sentence. When you hear the sentence, you can either give a "thumbs up" which means you agree with the sentence, or you can give a "thumbs down" which means you don't agree with the sentence. In this game, it's OK to try to trick us or tell the truth—you decide! Then the rest of us will decide whether we think you're telling the truth or not. If we think you're telling the truth, we'll run to the "yes" paper. If we think you're not telling the truth, we'll run to the "no" paper. Then you can use your other thumb to tell us the real answer.**

For example, if I say, "I like ice cream and pickles," I'll give a thumbs up or thumbs down. Run to "yes" if you think I really like pickles and ice cream or to "no" if you think I'm denying it. Then I'll give you the real answer with my other thumb.

Use the following statements. Let children run to the "yes" or "no" papers and then return to the center. Continue until each child's had a chance to agree with or deny a statement.

- **You like broccoli.**
- **You're six years old.**
- **You like the color orange.**
- **Riding a bike is your favorite hobby.**
- **You have three sisters.**
- **Your parents drive a green car.**
- **You want to be a tennis star when you grow up.**
- **You like to swim.**

Ask:

- **How did it feel to deny something that was true?** (It felt funny; I felt like I was lying.)
- **What made you decide whether to agree or disagree?** (I wanted to tell the truth; I wanted to trick you.)

Say: **In our game, it was OK to trick class members, but in real life it's not. To deny something means choosing to lie. It's like forgetting something on purpose. Sometimes it's hard to tell the truth. Let's hear a story about a time one disciple lied and said he didn't know that ✎Jesus is our Lord.**

Bible Song and Prayer Time (up to 5 minutes)

Before class, make surprise cards for this activity by cutting construction paper into two-by-six-inch strips. Prepare a surprise card for each child plus a few extras for visitors. Fold the cards in half, then stamp the *cross stamp* inside

◉ The Point

one of the surprise cards. Place a marker at Mark 14:53-72; 15:21-41 in the Bible you'll be using.

Have children sit in a circle. Say: **Now it's time to choose a Bible person to bring me the Bible marked with today's Bible story. As we sing our Bible song, I'll pass out the surprise cards. Don't look inside your card until the song is over.**

Lead the children in singing "God's Book" (track 3) with the *CD* to the tune of "Old MacDonald Had a Farm." As you sing, pass out the surprise cards. If you want to include the names of all the children in your class, sing the song without the *CD*, and repeat the naming section. If you choose to use the *CD*, vary the names you use each week.

Sing

Now it's time to read God's Book
And hear a Bible story.
It's fun to be here with my
   friends
And hear a Bible story.

(Name)**'s here.**
(Name)**'s here.**
Here is (name).
Here is (name).
**Now it's time to read God's Book
And hear a Bible story.**

Now it's time to read God's Book
And hear a Bible story.
It's fun to be here with my
   friends
And hear a Bible story.

(Name)**'s here.**
(Name)**'s here.**
Here is (name).
Here is (name).
**Now it's time to read God's Book
And hear a Bible story.**

After the song, say: **You may look inside your surprise cards. The person who has the cross stamped inside his or her card will be our Bible person for today.**

Identify the Bible person, then have the rest of the children clap for him or her. Ask the Bible person to bring you the Bible. Help the Bible person open the Bible to the marked place and show the children where your story comes from. Then have the Bible person sit down.

Say: (Name) **was our special Bible person today. Each week, we'll have only one special Bible person, but each one of you is a special part of our class! Today we're all learning that ● Jesus is our Lord.**

● The Point

Let's say a special prayer now and ask God to help us learn more about Jesus. I'll pass around this basket. When the basket comes to you, put your surprise card in it and say, "God, please help me know that ● Jesus is our Lord."

● The Point

Pass around the basket or box. After you've collected everyone's surprise card, set the basket aside, and pick up the Bible. Lead children in this prayer: **God, thank you for the Bible and for all the stories in it. Teach us today that ● Jesus is our Lord. In Jesus' name we pray, amen.**

● The Point

Hear the Bible Story (up to 10 minutes)

Before class, gather the following items and place them in a box: a thorny rose stem, a nail, and a stone.

Bring out the *Bible Big Book: Peter Tells the Easter Story.*

Say: **Let's see if you can find things in the pictures of our Big Book to** help us review the story. When I ask if you can find something in the picture, put your hand on your head. I'll choose someone to point to the picture and answer a question.

Hold up the open *Bible Big Book* to page 1. Ask the following questions:

● **Find the water in the picture. What did Jesus do with the water?** (He washed his disciples' feet.)

● **Find Peter. How did he feel about Jesus washing his feet?** (Peter was embarrassed; he thought Jesus shouldn't wash his feet.)

Fold back the *Bible Big Book* so children see only page 2.

● **Find Jesus. Why was he praying to God?** (He needed strength; he knew he was going to die.)

● **Find Peter. What did Jesus say Peter would do?** (Say he didn't know Jesus.)

Fold back the *Bible Big Book* so children see only page 3.

● **Find the guards. What did they do in the garden?** (Arrested Jesus.)

● **Find Peter. Why did he fight the guards?** (He was afraid; he wanted to help Jesus.)

Say: **Good job! Now let's hear the next part of the story. It's a very sad part about Peter saying he didn't know Jesus and about how Jesus followed God's plan even though it was hard. You can help me tell the story. I have some things for you to touch and look at as we listen to the story. I'll pass them to you when it's time.**

Open the *Bible Big Book* to page 4. Remind children that Peter is doing the talking in the story. Read the story below, and lead children in the accompanying actions.

I didn't know where the other disciples ran. I was afraid, but I *had* to know what was happening to Jesus. I quietly followed the crowd back to Jerusalem. Stand and tiptoe around the Big Book one time. **They took Jesus to the house of the high priest. I could see people being mean to Jesus. I was afraid.**

I sat by a fire with some of the guards. Sit down and warm your hands. **A servant girl said, "You were with Jesus." I was scared, so I said, "No! I don't know Jesus!" Two more times people asked if I knew Jesus, and I said, "No!" Then the rooster crowed. Can you show me what a rooster sounds like?** Pause for children to crow like roosters. Then clap your hands for quiet, and wait for children to respond. **I remembered what Jesus told me—before the rooster crowed, I would say I didn't know him three times. I started to cry.**

Lay the Big Book down. Ask:

● **What would you say if someone asked if you knew Jesus?** (Yes; I'm not sure.)

Say: **Peter was afraid. It was hard for him to follow Jesus. Peter said he didn't know Jesus because Peter didn't want to be arrested by the guards who arrested Jesus.** Ask:

● **How did Peter feel?** (Bad; sad; rotten because he lied.)

Let's see what happens next.

Hold the Big Book open to page 5. Continue reading the story below.

There was a trial, and the temple leaders told lies about Jesus. The angry crowd believed the lies. So even though Jesus hadn't done anything wrong, they condemned him to die.

They put a crown of thorns on Jesus' head. Hold the rose stem and let each child gently feel the thorns, then continue reading. **They made Jesus carry a heavy wooden cross up the hill. Then the soldiers nailed Jesus' hands and feet to the cross.** Have the children feel the nail. **I cried because I loved Jesus—and because I'd said I didn't know him. And as we watched, Jesus, our Lord, died on the cross. The sky turned dark and the earth shook. I didn't know what to do.**

They carried Jesus away and laid him in a tomb. Then the soldiers sealed the tomb with a huge stone. Pass the stone around the circle.

Close the Big Book. Wait a few moments before you continue. Ask:

● **How does this story make you feel?** (Sad; not good; I feel bad that the people killed Jesus.)

● **We learned that Jesus can do miracles. Why didn't he use a miracle to escape?** (Jesus knew he had to die so we could be forgiven; it wasn't in God's plan.)

✏ The Point

Say: ✏**Jesus is our Lord, and Jesus followed God even when it was hard. God had a plan. If Jesus died for us, God could forgive our sins. Then we could live in heaven with Jesus.** Ask:

● **How do you think Peter felt when Jesus died?** (Bad; really sad; he cried a lot.)

● **Do you think Peter wanted to tell Jesus he was sorry? Explain.** (Yes, because Peter loved Jesus; no, it wouldn't do any good.)

✏ The Point

Say: **We've learned that** ✏ **Jesus is our Lord and that Jesus can do anything. Next week we'll hear how Jesus rose from the dead and is alive today!**

The disciples didn't understand yet why God let Jesus die on the cross. Let's sing a song to help us remember why Jesus died for us.

Do the Bible Story (up to 10 minutes)

Lead the children in singing "That's Why He Died" (track 5) with the *CD* to the tune of "Jesus Loves Me."

Sing 🎵

On a cross, my Jesus died.
His disciples stood and cried
Because they could not under-
   stand
That this was part of God's
   good plan.
Yes, Jesus loves me.
Yes, Jesus loves me.
Yes, Jesus loves me.
That's why he died for me.

Jesus gave his life that day
So he could take my sins away.
Now I'll live as God's true
   friend.
In heaven, my life will never
   end.
Yes, Jesus loves me.
Yes, Jesus loves me.
Yes, Jesus loves me.
That's why he died for me.

Turn off the CD player. Ask:

● **Why did Jesus die?** (Because he loved us; because it was God's plan; to take my sins away.)

Say: **You sang so well. I have something for you.** Put a *cross stamp* on each child's hand. Say: **The cross will help you remember that** ✏**Jesus is our**

✏ The Point

Lord. I'm very sad when I think of Jesus dying. But it makes me happy to remember that he rose again. We'll find out about that next week.

Practicing The Point

Some Friend (up to 5 minutes)

Before this activity, tape a facial tissue to Pockets' paw. Bring out Pockets the Kangaroo. Go through the following script. After you finish the script, put Pockets away and out of sight.

Some Friend

PUPPET SCRIPT

(Pockets comes in sniffling softly and dabbing her nose.)

Teacher: Pockets, what seems to be the matter? You look very unhappy.

Pockets: Oh, I did something wrong, and now I don't know what to do. *(Sniffles.)*

Teacher: If you tell us what's wrong, maybe we can help. We're your friends, and we like helping you.

Pockets: *(Moaning loudly)* Ooohhh!

Teacher: *(Patting Pockets lovingly)* But Pockets, you <u>are</u> our friend.

Pockets: I know—you're <u>my</u> friends, too. But I told some people at school that Sarah wasn't my friend and that I didn't know her.

Teacher: But I thought you and Sarah were good friends. Why would you say those things?

Pockets: Well, Sarah had her hair fixed a different way, and lots of the kangaroos at school were laughing at her. They asked me if Sarah and I were friends. I didn't want to be laughed at, too, so I said that we weren't friends and that I didn't know her. *(Sobs.)* Now I feel real bad, and I don't know what to dooo, boo hoo!

Teacher: Maybe we can help. We heard a story today about how Peter told some people he didn't know Jesus. Let's tell Pockets about the day that Peter denied that Jesus was his friend. *(Encourage children to retell the Bible story of how Peter denied Jesus. Have them point out that Peter cried because he'd been untruthful.)* Peter said he didn't know Jesus, just as you denied knowing Sarah. But guess what? Jesus is our Lord and because he loved Peter so much, Jesus forgave Peter! I think Sarah would forgive you, too, if you ask her.

(Continued)

The Point

Pockets: Do you really think so? (Pause for their response.) Thanks for telling me the Bible story about Peter. If Jesus forgave Peter, maybe Sarah will forgive me, too. I'm going to hop right over to her house! 'Bye!

TODAY I LEARNED...

We believe that Christian education extends beyond the classroom into the home. Photocopy the "Today I Learned..." handout (p. 57) for this week, and send it home with your children. Encourage parents to use the handout to plan meaningful family activities to reinforce this week's topic. Follow up the "Today I Learned..." activities next week by asking children what their families did.

Closing

Crisscross (up to 5 minutes)

Gather children at a table. Hand each child three pretzel sticks. Tell children to make a cross using all three of the sticks. They may use two sticks for either the vertical or horizontal branch. When the crosses have been made, ask:

● **How many times did Peter deny he knew Jesus?** (Three.)

● **The Point**

Say: **Each time I ask you if you know Jesus, shout ✏ "Jesus is our Lord!" and eat one pretzel stick.**

When all of the pretzel sticks have been eaten, say: **We're glad Jesus always followed God—even when it was hard. Let's say a prayer and thank God for Jesus.** Pray: **Dear God, thank you for Jesus. His love was so great that he died for us. Thank you for helping Jesus follow you even when it was hard. Please help us follow you, too. In Jesus' name, amen.**

● **The Point**

Say: **Even though we're sad that Jesus died, we know that he rose again. We can trust God to make things work out for the best. We can be happy that God loves us and that ● Jesus is our Lord!**

For Extra Time

If you have a long class time or want to add additional elements to your lesson, try one of the following activities.

LIVELY LEARNING: Jesus Is Lord!

Gather children in a circle on the floor. Choose one child to be the Tapper. Have that child walk around the circle, touching each child lightly on the head and saying "Peter." When the Tapper touches a child and says, "Jesus is Lord!" that child jumps up and chases the Tapper around the circle. If the Tapper is tagged, he or she must go again. If the Tapper makes it safely to the empty place in the circle, the child who was tapped becomes the Tapper.

MAKE TO TAKE: Nail Crosses

Before this activity, cut one six-inch length and one twelve-inch length of thin-gauge wire for each child. File the ends of the nails with a rasp to make them dull.

Have children get with a partner. Hand each child two three-inch nails and a short piece of wire. Have one partner hold two nails in a cross shape while the other person wraps the wire around the nails in a crisscross pattern to secure the nails together. Demonstrate how to twist the ends of the long piece of wire around the cross to make a necklace. As the children work, tell them that when they wear a cross, it tells others that ✏ Jesus is our Lord.

● **The Point**

TREAT TO EAT: Cracker Crosses

Hand each child four long, rectangular-shaped crackers. Show children how to create a cracker cross by spreading peanut butter in the center of a cracker. Lay a second cracker lengthwise on top. Let each child make two cracker crosses to eat. While they enjoy their treats, ask questions such as "Why is the cross so important to Christians?" and "Why did Jesus die?" Remind children that ✏ Jesus is our Lord and that he died because he loves us and wants us to be God's friends.

● **The Point**

STORY PICTURE: Peter Denies Jesus

Hand each child a photocopy of the "Today I Learned..." handout from page 57. Set out crayons, glue, and craft feathers. Tell children to color the picture, then glue feathers on the rooster's tail. As children work, tell them that ✏ Jesus is our Lord and that we want to tell everyone we know about Jesus.

● **The Point**

Start

Follow Me!

Home

Place a bean as a game marker at START. Flip a penny for your move. Heads, go ahead two spaces. Tails, go back one space. Follow the arrows, and play until everyone makes it HOME.

Jesus is our Lord.

TODAY I LEARNED...

The Point 🖊 Jesus is our Lord.

Today your child learned that Jesus is our Lord. Children learned about Peter's denial and how Jesus died on the cross because he loves us. They talked about the fact that following God isn't always easy.

Verse to Learn

"And every tongue confess that Jesus Christ is Lord" (Philippians 2:11a).

Ask Me...

● Why did Peter say he didn't know Jesus?

● How can you let others know that Jesus is our Lord?

● What are some ways our family can follow Jesus?

Family Fun

● Go for a walk in the woods or a park, and let your child collect two small tree branches. Help your child tie twine or yarn in a crisscross pattern around the branches to create a cross. Write "Jesus is our Lord" on an index card. Help your child attach the card to the center of the cross with tape or staples. Hang the cross beside your doorway to let people know your family knows Jesus.

Peter Denies Jesus (Mark 14:53-72; 15:21-41)

Celebrate Jesus

The Point
🖎 Jesus is our Lord.

The Bible Basis

John 20:1-9. Mary found the stone rolled away—and Jesus was alive!

Imagine Mary Magdalene's thoughts as she sadly made her way to the tomb where Jesus had been laid three days earlier. The stone that she'd thought would bar her entrance had been rolled away! Shock and surprise sent her rushing to find Peter and the other disciples. Most of the disciples were skeptical of her report, but Peter and John raced to see for themselves. When they peered into the tomb, the only thing they found was the linen shroud Jesus had been wrapped in. The tomb was empty—Jesus was risen and alive!

Kindergartners love the thrill of Easter morning with colorful eggs, candies, and the freshness of spring in the air. But the focus of their happiness often isn't the true reason for Easter joy. We want to refocus their hearts and minds on the real meaning of this most joyous day of all Christendom. Using an egg as an example, we can help young children see that the important thing isn't the shell, but rather the life inside. In the same way, the empty tomb isn't what's important, but rather the life that came from it. Use this lesson to teach children that Easter is when we celebrate Jesus' victory over death and that his victory means we can be forgiven and live as God's friends forever.

Getting The Point

🖎 **Jesus is our Lord.**

It's important to say The Point just as it's written in each activity. Repeating The Point again and again will help the children remember it and apply it to their lives.

Children will
● celebrate the joy of Easter,
● know that Jesus is always with us,
● understand that Jesus' death and resurrection were part of God's plan, and
● teach Pockets the real meaning of Easter.

🖎 **The Point**

This Lesson at a Glance

Before the lesson, collect the necessary items for the activities you plan to use. Refer to the Classroom Supplies and Learning Lab Supplies columns to determine what you'll need. Remember to make photocopies of the "Today I Learned..." handout (p. 70) to send home with your children.

Section	Minutes	What Children Will Do	Classroom Supplies	Learning Lab Supplies
Welcome Time	up to 5	**Welcome!**—Receive name tags and be greeted by the teacher.	"Cross Name Tags" handouts (p. 30), markers, pins or tape	
Let's Get Started Direct children to one or more of the Let's Get Started activities until everyone arrives.	up to 10	**Option 1: Jingle Bracelets**—Make musical instruments to celebrate Easter.	Jingle bells, elastic thread, scissors, beads	
	up to 10	**Option 2: Rock 'n' Roll**—Roll stones into "caves."	Stones, paper cups	
	up to 10	**Option 3: Celebration Station**—Decorate the room for a party.	Balloons, crepe paper, scissors, tape	
Pick-Up Song	up to 5	**We Will Pick Up**—Sing a song as they pick up toys and gather for Bible-Story Time.	CD player	CD: "We Will Pick Up" (track 2)
Bible-Story Time	up to 5	**Setting the Stage**—Sing and move to a new song.	CD player, crepe paper, scissors, tape, jingle bracelets	CD: "Jesus Is Alive!" (track 6)
	up to 5	**Bible Song and Prayer Time**—Sing a song, bring out the Bible, and pray together.	Bible, construction paper, scissors, basket or box, CD player	CD: "God's Book" (track 3), cross stamp and ink pad
	up to 10	**Hear the Bible Story**—Hear the exciting story of Jesus' resurrection from John 20:1-9.	Bible, CD player	Bible Big Book: Peter Tells the Easter Story, CD: "Peter Tells the Easter Story, Part II" (track 7)
	up to 10	**Do the Bible Story**—Act out the story of the first Easter morning.		
Practicing The Point	up to 5	**It's What's Inside That Counts**—Help Pockets learn the real joy of Easter.	Pockets the Kangaroo, small Easter egg, large plastic egg, stone, cross, paper or candy heart, paper	
Closing	up to 5	**Jesus Is Alive!**—Celebrate Jesus' life with a song and say a prayer.	CD player, celebration streamer from "Setting the Stage," jingle bracelets from Option 1, tape	CD: "Jesus Is Alive!" (track 6)
For Extra Time		For extra-time ideas and supplies, see page 69.		

Welcome Time

Welcome! (up to 5 minutes)

- Bend down and make eye contact with children as they arrive.
- Greet each child individually with an enthusiastic smile.
- Thank each child for coming to class today.
- As children arrive, ask them about last week's "Today I Learned…" discussion. Use questions such as "What was one way you followed God last week?" and "What's your favorite holiday?"
- Say: **Today we're going to learn that ● Jesus is our Lord.**
- Hand out the cross name tags children made during Lesson 1, and help them attach the name tags to their clothing. If some of the name tags were damaged or if some of the children weren't in class that week, have them make new name tags using the photocopiable handout on page 30.
- Direct the children to the Let's Get Started activities you've set up.

● The Point

Let's Get Started

Set up one or more of the following activities for children to do as they arrive. After you greet each child, invite him or her to choose an activity.

Circulate among the children to offer help as needed and to direct their conversation toward today's lesson. Ask questions such as "Isn't it fun to make music?" and "Why are parties fun?"

✔ Create a mood of celebration in your room as children arrive. To help set the mood, play an upbeat musical CD of your choice in the background. Hand out colorful treats such as little cards with "Jesus is risen!" printed on them and a wrapped candy stapled to each card. This lesson is about celebration, so smile, have fun, and *feel the joy of our risen Lord* with your children!

OPTION 1: Jingle Bracelets (up to 10 minutes)

Set out jingle bells, beads, elastic thread, and scissors. Invite children to work with a friend. Tell them they'll be making musical instruments to help in a special celebration. Measure and cut a length of elastic thread to fit around each child's wrist or ankle. Let children help each other string three bells and three small beads on the elastic thread, then tie the ends together. As children make their anklets or bracelets, remind them they've been learning that ● Jesus is our Lord and that today they'll celebrate a special day for Jesus and for everyone. Allow children to wear their jingle bracelets until after the "Setting the Stage" activity. If you don't choose Option 1, be sure to bring jingle bells or other noise-makers for children to use during "Setting the Stage."

● The Point

☐ OPTION 2: Rock 'n' Roll (up to 10 minutes)

🔴 **The Point**

Hand each pair of children two paper cup "caves" and one round, smooth stone. Have children sit four feet apart on the floor and set the cups in front of them with the cups' openings facing each other. Tell children to roll the stones back and forth and try to get them in their partners' caves to score points. Have each pair play until one partner has three points. Remind children that 🔴 Jesus is our Lord and that they'll hear a story about a cave, a big stone, and a wonderful celebration!

☐ OPTION 3: Celebration Station (up to 10 minutes)

Set out crepe paper, scissors, tape, and balloons that have been blown up and tied.

Ask the children to think about how they'd decorate the room for a special party or celebration. Then let them work together to transform the room into a colorful party area. Suggest tying crepe paper streamers to the balloons and taping them to the walls. Help children string crepe paper across the doorway and tape it in place. Encourage children to work together and be creative. Make comments such as "My, it looks festive in our room!" and "Why are we so happy?" and "What's the celebration about?" Mention that children will hear a story about a special morning when Jesus' followers knew that 🔴 Jesus is our Lord now and forever.

🔴 **The Point**

After everyone has arrived and you're ready to move on to Bible-Story Time, encourage the children to finish what they're doing and get ready to clean up.

Pick-Up Song

We Will Pick Up (up to 5 minutes)

Lead children in singing "We Will Pick Up" (track 2) with the *CD* to the tune of "London Bridge." Encourage the children to sing along as they help clean up the room.

If you want to include the names of all the children in your class, sing the song without the *CD*, and repeat the naming section. If you choose to use the *CD*, vary the names you use each week.

Sing

We will pick up all our toys,
All our toys, all our toys.
We will pick up all our toys
And put them all away.

I see (name) picking up,
Picking up, picking up.
I see (name) picking up
And putting toys away.

(Repeat)

Bible-Story Time

Setting the Stage (up to 5 minutes)

Tell the children you'll clap your hands to get their attention. Explain that when you clap, children are to stop what they're doing, raise their hands, and focus on you. Encourage children to respond quickly so you'll have time for all the fun activities you've planned.

Before class, cut two twelve-inch streamers of crepe paper for each child.

Hand each child two streamers. Choose a couple of children to pass out the jingle bracelets made in Option 1. Say: **I'm so happy today. I feel like singing. Let's start off our time together with a fun song. While we sing, let's march and jingle our bracelets and wave our streamers.**

Join children in singing "Jesus Is Alive!" (track 6) with the *CD* to the tune of "This Old Man." Encourage children to wave their streamers and jingle their bracelets in time to the music as they march around the room.

Sing

At the tomb,	**Jesus died**
Mary stared	**For our sins.**
'Cuz our Jesus wasn't there.	**Now he's back with us again.**
He had risen!	**He has risen!**
Jump and shout, "Hooray!	**Jump and shout, "Hooray!**
Jesus is alive today!"	**Jesus is alive today!"**

After you're finished singing, ask children to remove their jingle bracelets, and set them aside until later. Have children sit in a circle with their streamers. Say: **That song was such fun—just like a party! When we're very happy about something, we celebrate.** Ask:

● **What are some special days when we have celebrations?** (Help children name holidays, such as Christmas, Easter, Thanksgiving, their birthdays, Valentine's Day, New Year's Eve, and the Fourth of July.)

Say: **Think of your favorite celebration. We'll take turns going around the circle. You can name your favorite celebration and why it's your favorite. Then tie your two streamers together.**

Continue around the circle until each child has tied his or her own streamers together. Say: **Easter is the best celebration of all! We celebrate Easter because Jesus is alive, Jesus loves us, and ◖Jesus is our Lord. I'm going to say, ◖ "Jesus is our Lord" and then tie my streamers to someone else's. Then that person can say The Point and tie his or her streamers onto another person's streamers.**

● **The Point**

Continue until all the streamers have been joined into one long strand. Say: **I'm so glad that ◖Jesus is our Lord. He followed God's plan so we could all be part of God's family, just as our streamers are part of one big streamer. Let's hang up our celebration streamer to remind us that because Jesus is risen, we can all be part of God's family.** Tape the streamer along a wall.

● **The Point**

Bible Song and Prayer Time (up to 5 minutes)

Before class, make surprise cards for this activity by cutting construction paper into two-by-six-inch strips. Prepare a surprise card for each child plus a few for visitors. Fold the cards in half, then stamp the *cross stamp* inside one of the surprise cards. Mark John 20:1-9 in the Bible you'll be using.

Have the children sit in a circle. Say: **Now it's time to choose a Bible person to bring me the Bible marked with today's Bible story. As we sing our Bible song, I'll pass out the surprise cards. Don't look inside your card until the song is over.**

Lead the children in singing "God's Book" (track 3) with the *CD* to the tune of "Old MacDonald Had a Farm." As you sing, pass out the surprise cards. If you want to include the names of all the children in your class, sing the song without the *CD,* and repeat the naming section. If you choose to use the *CD,* vary the names you use each week.

Sing

Now it's time to read God's Book
And hear a Bible story.
It's fun to be here with my
    friends
And hear a Bible story.

(Name)**'s here.**
(Name)**'s here.**
Here is (name).
Here is (name).
Now it's time to read God's Book
And hear a Bible story.

Now it's time to read God's Book
And hear a Bible story.
It's fun to be here with my
    friends
And hear a Bible story.

(Name)**'s here.**
(Name)**'s here.**
Here is (name).
Here is (name).
Now it's time to read God's Book
And hear a Bible story.

After the song, say: **You may look inside your surprise cards. The person who has the cross stamped inside his or her card will be our Bible person for today.**

Identify the Bible person, then have the rest of the children clap for him or her. Ask the Bible person to bring you the Bible. Help the Bible person open the Bible to the marked place and show the children where your story comes from. Then have the Bible person sit down.

Say: (Name) **was our special Bible person today. Each week we'll have only one special Bible person, but each one of you is a special part of our class! Today we're all learning that ⬤Jesus is our Lord.**

Let's say a special prayer now and ask God to help us learn more about Jesus. I'll pass around this basket. When the basket comes to you, put your surprise card in it and say, "God, help me know that ⬤Jesus is our Lord."

Pass around the basket or box. After you've collected everyone's surprise card, set the basket aside, and pick up the Bible. Lead children in this prayer: **God, thank you for the Bible and for all the stories in it. Teach us today that ⬤Jesus is our Lord and that he's always with us. In Jesus' name we pray, amen.**

⬤ The Point

⬤ The Point

⬤ The Point

Hear the Bible Story (up to 10 minutes)

Bring out the *Bible Big Book: Peter Tells the Easter Story* and the *CD*. Have the children gather around you.

Say: **Before we listen to another part of the Bible story, let's review the story so far. Get with a friend.** Pause. **Decide which of you will be the Actor and which will be the Answerer. I'll whisper an action to the Actor, and he or she can act it out. Then the Answerer can tell what part that action played in the story. Then switch roles with your partner.**

Use the following actions for the Actors to act out. After each turn, be sure children switch roles.

● **Tiptoe, tiptoe, follow the soldiers.** (Peter followed the soldiers and Jesus after Jesus' arrest.)

● **Shake your head "no" three times.** (Peter denied knowing Jesus three times.)

● **Crow like a rooster.** (Peter denied Jesus three times before the rooster crowed.)

● **Stand like a cross with your arms straight out at the sides.** (The cross was where Jesus died.)

Say: **What a good job of acting and answering! You're all good at re-membering, but let's see if you can remember who's telling the story in our *Bible Big Book.*** Pause while children respond.

Say: **Peter's telling the story, and he has more to tell us today.** Hold up the Bible and say: **Our Bible story comes from the book of John.** Hold up the *Bible Big Book* and say: **Our Big Book shows us pictures of the story. Our story today is about the very first Easter morning and the surpris-ing and wonderful thing that happened.** Hold the book open to pages 6 and 7 so the children can see the picture. Say: **As you look at the pictures, I want you to listen for two things. Listen for what Mary saw in the tomb and for what Peter saw in the tomb. When you know the answer, put your hands on your heart.**

Turn on the *CD* (track 7), and listen to pages 6 and 7 of *Peter Tells the Easter Story.* When you're finished, close the *Bible Big Book,* and stop the CD player.

Say: **I see you have your hands on your hearts. Can you feel your heart beating? Your heart is beating because you're alive. And Jesus' heart was beating because he was alive again!** Ask:

● **What did Mary see at the tomb?** (An angel; she didn't find Jesus; she saw the stone rolled away from the tomb.)

● **How did Mary feel when she saw the empty tomb?** (Surprised; scared; happy that Jesus was alive.)

● **Why did Mary run to the disciples?** (She wanted to tell them the good news; she wanted to show them that Jesus had risen.)

● **What did Peter see?** (He saw cloth; he didn't see Jesus, but he saw the stone rolled away.)

Say: **When Mary saw that Jesus had risen, she ran to share the good news with Peter. You can share the good news that Jesus is alive too.** Ask:

● **Who would you like to tell that Jesus is alive?** (My neighbor; my friend at kindergarten; my Aunt Alice.)

Say: **Mary and Peter and Jesus' other friends were so happy when they found out Jesus had risen from the dead. Then they remembered how Jesus told them he'd be with them forever. When Peter realized Jesus was alive, he wondered if Jesus would forgive him.** Ask:

● **Do you remember why Peter needed to be forgiven?** (He said he didn't know Jesus.)

● **The Point**

Say: **Next week we'll find out how Jesus forgave Peter. I'm excited to find out what happens next, aren't you? I know that ◐ Jesus is our Lord, and I know that Jesus is alive! That's why we're celebrating today. Let's act out the Bible story to help us remember that first Easter morning.**

Do the Bible Story (up to 10 minutes)

As you read this interactive version of the Bible story, encourage the children to do the motions with you.

Jesus had been dead for three days. (*Softly make crying motions.*)
Then early on the third morning (*yawn and stretch*),
When the sun was barely up (*rub your eyes sleepily*),
Mary walked (*pat your knees in a slow, steady rhythm*)
Down to the garden to Jesus' tomb. (*Continue to pat your knees.*)
Little birds sang (*whistle or say "tweet-tweet" and flap your arms*),
And the wind whispered in the trees. (*Blow softly.*)
Mary wondered (*scratch your head*),
"How will I move the big stone?" (*Make a big circle with your arms.*)
But the stone was gone! (*Point and look surprised.*)
Mary looked into the tomb. (*Make peeking motions.*)
"Oh!" said Mary. (*Lay your hand by your cheek.*)
"Jesus isn't here!" (*Raise your hands in surprise.*)
Then a bright light appeared (*shield your eyes*),
And an angel spoke to Mary. (*Put your hands on your heart.*)
"Jesus is alive!" (*Clap your hands.*)
Mary ran quickly home. (*Pat your knees quickly.*)
She told the disciples the good news. (*Point back toward the tomb.*)
The disciples ran to see for themselves. (*Pat your knees quickly.*)
They peeked inside the tomb. (*Cup your hands around your eyes.*)
He's risen! (*Raise your hands above your head.*)
He's risen! (*Raise your hands above your head.*)
Jesus is alive! (*Clap.*)
And ◐ Jesus is our Lord! (*Shout "hooray!"*)

● **The Point**

Say: **On that first Easter morning, an angel told Mary that ◐ Jesus is our Lord and that Jesus is alive. She wanted to share that good news with the other disciples. Let's share the good news with Pockets!**

Practicing The Point

It's What's Inside That Counts (up to 5 minutes)

Before class, place the following items in a large plastic egg: a cross, a small stone, the number three on a square of paper, and a paper or candy heart. Place a pretty Easter egg in Pockets' pouch.

Bring out Pockets the Kangaroo. Go through the following script. After you finish the script, put Pockets away and out of sight.

It's What's Inside That Counts

PUPPET SCRIPT

Pockets: *(Sadly)* Hi, everyone. Happy Easter time.

Teacher: You don't seem very happy, Pockets. But you do have a pretty egg.

Pockets: *(Sighing)* It's pretty. But I see all of you smiling and happy, and I don't feel that way. I have an Easter egg—I'm s'posed to be happy, aren't I?

Teacher: Well, Pockets, maybe it's because you don't know what Easter is really about. Children, can you share the Bible story we heard today and help Pockets learn what Easter's all about? We'll use this special egg to help. I'll hand you things from inside the egg to help tell the story. *(Choose two children to help you open the egg. Hold up the cross, and have children tell that Jesus died on a cross. Hold up the number three, and let children tell how Jesus had been dead for three days in the tomb. Hold up the stone, and have them tell about Mary seeing the stone rolled away and the angel proclaiming, "Jesus is alive." Hold up the heart, and have children tell that Jesus is alive and that he'll always be with us.)* See, Pockets? The real meaning of Easter is the fact that Jesus is risen and he's alive! <u>That's</u> why we're happy. The joy of Easter isn't in your Easter egg; it's in knowing Jesus rose from the tomb!

Pockets: *(Patting her egg)* Just like a chick comes out of an egg?

Teacher: Almost, Pockets. ✏ Jesus is our Lord, and Jesus died because he wanted us to be forgiven for the wrong things we do so we can be friends with God. And when we ask Jesus to live in our hearts, he'll be with us forever! <u>That's</u> the joy of Easter!

Pockets: *(Excited and hopping up and down.)* I <u>am</u> happy now! Jesus is alive, and I feel like celebrating! Thanks, everyone, for teaching me what Easter's really about! 'Bye!

⚫ **The Point**

TODAY I LEARNED . . .

We believe that Christian education extends beyond the classroom into the home. Photocopy the "Today I Learned..." handout (p. 70) for this week, and send it home with your children. Encourage parents to use the handout to plan meaningful family activities to reinforce this week's topic. Follow up the "Today I Learned..." activities next week by asking children what their families did.

Closing

Jesus Is Alive! (up to 5 minutes)

The Point

The Point

Have children put on their jingle bracelets.

Say: **We've been learning that** **Jesus is our Lord. And we've been celebrating the fact that Jesus is alive. Let's get our celebration streamer and tape it in a big circle.** Have children help hold the streamer and tape the ends together. Say: **Find a place to hold the streamer. We're standing in a circle that surrounds us just as Jesus' love surrounds us. Jesus' love was so great that he died for us. Jesus took our sins away and helped us be God's friends again. When we pray and ask Jesus to live in our hearts, we'll be with him forever. Let's pray and thank God that Jesus is alive.**

Pray: **Dear God, we thank you that Jesus is alive. We're so happy to know that Jesus is our Lord. Thank you. In Jesus' name, amen.**

Now let's take turns going around our circle of love. Say, "Jesus is always with you" to the person on your left. Have one child at a time repeat the sentence. When the message has traveled around the circle, say: **Don't you feel like celebrating? Let's end our time together with our celebration song. While we sing, hold the celebration streamer and walk around in our circle of love.**

Lead the children in singing "Jesus Is Alive!" (track 6) with the *CD* to the tune of "This Old Man." Encourage them to jangle their jingle bracelets as they hold the streamer and sing.

Sing

At the tomb,	Jesus died
Mary stared	For our sins.
'Cuz our Jesus wasn't there.	Now he's back with us again.
He had risen!	He has risen!
Jump and shout, "Hooray!	Jump and shout, "Hooray!
Jesus is alive today!"	Jesus is alive today!"

The Point

Say: **Jesus is alive, and he's with us forever. What a celebration! Wear your jingle bracelets home, and each time they ring, remember that Jesus is our Lord and that he's alive!**

For Extra Time

If you have a long class time or want to add additional elements to your lesson, try one of the following activities.

LIVELY LEARNING: Push That Stone!

You'll need two medium-sized boxes for this game. Form two groups with the children, and hand each group a box. Have a child from each group sit in the box. When you clap, the rest of the group will push the "stone" to the other end of the room. Then have another child trade places with the child in the box. After everyone's had a turn to sit in a box and be pushed, ask children questions such as "Who rolled the stone away from Jesus' tomb?" and "Why couldn't a heavy stone stop Jesus from rising from the tomb?" Remind children that ⬤ Jesus is our Lord and that we can celebrate the fact that Jesus is alive today.

The Point

MAKE TO TAKE: Stone Paperweight

Before this activity, collect a smooth, medium-sized stone for each child to paint.

Set out tempera or acrylic paints, paintbrushes, water, and a fine-tipped permanent marker. Hand each child a stone. Let children paint their stones and then blow on them to help them dry. When the stones are dry, use the marker to help children write, "Jesus is alive!" on their stones. As children paint, explain that the stone is a paperweight; also remind them that ⬤ Jesus is our Lord and that the stone was rolled away from his tomb. Remind them that Jesus is alive and that's why we celebrate Easter.

The Point

TREAT TO EAT: Easter Butterflies

Let children make delicious celebration snacks. Set out butterfly-shaped crackers, canned icing, plastic knives, and a candy gummy worm (caterpillar) for each child. Let children frost their butterflies and then lay a gummy caterpillar down the center. Point out how caterpillars wrap themselves in cocoons before they turn to butterflies just as Jesus laid in the tomb before he rose. Remind them that ⬤ Jesus is our Lord and that he's alive, and that's why we celebrate Easter.

The Point

STORY PICTURE: Jesus Is Alive!

Before this activity, crumple a sheet of construction paper, then smooth it out. Cut a three-inch round "stone" from the crumpled paper for each child.

Hand each child a photocopy of the "Today I Learned..." handout from page 70. Set out crayons and a paper fastener for each child. Have children color the picture. Help them attach the stone to the tomb by poking the paper fastener through the edge of the stone and through the dot on the picture. Let children "roll" the stone away from the tomb. Remind them that ⬤ Jesus is our Lord and that he's alive and with us forever.

The Point

TODAY I LEARNED...

The Point ✏️ Jesus is our Lord.

Today your child learned that Jesus is our Lord. Children learned that Jesus is alive and with us all the time. They talked about the fact that Jesus died so we could be God's friends.

Verse to Learn

"And every tongue confess that Jesus Christ is Lord" (Philippians 2:11a).

Ask Me...

● What happened that first Easter morning?
● Why did Jesus die for you?
● What are ways our family can tell others that Jesus is alive?

Family Fun

● Take a walk with your child, and have him or her choose a pretty stone along the way. Set the stone in the center of your table as a reminder of the stone that was rolled away on the first Easter morning.
● Fill a plastic egg with a cross, a stone, a paper heart, and a number three written on a small square of paper. Let your child open the egg and tell you the story of Easter using the items inside.

Jesus Is Alive! (John 20:1-9)

I'm Forgiven!

The Bible Basis

John 21:4-17. Jesus appears to his followers and demonstrates his love and forgiveness to Peter.

Jesus' disciples must have been puzzled after they discovered that the stone at the tomb had been rolled away and that Jesus' body was nowhere to be found. Could Jesus truly be risen as the angel said? And if Jesus *was* alive, where was he? The disciples didn't need to look far; Jesus came to them. In fact, he appeared to his followers several times. John records that early one morning when the disciples were hungry and frustrated from poor fishing, a man on the shore told them to toss their nets on the other side of the boat. When they did, their nets suddenly overflowed with a great catch. The disciples hurried to shore, realizing that the man who was cooking fish for their breakfast was none other than Jesus himself. Three times Jesus turned to Peter and asked, "Peter, do you love me?" And purging each denial he'd made earlier, Peter affirmed his love for Jesus three times. Jesus followed each confession of love with the charge to care for his sheep. Jesus' commands were Peter's confirmation that he'd been forgiven and reinstated. With a jubilant sense of relief and release, Peter felt the mercy and forgiveness only Jesus can give.

Kindergartners often need reassurance that they're still loved after they do or say something wrong. Offering forgiveness is a loving way to reassure young children that the "slate is clean" and that it's time for a fresh, new start. It's important for children to know that we all do and say wrong things and that Jesus is willing to forgive us as readily as he forgave Peter. Use this lesson to help children understand that Jesus is a loving Lord who freely offers forgiveness when we ask.

Getting The Point

⬤ Jesus is our Lord.

It's important to say The Point just as it's written in each activity. Repeating The Point again and again will help the children remember it and apply it to their lives.

Children will
● know that Jesus forgave Peter,
● discover that Jesus forgives them,
● help Pockets learn that forgiveness is important, and
● understand that Jesus wants us to care for others.

⬤ The Point

This Lesson at a Glance

Before the lesson, collect the necessary items for the activities you plan to use. Refer to the Classroom Supplies and Learning Lab Supplies columns to determine what you'll need. Remember to make photocopies of the "Today I Learned..." handout (p. 82) to send home with your children.

Section	Minutes	What Children Will Do	Classroom Supplies	Learning Lab Supplies
Welcome Time	up to 5	**Welcome!**—Receive name tags and be greeted by the teacher.	"Cross Name Tags" handouts (p. 30), markers, pins or tape	
Let's Get Started Direct children to one or more of the Let's Get Started activities until everyone arrives.	up to 10	**Option 1: Fishing Buddies**—Fish with a partner for an unusual catch.	Construction paper, scissors, yarn, straws, tape, paper clips, magnets, box, marker	
	up to 10	**Option 2: Toes in the Sand**—Use their toes and fingers to create story pictures in damp sand.	Damp sand, cookie sheets, newspaper	
	up to 10	**Option 3: Tuna Treats**—Help each other make tuna treats to enjoy.	Bread, tuna salad, plastic knives, paper plates, heart-shaped cookie cutter, plastic wrap, bowl	
Pick-Up Song	up to 5	**We Will Pick Up**—Sing a song as they pick up toys and gather for Bible-Story Time.	CD player	CD: "We Will Pick Up" (track 2)
Bible-Story Time	up to 5	**Setting the Stage**—Mend broken cups and learn about forgiveness.	Paper cups, scissors, tape	
	up to 5	**Bible Song and Prayer Time**—Sing a song, bring out the Bible, and pray together.	Bible, construction paper, scissors, basket or box, CD player	CD: "God's Book" (track 3), cross stamp and ink pad
	up to 10	**Hear the Bible Story**—Review the Easter story and learn from John 21:4-17 how Jesus forgave Peter.	CD player	*Bible Big Book: Peter Tells the Easter Story,* CD: "Peter Tells the Easter Story, Part III" (track 8)
	up to 10	**Do the Bible Story**—Play a game and be the Fish or the Fisherman.	Bedsheet	
Practicing The Point	up to 5	**Forgiving Friends**—Help Pockets understand that forgiving someone is part of caring for them.	Pockets the Kangaroo, sunglasses	
Closing	up to 5	**ForG-I-V-E**—Sing a song and say a prayer.	CD player	CD: "G-I-V-E" (track 9)
For Extra Time		For extra-time ideas and supplies, see page 81.		

Jesus is our Lord.

Welcome Time

Welcome! (up to 5 minutes)

- Bend down and make eye contact with children as they arrive.
- Greet each child individually with an enthusiastic smile.
- Thank each child for coming to class today.
- As children arrive, ask them about last week's "Today I Learned…" discussion. Use questions such as "Who did you tell about Jesus?" and "Do you think Jesus will forgive Peter? Explain."
- Say: **Today we're going to learn that ✎ Jesus is our Lord.**
- Hand out the cross name tags children made during Lesson 1, and help them attach the name tags to their clothing. If some of the name tags were damaged or if some of the children weren't in class that week, have them make new name tags using the photocopiable handout on page 30.
- Direct children to the Let's Get Started activities you've set up.

✎ **The Point**

Let's Get Started

Set up one or more of the following activities for children to do as they arrive. After you greet each child, invite him or her to choose an activity.

Circulate among the children to offer help as needed and to direct their conversation toward today's lesson. Ask questions such as "Have you ever forgiven anyone?" or "When's a time someone forgave you?"

OPTION 1: Fishing Buddies (up to 10 minutes)

Before class, cut ten simple fish shapes from construction paper. Draw sad faces on five fish and smiley faces on the other five. Slide a paper clip onto each fish. Make a simple fishing pole by taping the end of an eight-inch piece of yarn to a drinking straw. Tape a small refrigerator magnet to the other end of the yarn.

Place the fish in a large box or bucket in one corner of the room. As children arrive, point out the fishing pond. Invite children to find a fishing buddy. Have partners take turns using a fishing pole to catch a fish. (The magnet "hook" will stick to the paper clips on the fish.) If a child catches a sad fish, the child should tell when another person made him or her sad. If a child catches a smiley fish, the child should tell about a time someone helped him or her feel better. Tell children they'll hear a story today about a fisherman who felt better because Jesus forgave him.

✔ A super-fast way to cut multiple shapes is to fold your paper three or four times, then trace a shape on the top. When you cut along the outline, you'll be cutting three or four shapes simultaneously.

OPTION 2: Toes in the Sand (up to 10 minutes)

Spread newspaper on the floor. Pour damp sand into cookie sheets or baking pans, and set them on the newspaper. As children arrive, tell them they'll be making pictures in the sand to help tell the Easter story. Let each child remove a shoe and a sock and take turns drawing crosses, hearts, roosters, and stones in the sand with their toes or fingers. As they draw, ask story questions such as "What part did a rooster play in the Easter story?" and "How is a heart of love part of the Easter story?"

Tell children they'll hear a story that happened on a sandy beach after Jesus helped his disciples catch fish one special morning. Then show the children how to draw a simple Christian fish in the sand. Explain that ● Jesus is our Lord and that his followers had a special way of telling each other they loved Jesus. They drew fish in the sand to show they followed Jesus. Encourage the children to draw simple Christian fish in the damp sand along with other story pictures.

● **The Point**

OPTION 3: Tuna Treats (up to 10 minutes)

Before class, prepare a bowl of simple tuna fish salad using drained tuna and mayonnaise. Cover the bowl, and keep it well-chilled until class time.

Set out tuna salad, bread, plastic knives, a heart-shaped cookie cutter, and paper plates. Let children work cooperatively to make snacks to share. Have some children cut heart shapes from bread. A couple of children can spread tuna salad on the hearts. Other children can arrange the treats on paper plates.

As children work, ask questions such as "What's your favorite food for breakfast?" and "Would you eat fish for breakfast? Why or why not?" Tell children they'll learn that ● Jesus is our Lord and that they'll hear about a time Jesus prepared a special breakfast for his disciples.

● **The Point**

Be sure children make a tuna treat for each person in the class. Cover the treats with plastic wrap, and set them aside for the "Hear the Bible Story" activity.

✔ When you're making food projects that contain mayonnaise, be sure the treat is eaten within one hour of preparation unless you have access to a refrigerator.

✔ If you don't choose Option 3, make a small tuna sandwich for each child before class.

After everyone has arrived and you're ready to move on to Bible-Story Time, encourage the children to finish what they're doing and get ready to clean up.

Pick-Up Song

We Will Pick Up (up to 5 minutes)

Lead children in singing "We Will Pick Up" (track 2) with the *CD* to the tune of "London Bridge." Encourage the children to sing along as they help clean up the room.

If you want to include the names of all the children in your class, sing the song without the *CD*, and repeat the naming section. If you choose to use the *CD*, vary the names you use each week.

Sing

We will pick up all our toys,
All our toys, all our toys.
We will pick up all our toys
And put them all away.

I see (name) **picking up,**
Picking up, picking up.
I see (name) **picking up**
And putting toys away.

(Repeat)

Bible-Story Time

Setting the Stage (up to 5 minutes)

Tell the children you'll clap your hands to get their attention. Explain that when you clap, children are to stop what they're doing, raise their hands, and focus on you. Encourage children to respond quickly so you'll have time for all the fun activities you've planned.

Before this activity, cut paper cups into three or four large pieces. Cut a cup apart for every two children, but keep the pieces from each cup together.

Help children form pairs. Say: **I'm going to give each pair a broken cup. Work together to mend the cup with tape. When you're finished, hold the cup in the air.**

Give each pair the pieces of one cup. Set tape in the center of the floor. As children work, circulate and ask questions such as "When was a time you broke something?" and "How did you feel when it was mended?"

When all the cups are in the air, say: **I'm glad to see all those mended cups. You may set them down for a moment.** Ask:

● **How did it feel to receive a broken cup?** (Funny; I wanted it whole again.)

● **Why isn't a broken cup good?** (It leaks; it doesn't work.)

● **Why is it important to mend something that's broken?** (So it's like new again; so people can use it.)

Say: **Mending something that's broken is a lot like forgiving someone when they've done something wrong. When a person does a wrong thing, he or she feels broken and bad and needs forgiveness to feel good and new again.** Ask:

● **Who can tell about a time when you were forgiven after you broke something or did something wrong? How did you feel?** Allow time for

Jesus is our Lord.

children to tell about their experiences.

Say: **Peter did a wrong thing when he lied and said he didn't know Jesus.** Ask:

● **How do you think Peter felt after denying Jesus?** (Bad; he was ashamed; he felt awful.)

● The Point

Say: **Peter's heart was broken because he'd done something wrong. Peter knew that ● Jesus is our Lord and yet he said he didn't know Jesus.** Ask:

● **How could Peter feel better?** (Ask Jesus' forgiveness; to be forgiven.)

Say: **Peter needs someone to forgive him and mend his heart just as you mended the broken cups. Our Bible story is about forgiveness. Let's hear what happened.**

Bible Song and Prayer Time (up to 5 minutes)

Before class, make surprise cards for this activity by cutting construction paper into two-by-six-inch strips. Prepare a surprise card for each child plus a few extras for visitors. Fold the cards in half, then stamp the *cross stamp* inside one of the surprise cards. Mark John 21:4-17 in the Bible you'll be using.

Have the children sit in a circle. Say: **Now it's time to choose a Bible person to bring me the Bible marked with today's Bible story. As we sing our Bible song, I'll pass out the surprise cards. Don't look inside your card until the song is over.**

Lead the children in singing "God's Book" (track 3) with the *CD* to the tune of "Old MacDonald Had a Farm." As you sing, pass out the surprise cards. If you want to include the names of all the children in your class, sing the song without the *CD,* and repeat the naming section. If you choose to use the *CD,* vary the names you use each week.

Sing

Now it's time to read God's Book
And hear a Bible story.
It's fun to be here with my
    friends
And hear a Bible story.

(Name)**'s here.**
(Name)**'s here.**
Here is (name).
Here is (name).
Now it's time to read God's Book
And hear a Bible story.

Now it's time to read God's Book
And hear a Bible story.
It's fun to be here with my
    friends
And hear a Bible story.

(Name)**'s here.**
(Name)**'s here.**
Here is (name).
Here is (name).
Now it's time to read God's Book
And hear a Bible story.

After the song, say: **You may look inside your surprise cards. The person who has the cross stamped inside his or her card will be our Bible person for today.**

Identify the Bible person, then have the rest of the children clap for him or her. Ask the Bible person to bring you the Bible. Help the Bible person open the Bible to the marked place and show the children where your story comes from. Then have the Bible person sit down.

Say: (Name) **was our special Bible person today. Each week, we'll have** only one special Bible person, but each one of you is a special part of our class! Today we're all learning that Jesus is our Lord.

● The Point

Let's say a special prayer now and ask God to help us learn more about Jesus. I'll pass around this basket. When the basket comes to you, put your surprise card in it and say, "God, please help me remember that ●Jesus is our Lord."

● The Point

Pass around the basket or box. After you've collected everyone's surprise card, set the basket aside, and pick up the Bible. Lead the children in this prayer: **God, thank you for the Bible and for all the stories in it. Teach us today that ●Jesus is our Lord and that he always forgives us. In Jesus' name we pray, amen.**

● The Point

Hear the Bible Story (up to 10 minutes)

Bring out the *Bible Big Book: Peter Tells the Easter Story* and the *CD*. Hold up the Big Book and say: **We've been learning that ●Jesus is our Lord. Today we'll hear the last part of the Easter story, but first let's play a review game. I'll ask a story question. If you know the answer, clap your hands two times. I'll call on someone to answer and another person to find the picture that tells about that part of the story. Ready?**

● The Point

Use the following questions. Allow the children who locate the story picture to hold up the Big Book so everyone can see the picture.

● **Why did Jesus wash his followers' feet?** (Page 1, because Jesus wanted to teach us about serving each other.)

● **What did Jesus do in the garden?** (Page 2, Jesus prayed.)

● **How did Jesus know he'd be arrested by soldiers?** (Page 3, God told him; he's our Lord and knows everything.)

● **What did Peter do three times?** (Page 4, he said he didn't know Jesus.)

● **Why did Jesus die on the cross?** (Page 5, it was God's plan; Jesus died for us because he loved us; Jesus died to take away our sins.)

● **What happened when Mary went to the tomb?** (Pages 6-7, she found an angel; she talked to an angel; Jesus wasn't there; the stone was rolled away.)

● **What did Peter find at the tomb?** (Pages 6-7, Peter found cloth but not Jesus; an empty tomb.)

● **Which picture shows the first Easter morning? What happened that morning?** (Pages 6-7, Easter is when Jesus wasn't dead anymore; Jesus had risen; Jesus wasn't in the tomb anymore.)

Close the Big Book. Say: **Good job. Well, last time together we learned that ●Jesus is our Lord and that he had risen from the dead. Jesus is alive! But Peter was worried.** Ask:

● The Point

● **Why was Peter worried?** (He didn't think Jesus would forgive him; he felt bad because he denied Jesus; he was afraid Jesus didn't love him anymore.)

● **How would it feel to know that Jesus was alive but you'd lied about him?** (It'd feel awful; I'd want to say, "I'm sorry"; I wouldn't want to see him because I'd be scared.)

Say: **Let's listen to the last part of "Peter Tells the Easter Story."**

Hand each child a tuna treat from Option 3. When each child has a treat, say: **We can share a fish breakfast with Jesus and the disciples. When**

the story tells about fish for breakfast, quietly nibble your treats. Then listen carefully to the rest of the story.

Open the *Bible Big Book* to page 8, and hold it up so children can see the story picture. Play the *CD,* and listen to "Peter Tells the Easter Story, Part III" (track 8). When you're done, turn off the CD player.

Close the Big Book and ask:

● **Why did Jesus help his disciples catch fish?** (He wanted them to know he was Jesus; he wanted to help them.)

● **How do you think the disciples felt when they realized it was Jesus?** (Surprised; they were happy to see Jesus again.)

● **What question did Jesus ask Peter three times?** (Do you love me?)

● **Why did Jesus ask Peter the same thing three times?** (To make sure Peter meant it; because Peter had denied Jesus three times.)

● **Do you think Peter was honest when he said, "I love you, Lord"? Why or why not?** (Yes, Peter learned not to lie about Jesus; yes, Peter always loved Jesus.)

● **Why did Jesus forgive Peter?** (Because Jesus loved Peter; because Jesus forgives us when we do wrong things.)

● **How did Peter feel by the end of the story?** (Happy that Jesus still loved him; glad that Jesus forgave him; happy that Jesus wanted him to care for others.)

● **The Point**

Say: **When Jesus asked Peter to care for his sheep, Jesus meant for Peter to care for Jesus' followers. ●Jesus is our Lord. He wants us to care for others and tell all about him. Just as Jesus fed and cared for his followers by helping them catch fish, we can help care for others every day.** Ask:

● **How can we care for others?** (By helping; by telling them about Jesus; by offering food or money or clothing.)

● **The Point**

Say: ●**Jesus is our Lord, and he came to love us and forgive us and teach us how to love others. When we care for others as Jesus did, we spread his love. Isn't it great to be forgiven and loved by Jesus?**

Do the Bible Story (up to 10 minutes)

Spread a bedsheet in the center of the floor as a fishing net. Gather children at one end of the room. Say: **This fun game will remind us how Jesus fed his disciples by helping them catch fish when they were hungry. We'll need a Fisherman to stand on the far side of the fishing net. The rest of you will be Fish. The Fisherman will call out a color. If you're wearing that color, "swim" across the net to the other side of the room. If you're tagged by the Fisherman as you swim out of the net, you're caught. Then you may join the Fisherman and help catch Fish.**

Continue playing until all the Fish have been caught. If there's time, play with two other Fishermen. When you're finished, say: **Now swim to the net and find a place to sit.** Pause for children to sit down. Ask:

● **Why did Jesus feed his disciples?** (He wanted to show that he cared for them; he wanted to help them because they were hungry.)

● **What did Jesus ask Peter to do?** (Feed my sheep; care for his sheep.)

Say: **Jesus asked Peter to care for his sheep. Jesus wants us to care for people, too.** Ask:

● **How can we care for others?** (By feeding them if they're hungry; by being kind and helpful; by giving money; by praying.)

Say: **It's important to know that**  **Jesus is our Lord and that we can care for others as Jesus cared. When we know we're loved and forgiven, we want to spread Jesus' love to others.**

🖊 **The Point**

Practicing The Point

Forgiving Friends (up to 5 minutes)

Before this activity, put a pair of sunglasses on Pockets.

Take out Pockets the Kangaroo, and go through the following script. After you finish the script, put Pockets away and out of sight.

Forgiving Friends

PUPPET SCRIPT

Pockets: *(Looks all around—over teacher's shoulder, under the table, behind a child's ear.)*

Teacher: Pockets, is that you? Is something lost?

Pockets: *(Still searching)* No, I just don't want to be <u>found!</u>

Teacher: What do you mean? Are you playing a game of Hide-and-Seek with someone?

Pockets: Sort of—I'm trying to hide from Pointer, but I don't think Pointer wants to find me anyway.

Teacher: Why are you hiding from your best friend?

Pockets: Well . . . *(Stops searching and hangs her head.)* I got mad at Pointer yesterday for spilling my milk, and I called him a "goosey-goose." *(Excitedly making excuse)* I didn't mean to say it; I was just mad. Now Pointer's probably mad at me and won't want to be friends.

Teacher: Today we heard a story about how Jesus forgave Peter for something that Peter said. Children, can you tell Pockets about the time Jesus forgave Peter? *(Allow children time to tell the Bible story in their own words.)* You see, Pockets, sometimes we say or do things we don't mean. That's when we need to be forgiven. And we want to forgive others when they do something wrong, too. Then we can show that we still care about them. Jesus loved and forgave Peter, even when Peter told an awful lie. I'm sure Pointer will forgive you, too.

Pockets: Boys and girls, do you think Pointer will forgive me if I ask him to forgive me? *(Allow children to respond.)* Guess I won't need these glasses then. I want to get <u>found!</u> I'm so glad that 🖊 Jesus is our Lord and that he wants us to forgive and care for each other! I'm going to find Pointer! 'Bye, kids!

🖊 **The Point**

TODAY I LEARNED...

We believe that Christian education extends beyond the classroom into the home. Photocopy the "Today I Learned..." handout (p. 82) for this week, and send it home with your children. Encourage parents to use the handout to plan meaningful family activities to reinforce this week's topic. Follow up the "Today I Learned..." activities next week by asking children what their families did.

Closing

ForG-I-V-E (up to 5 minutes)

● **The Point**

Say: ● **Jesus is our Lord, and just as Jesus forgave Peter, Jesus is willing to forgive us. And when we're forgiven, we can start giving love to others. Peter couldn't help others when he felt so bad after denying he knew Jesus. But when Jesus forgave Peter, Peter could give love to others. Let's sing a song about putting the "give" back in the word "forgive."**

Lead children in singing "G-I-V-E" (track 9) with the *CD* to the tune of "Old MacDonald."

Sing

Put the g-i-v-e back	Put the g-i-v-e back
Into the word "forgive."	Into the word "forgive."
That's the way my Jesus wants	That's the way my Jesus wants
M-e, me, to live.	M-e, me, to live.
I will care.	I will care.
I will share.	I will share.
Spread his love	Spread his love
Everywhere!	Everywhere!
Put the g-i-v-e back	Put the g-i-v-e back
Into the word "forgive."	Into the word "forgive."

● **The Point**

Say: **It's wonderful to be forgiven! Jesus is willing to forgive us just as he forgave Peter. Let's thank Jesus for that.** Pray: **Dear God, thank you that ●Jesus is Lord and that he forgave Peter. Thank you for being willing to forgive the wrong things we do. We want to be forgiven so we can care for others just as Peter did. In Jesus' name we pray, amen.**

For Extra Time

If you have a long class time or want to add additional elements to your lesson, try one of the following activities.

LIVELY LEARNING: *Bible Big Book* Listening Center

Let your children enjoy listening to the *Bible Big Book* story. Set the *Bible Big Book* and the CD player in a corner of the room. Choose one child to be the Book-Holder and one to be the Page-Turner. Assure the other children that they'll have chances to be helpers another time. (You may wish to keep a record of the children who've been the Holder and Page-Turner.) Be sure to tell children to listen for the sound of the chime and to turn the page when they hear it. The complete version of "Peter Tells the Easter Story" is track 10 on the *CD*.

MAKE TO TAKE: Sand Painting

Before this activity, cut one six-by-six-inch poster board square for each child. Cover a table with newspaper. Set out glue, sand, and crayons. Hand each child a poster board square. Show children how to draw a simple fish shape. Let each child draw a fish outline on his or her paper, trace along the fish outline with glue, then sprinkle sand on the glue. Shake excess sand onto newspaper.

As children work, tell them how Jesus' followers often used the sign of a fish to tell other followers that ⬤ Jesus is our Lord.

⬤ **The Point**

TREAT TO EAT: Fishy Snacks

Pour fish-shaped crackers into a large fishbowl. Provide a small measuring cup as a scoop. Hand each child a plastic sandwich bag, and let children go fishing with the scoop (one scoop of crackers per child). As the children eat their treats, remind them that ⬤ Jesus is our Lord and that Jesus and his followers often ate fish for breakfast. Take turns creating humorous recipes for fishy breakfast foods, such as scrambled fish, fish cereal with milk and sugar, and fried fish with blueberry syrup.

⬤ **The Point**

STORY PICTURE: Jesus Forgives Peter

Hand each child a photocopy of the "Today I Learned..." handout from page 82. Set out red, yellow, and orange tissue paper or construction paper. Let children glue paper flames to the fire. Ask children if any of them have eaten fish for breakfast. Remind them that ⬤ Jesus is our Lord and that he cared for his disciples when he helped them catch fish.

⬤ **The Point**

TODAY I LEARNED...

The Point ✏ Jesus is our Lord.

Today your child learned that Jesus is our Lord. Children learned how Jesus forgave Peter and asked him to care for the people Jesus loved. They talked about how we can be forgiven and then move on to care for others as Peter did.

Verse to Learn

"And every tongue confess that Jesus Christ is Lord" (Philippians 2:11a).

Ask Me...

● What did Jesus ask Peter three times?
● How can you care for others?
● How can our family thank Jesus for his forgiveness?

Family Fun

● Let your child experience caring for others in a firsthand way. Decorate a large box with construction paper and markers. Work with your child to create a list of items needed around the house, such as cleaning supplies, paper products, soap, and toothpaste. Gather as many of the items on your list as possible. Donate the box to a county rest home or homeless shelter. Talk about how Jesus asked Peter to care for others and how we can care for others, too.

Jesus Forgives Peter (John 21:4-17)

Permission to photocopy this handout from Group's Hands-On Bible Curriculum™ for Pre-K & K granted for local church use. Copyright © Group Publishing, Inc., P.O. Box 481, Loveland, CO 80539.

Jesus Helps Us Follow Him

The events following Jesus' resurrection demonstrate how completely God enables us to follow our Lord. Through the stories of Thomas and the two followers on the road to Emmaus, we learn that Jesus helps us follow him when we're confused or doubtful. At his ascension, Jesus commissioned his followers, then and now, to put their faith into action and teach the world about him. The story of Pentecost dramatically demonstrates how the Holy Spirit enables, teaches, and guides Jesus' followers as they carry out that great commission.

When a path is strewn with questions and doubts, most of us would choose not to travel that path. Though most kindergartners are quite trusting, they're also curious and have many questions. Jesus wants children to know he's cleared the way for them to follow through the guidance of the Holy Spirit. The lessons in this module will help children understand that Jesus helps us follow him all the time.

Four Lessons on How Jesus Helps Us Follow Him

	Page	Point	Bible Basis
Lesson 6 **The Road to Emmaus**	89	Jesus helps us follow him when we don't understand.	Luke 24:13-35
Lesson 7 **Thomas Believes**	101	Jesus helps us follow him when we have questions.	John 20:24-29
Lesson 8 **Heaven Bound**	113	Jesus helps us follow him.	Matthew 28:16-20; Acts 1:6-11
Lesson 9 **Pentecost Praise**	127	Jesus helps us follow him by giving us the Holy Spirit.	Acts 2:1-13, 38-41

Time Stretchers

"I'm Going to Emmaus"

Children will enjoy this memory game. Form a circle, and hand a child a small suitcase or backpack. Have the child say, "I'm going to Emmaus and I'll take (the name of a favorite toy, food, animal, or object)." The child then passes the suitcase to the next person who repeats what's been said and adds an item of his or her own. Continue until you've traveled all the way around the circle. Mention that two friends of Jesus, who were traveling on the road to Emmaus, met another traveler who surprised them.

Follow Me Along the Way

Before this activity, use masking tape to make a path on the floor. Make sure it's an interesting path that curves and winds around the room. Tell kids you'll play a game like Follow the Leader, only they must stay on the path as they follow. Choose a child to be the leader. Encourage him or her to move along the path in unusual ways such as hopping or crawling or walking backward. Switch leaders often so each child has a turn to be the leader. Tell children they'll hear a story about two of Jesus' followers who were traveling on a road. Explain that they met an amazing man who followed them to Emmaus.

Remembering God's Word

Each four- and five-week module focuses on a key Bible verse. The key verse for this module is "Believe in the Lord Jesus, and you will be saved—you and your household" (Acts 16:31).

This module's key verse will teach children that believing in Jesus is important and that when we believe, Jesus helps us follow him. Have fun using these ideas any time during the lessons on following Jesus.

Believe It or Not . . .

Before this activity, tape a sheet of paper with the words "I Believe It" on one wall. Tape a second sheet of paper with the word "Not!" to the opposite wall.

Read Acts 16:31 aloud from an easy-to-understand Bible translation. Ask:
● **What does it mean to believe in something?** (To know that it's true; to have faith.)
● **What things do you believe about Jesus?** (That he's powerful; that he's God's Son; that he died for my sins.)

Say: **Jesus wants us to believe that he's God's Son, that he loves us, and that he died for our sins. Let's play a game about believing to understand what that means.**

Have children sit in the center of the room. Choose a child to tell the class something he or she can do, such as balancing a book on his or her finger or hopping backward on one foot. The child then says, "Believe it or not." Children choose whether they believe the person can really do what he or

84 ● Introduction

she said. Have them stand by the paper that tells whether they believe or don't believe. Then let the child show if he or she can do the action. Continue until each child gets to tell something he or she can do. Explain that one of Jesus' disciples had a hard time believing Jesus was alive until he saw Jesus for himself.

Our House

Read the key verse (Acts 16:31) aloud. Ask:
● **What does Jesus save us from?** (Sin; bad things; being alone.)
● **Who are the people in your house?** (My mom; my dad; my brothers and sisters.)

Say: **When we believe that Jesus is God's Son, Jesus takes away the bad things we've done. Jesus wants everyone in our families to believe in him, too.**

Make copies of the "Our House" handout from page 87. Give each pair of children a copy of the handout. Set out tape, scissors, and crayons or markers. Encourage children to take turns cutting on dotted lines so that the door and the windows will open. Then have children fold the house in half and tape the edge. Fold open the door and windows. Partners take turns repeating the key verse to each other. Each time children repeat the verse, they draw a member of their family in a window or door. Continue until each child has drawn all of his or her family members. Draw family members outside the house if you run out of windows and doors. Make extra copies of the handout so both partners can create a house.

Story Enhancements

Make Bible stories come alive in your classroom by bringing in Bible costumes, by setting out sensory items that fit with the story, or by creating bulletin boards to stimulate interest. When children learn with their five senses as well as with their hearts and minds, lessons come alive and children remember them. Each week, bring in one or more of the following items to help motivate and involve children in the Bible lessons they'll be learning. The following ideas will help get you started.

Module Bulletin Board

Before class, cover the bottom third of a bulletin board or wall with green or brown paper. Cover the top two-thirds with blue paper for the sky. Make a large church from poster board. Use construction paper to cut rectangles for windows and doors, and tape one side of each shape to the house. Fold back the flaps so they open and close.

Each week the children will add a part to the bulletin board which illustrates The Point for that lesson.

Lesson 6
● Bring in leather sandals, a bowl of water, and paper towels. Talk about how people in Jesus' day traveled by foot and wore sandals. Explain that

when travelers or guests came to visit, servants washed their feet. Let children take turns washing each other's hands or feet.

● Bring in a variety of pebbles. Let children touch the pebbles and use them to lay a path around the room. As children follow the path, tell them they'll hear a story about a road and the amazing thing that happened there.

● Let children draw and cut out figures of themselves. Tape the cutouts to the bulletin board.

Lesson 7

● Make a sensory box by cutting a fist-sized hole in the end of a shoe box with a lid. Place various sensory items in the box such as feathers, stones, sandpaper, marbles, and sponges. Invite children to feel and identify the items. Then open the box and see how many items the children correctly identified. Point out that when we touch things they seem more real.

● Put tempera paint in a pie pan and let children make prints of their hands. Have children take turns guessing which hand print belongs to what person. Explain that children will hear a story about a man who didn't believe Jesus was alive until he saw Jesus' hands.

● Have children draw their family members' faces in the windows of the church on the bulletin board.

Lesson 8

● Bring in pictures of missionaries and the places where they serve, or invite a missionary to tell a little bit about his or her work. Explain that Jesus wants us to follow and serve him wherever we are—in our own neighborhoods or around the world.

● Bring in foods from different countries for the children to taste. You might want to include bean sprouts from China, tortillas from Mexico, or pineapples from Hawaii. Talk about the fact that people who serve God all over the world have to get used to different foods and customs.

● Let children place a cross on top of the bulletin board church.

Lesson 9

● Bring in different kinds of whole-grain bread and honey to spread on the bread. Invite children to taste the bread and honey. Explain that the Feast of Pentecost was a celebration of the grain harvest, and that during the feast many people gathered together to enjoy food and friendship. Tell children they'll hear a story about something amazing that happened at the Feast of Pentecost.

● Invite church members who speak foreign languages to share with the class. Have them teach children how to say "Jesus loves me" or "Hello" in another language.

● On the bulletin board, have children tape the cutouts of themselves spreading out from the church. Explain that Jesus wants us to go into all the world and tell others about him.

Our House

Photocopy and cut out the pattern. Cut on the dotted lines. Fold back along the center line and tape the house halves together. Fold back the windows and door. Draw your family members in the windows and doorway.

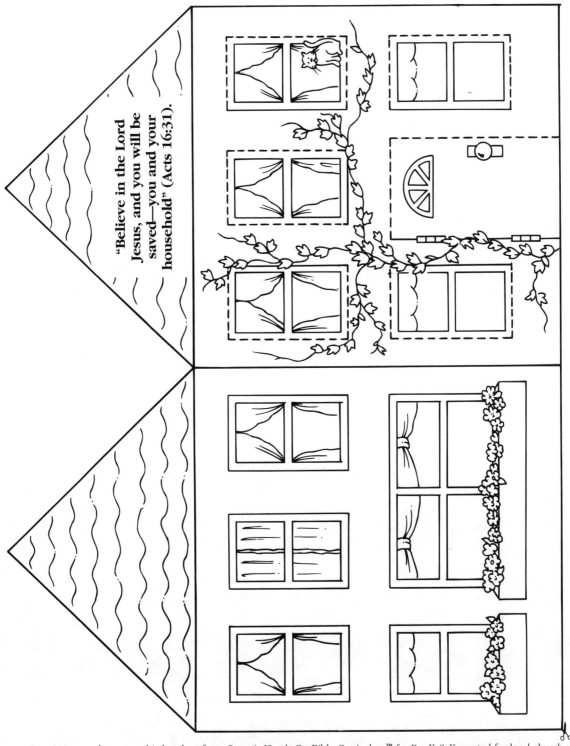

"Believe in the Lord Jesus, and you will be saved—you and your household" (Acts 16:31).

Jesus helps us follow him. ●

The Road to Emmaus

The Point

✎ Jesus helps us follow him when we don't understand.

The Bible Basis

Luke 24:13-35. Jesus walked with the men toward Emmaus.

Three days after Jesus' death, Cleopas and his friend walked from Jerusalem to Emmaus. Confused and sad, their minds echoed the same haunting questions: Why did Jesus die? Why did angels say he was alive? How could his tomb be empty? Where is Jesus now? They didn't understand or perhaps *couldn't* understand until a stranger who joined them on their journey dispelled their confusion by explaining the prophecies and promises concerning Jesus. When the stranger broke bread at dinner, the men recognized Jesus. For Jesus' friends, joy and understanding replaced the muddle of confusion—Jesus was alive and now they truly understood.

Five- and six-year-olds have a difficult time understanding many things in their world. Questions such as "*Why* do I have to eat spinach?" "*Why* can't I go to the movies?" or "*Why* do I have to go to bed now?" echo young children's desire to understand the reasons behind everything. But through those whys, children become wise and trust Jesus to lead the way. It's important for children to realize that Jesus helps us understand all we need to know. Use this lesson to help children trust Jesus and follow him more closely.

Getting The Point

✎ **Jesus helps us follow him when we don't understand.**

It's important to say The Point just as it's written in each activity. Repeating The Point again and again will help the children remember it and apply it to their lives.

Children will
● learn that sometimes we need help understanding things,
● ask for help when they need it,
● help Pockets learn that it's important to follow Jesus, and
● make reminders that Jesus helps us follow him.

● **The Point**

This Lesson at a Glance

Before the lesson, collect the necessary items for the activities you plan to use. Refer to the Classroom Supplies and Learning Lab Supplies columns to determine what you'll need. Remember to make photocopies of the "Today I Learned..." handout (p. 100) to send home with your children.

Section	Minutes	What Children Will Do	Classroom Supplies	Learning Lab Supplies
Welcome Time	up to 5	**Welcome!**—Receive name tags and be greeted by the teacher.	"Cross Name Tags" handouts (p. 30), markers, pins or tape	
Let's Get Started Direct children to one or more of the Let's Get Started activities until everyone arrives.	up to 10	**Option 1: Follow Flowers**—Understand and follow directions for making pretty flowers.	Pipe cleaners, facial tissues	
	up to 10	**Option 2: A Puzzler**—Solve a confusing puzzle.	Three blocks, three crayons, three books	
	up to 10	**Option 3: On the Road**—Paint cobblestones and trace footsteps along the road to Emmaus.	Paper grocery sacks, markers, scissors, tape, potatoes, white tempera paint, newspapers, cake pan, knife	
Pick-Up Song	up to 5	**We Will Pick Up**—Sing a song as they pick up toys and gather for Bible-Story Time.	CD player	CD: "We Will Pick Up" (track 2)
Bible-Story Time	up to 5	**Setting the Stage**—Sing a funny song and learn that sometimes we need help understanding things.		
	up to 5	**Bible Song and Prayer Time**—Sing a song, bring out the Bible, and pray together.	Bible, construction paper, scissors, basket or box, CD player	CD: "God's Book" (track 3), flame stamp and ink pad
	up to 10	**Hear the Bible Story**—Help tell the story of Jesus and his friends on the road to Emmaus from Luke 24:13-35.	Bible, green construction paper, glue stick, brown crayons, cotton balls	Learning Mat: Follow Jesus, sandpaper square
	up to 10	**Do the Bible Story**—Follow a pretend road to Emmaus and tell everyone that Jesus is alive.	Graham crackers, a paper plate, road from Option 3	
Practicing The Point	up to 5	**Carrot Caper**—Teach Pockets that Jesus helps us understand when we're confused.	Pockets the Kangaroo, carrot, rubber band	
Closing	up to 5	**Follow the Leader**—Sing a song and pray.	CD player	CD: "Jesus Knows" (track 11)
For Extra Time		For extra-time ideas and supplies, see page 99.		

Jesus helps us follow him when we don't understand.

Welcome Time

Welcome! (up to 5 minutes)

- Bend down and make eye contact with children as they arrive.
- Greet each child individually with an enthusiastic smile.
- Thank each child for coming to class today.
- Say: **Today we're going to learn that** 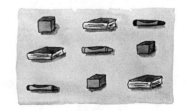 **Jesus helps us follow him when we don't understand.**
- Hand out the cross name tags children made in Lesson 1, and help them attach the name tags to their clothing. If some of the name tags were damaged or if children weren't in class that week, have them make new name tags using the photocopiable patterns on page 30.
- Direct children to the Let's Get Started activities you've set up.

● The Point

Let's Get Started

Set up one or more of the following activities for children to do as they arrive. After you greet each child, invite him or her to choose an activity.

Circulate among the children to offer help as needed and to direct children's conversation toward today's lesson. Ask questions such as "Who can tell about a time when you were confused and didn't know what to do?" or "Who helps you find good answers to questions?"

OPTION 1: Follow Flowers (up to 10 minutes)

Set out pastel colored facial tissues and pipe cleaners. Tell children you'll give them directions for making flowers, then they'll each have a chance to make one. Demonstrate how to lay four facial tissues on top of one another. Poke your finger in the center of the tissues, and twist a pipe cleaner around the bunch to secure the flower. Fluff out the tissue "petals." Ask children if they understand the directions, then let them begin making their own flowers.

Encourage children to ask if they need help. Circulate and make comments such as "It's good to ask questions when we don't understand something" and "Who helps you when you don't know what to do?" Mention that they'll hear a story about two men who didn't understand that Jesus was alive. Tell children that Jesus helped the men understand. Point out that ● Jesus helps us follow him when we don't understand.

● The Point

OPTION 2: A Puzzler (up to 10 minutes)

Set out three blocks, three crayons, and three books. As children arrive, invite them to help solve a puzzle. Have children work together to lay the items in rows of three so there's no more than one block, book, and crayon in each row going across and up and down. As children work together, ask questions such as "Is this puzzle difficult to understand?" and "What can you do if you don't understand something?" If children need help, show them the

● The Point

pattern on the previous page and let them try again. Point out that even when things are hard to understand, there's help. Tell children that ● Jesus helps us follow him when we don't understand. Explain that they'll hear a story about two men who didn't understand something, but Jesus helped them solve the puzzle.

OPTION 3: On the Road (up to 10 minutes)

Before class, cut the bottoms from three or four large paper grocery sacks. Cut up one side of the bags, then open the bags and tape them end to end to form a "road." Cut two potatoes in half widthwise to use as stampers.

Cover the floor in one corner of the room with newspapers. Lay the grocery bag road on the newspapers. Set out potato halves and a cake pan with one-quarter-inch of white tempera paint in the bottom. Use markers to trace children's footprints along the road as if they're following someone. Then have children take turns using the potatoes to stamp white cobblestones along the road. As children paint, make comments such as "Let's pretend this road starts at Jerusalem" and "In Bible times most people walked from city to city." Tell children that ● Jesus helps us follow him when we don't understand where to go or what to do. Explain that children will hear a story about two friends on a road and about the amazing traveler they met.

● The Point

When children finish, put the paint away and set the road in a corner to dry. You'll use the road in a later activity.

When everyone has arrived and you're ready to move on to the Bible-Story Time, encourage the children to finish what they're doing and get ready to clean up.

Pick-Up Song

We Will Pick Up (up to 5 minutes)

Lead children in singing "We Will Pick Up" (track 2) with the *CD* to the tune of "London Bridge." Encourage children to sing along as they help clean up the room.

If you want to include the names of all the children in your class, sing the song without the *CD* and repeat the naming section. If you choose to use the *CD*, vary the names you use each week.

Sing

We will pick up all our toys,
All our toys, all our toys.
We will pick up all our toys
And put them all away.

I see (name) picking up,
Picking up, picking up.
I see (name) picking up
And putting toys away.

(Repeat)

Jesus helps us follow him when we don't understand.

Bible-Story Time

Setting the Stage (up to 5 minutes)

Tell the children you'll clap your hands to get their attention. Explain that when you clap, the children are to stop what they're doing, raise their hands, and focus on you. Encourage children to respond quickly so you'll have time for all the fun activities you've planned.

Gather the children in a large circle and say: **Let's play a game! Listen carefully and follow my directions.** (Give the directions in a steady pace, slow enough for the children to follow, but fast enough to be confusingly fun.)

Skip in a circle to and fro.
Bend way down and touch your toe.
Take three steps and hum a tune.
Stand on tiptoe; reach for the moon.

Greet your neighbors, say "Hello!"
Nod your head, yes and no.
With a partner twirl around.
Now close your eyes and all sit down!

Say: **Good job! That was fun.** Ask:

● **Did you like the game? Why or why not?** (Yes, we moved around a lot; no, it was silly and I didn't understand it.)

● **Why did we play this game?** (I don't know; just for fun.)

● **This game seemed hard to figure out and even a little silly—why did you follow along?** (You said to; everyone else was playing; I don't know.)

Say: **It can be hard to follow when we don't understand what we're doing or why we're doing it. Today we'll hear a story about two friends who learned to follow Jesus when they didn't understand. We know that Jesus has reasons for us to follow him and that ◐ Jesus helps us follow him when we don't understand.**

We had a good reason for playing the game earlier—it was to help get some of our wiggles out so we can listen to the Bible story. Let's play the game again and lose the rest of our wiggles! Repeat the rhyme game from the start of the activity.

Bible Song and Prayer Time (up to 5 minutes)

Before class, make surprise cards for this activity by cutting construction paper into two-by-six-inch slips. Prepare a surprise card for each child plus a few extras for visitors. Fold the cards in half, then stamp the *flame stamp* inside one of the surprise cards. Mark Luke 24:13-35 in the Bible you'll be using.

Have children sit in a circle. Say: **Now it's time to choose a Bible person to bring me the Bible marked with today's Bible story. As we sing our Bible song, I'll pass out the surprise cards. Don't look inside your card until the song is over.**

Lead children in singing "God's Book" (track 3) with the *CD* to the tune of "Old MacDonald Had a Farm." As you sing, pass out the folded surprise cards.

◐ The Point

Note:
If the ink pad is dry, moisten it with three to five drops of water.

If you want to include the names of all the children in your class, sing the song without the *CD*, and repeat the naming section. If you choose to use the *CD*, vary the names you use each week.

Sing

Now it's time to read God's Book
And hear a Bible story.
It's fun to be here with my
**   friends**
And hear a Bible story.
(Name)**'s here.**
(Name)**'s here.**
Here is (name).
Here is (name).
Now it's time to read God's Book
And hear a Bible story.

Now it's time to read God's Book
And hear a Bible story.
It's fun to be here with my
**   friends**
And hear a Bible story.
(Name)**'s here.**
(Name)**'s here.**
Here is (name).
Here is (name).
Now it's time to read God's Book
And hear a Bible story.

After the song, say: **You may look inside your surprise cards. The person who has the flame stamped inside his or her card will be our Bible person for today.**

Identify the Bible person, then have the rest of the children clap for him or her. Ask the Bible person to bring you the Bible. Help the Bible person open the Bible to the marked place, and show children where your story comes from. Then have the Bible person sit down.

Say: (Name) **was our special Bible person today. Each week, we'll have only one special Bible person, but each one of you is a special part of our class! Today we're all learning that** 🖊 **Jesus helps us follow him when we don't understand.**

🖊 **The Point**

Let's say a special prayer now and ask God to help us follow Jesus. I'll pass around this basket. When the basket comes to you, put your surprise card in it and say, "God, please help us follow Jesus."

Pass around the basket or box. When you've collected everyone's surprise card, set the basket aside, and pick up the Bible. Lead children in this prayer: **God, thank you for the Bible and all the stories in it. Teach us today that** 🖊 **Jesus helps us follow him when we don't understand. In Jesus' name, amen.**

🖊 **The Point**

Hear the Bible Story (up to 10 minutes)

Bring out the *Learning Mat: Follow Jesus* and place it on the floor.

Open the Bible to the book of Luke. Point to the Bible and say: **Today's story is from Luke 24:13-35. It's about two friends who meet an amazing traveler along the road. The** *Learning Mat* **shows pictures of the Bible story.** Point to the picture of the road to Emmaus. **You can help me tell the story and add things to the** *Learning Mat.* **Since the story is about friends, find a friend to work with.** Pause while children get in pairs. Hand each pair one of the following items: the *sandpaper square* from the Learning Lab box, a three-by-five-inch piece of green construction paper, two brown crayons, and two cotton balls. (If you have more than four pairs of

Jesus helps us follow him when we don't understand.

children, hand out additional cotton balls or brown crayons.) Set a glue stick beside the *Learning Mat.*

Say: **Each set of friends has different items to add to the *Learning Mat.* As I tell the story, I'll tell you when it's time to add your part.**

Cleopas and his friend were walking from Jerusalem to the town of Emmaus (ee-MAY-us). **Let's say that together: Emmaus. The road to Emmaus was dusty and sandy. Let's add *sandpaper* to the road.** Have partners with the *sandpaper* glue it to the *Learning Mat.* Then continue. **The sad friends talked about what had happened to Jesus. Jesus had been killed on a cross and put in a tomb. Cleopas and his friend didn't understand why Jesus had to die. They missed him a lot as they walked on the road. Let's color the road to Emmaus.** Have the children with the brown crayons color the road.

Say: **A man appeared on the road beside them. Guess who it was?** Pause while children tell their ideas. **It was Jesus! But Jesus didn't want the men to recognize him yet.**

As Jesus walked with the men, he asked, "What are you talking about?" "Haven't you heard?" said the friends. "Three days ago our leaders had Jesus put to death. We hoped Jesus would set our country free, but then today some of the women saw *angels* at Jesus' empty tomb. The angels said Jesus is alive!" The two friends looked very sad and confused. They didn't know what to do.

So Jesus explained everything to them. He told them about God's promises and how Jesus was the Savior God promised. He told them that Jesus had to suffer before he went to live in heaven. Let's add some clouds to show Jesus' heavenly home. Pause while children glue stretched-out cotton balls to the sky.

Continue with the story. **The three men walked to Emmaus. Let's put leaves on the trees and color the buildings.** Have children tear green construction paper leaves and glue them to the trees. Invite children with crayons to color the buildings. Say: **It was getting late and the friends asked the man, who was really . . .** (pause for children to say "Jesus") **to stay for dinner. When the guest blessed and broke the bread, Cleopas and his friend realized it was Jesus! Think of their surprise! Then Jesus disappeared. Quickly, Cleopas and his friend ran back to Jerusalem to tell the good news to the disciples. Hop up and jog around the *Learning Mat.* When you get back to your place, shout "Jesus is alive!" and sit down.**

When all the children are seated, ask:

● **Who helped Cleopas and his friend understand about Jesus?** (Jesus helped them understand; Jesus helped explain things to the men.)

● **How did Jesus help them understand?** (He explained things to them; Jesus showed himself to the men and they saw Jesus.)

● **Do you think the men followed Jesus after Jesus helped them? Why or why not?** (Yes, they'll believe Jesus now; yes, they know Jesus is alive.)

Say: ✏**Jesus helps us follow him when we don't understand. He helped Cleopas and his friend by talking with them and showing them that he was Jesus. Jesus knew they could follow him better if they knew he was alive.**

● **How does Jesus help us follow him today?** (By praying; by reading the Bible; by listening in church; by obeying God's Word.)

● **The Point**

● The Point

Say: **Sometimes it's hard to follow Jesus because we don't understand what to do. It's important to know that ● Jesus helps us follow him when we don't understand. Just as he helped Cleopas and his friend on the road to Emmaus, we can trust Jesus to help us because he loves us all the time. Let's play a game on a road that's not always easy to follow.**

Fold the *Learning Mat* and return it to the Learning Lab box.

Do the Bible Story (up to 10 minutes)

Set the road children made during Option 3 in the center of the floor. If you chose not to do Option 3, children may hop around the edge of the *Learning Mat*. Set a plate of graham crackers at the end of the road. Ask:

● **Where were Cleopas and his friend going?** (To Emmaus; to town.)

Say: **We're going on the road to Emmaus too. Let's make two groups.** Help children form two groups and have them stand at the end of the road opposite the crackers. Say: **When I clap my hands, the first travelers from each group hop from cobblestone to cobblestone. Follow the stones to the end of the road. Because Jesus' friends recognized Jesus when he broke the bread, you'll pick up a graham cracker, break it in half, and say, "Jesus is alive." Then hop back with your crackers, and send the next two travelers down the road. Don't eat your crackers until everyone's had a chance to follow the road.**

When all the children have a graham cracker, ask:

● **Was the road easy or hard to follow? Explain.** (It was hard hopping only on the stones; it was easy because there are lots of stones to follow.)

● **What made it hard for people to follow Jesus after he died on the cross?** (They didn't know he would come back to life; they didn't know what to do next.)

● **What makes it hard to follow Jesus today?** (When I listen to my friends instead of to God; when I forget to pray or read the Bible.)

● **How does Jesus help us follow him?** (He gives us churches and teachers; the Bible tells us what to do; he gives us people who set a good example.)

● **What are some good ways to follow Jesus?** (Asking Jesus to help us; learning about Jesus; being kind to others.)

● The Point

Say: ● **Jesus helps us follow him when we don't understand, just as he helped Cleopas and his friend. He gives us pastors and teachers and parents and the Bible to guide us. Now, since I'm your teacher, I'd like you to pretend your graham crackers are roads and gobble them up.**

Practicing The Point

Carrot Caper (up to 5 minutes)

Before class, use a rubber band to fasten a carrot to Pockets' paw.

Bring out Pockets the Kangaroo and go through the following script. When you finish the script, put Pockets away and out of sight.

Jesus helps us follow him when we don't understand.

Carrot Caper

PUPPET SCRIPT

Pockets: *(Pockets comes in chanting a poem and looking at her carrot.)* Carrots and spinach and a to-ma-to; what they're good for I-don't-know.

Teacher: Well, Pockets, that's a funny rhyme. What's this all about?

Pockets: It's all about <u>vegetables!</u> *(Waving her carrot)* I don't like 'em and I don't <u>understand</u> why Mommy wants me to eat 'em. Daddy said I need to follow good health habits, but I don't understand <u>why</u> I have to eat carrots 'n' stuff.

Teacher: Sometimes it's hard to follow when we don't understand. We've been learning that 🖊 Jesus helps us follow him when we don't understand. Children, let's tell Pockets about the men on the road to Emmaus and how Jesus helped them. *(Encourage children to retell the Bible story. Have them point out that it's important to trust and follow Jesus even when it's hard.)* You see, Pockets, we can always trust Jesus and follow him even when we don't understand.

● **The Point**

Pockets: I want to follow Jesus, and I'm glad that 🖊 Jesus helps us follow him when we don't understand. But do you think he can help me understand why I need to eat my carrots?

● **The Point**

Teacher: God gives us good things to eat because he wants us to be healthy. Carrots are full of good vitamins so they give you lots of bounce. You wouldn't want to lose your bounce, would you?

Pockets: No way! What kind of kangaroo would I be if I couldn't bounce?

Teacher: So you see, Pockets, there's a good reason to eat your carrots. Just like there's good reasons to follow Jesus even when we're confused.

Pockets: Well, I <u>love</u> Jesus and . . . *(takes a nibble of carrot and acts surprised)* mmm, I guess I like <u>carrots,</u> too! Thanks for helping me learn that 🖊 Jesus helps us follow him when we don't understand. I <u>do</u> understand now! 'Bye, kids! *(Pockets leaves chanting this poem.)* Carrots and spinach and a to-ma-to; following Jesus is the way to go!

● **The Point**

TODAY I LEARNED...

We believe that Christian education extends beyond the classroom into the home. Photocopy the "Today I Learned..." handout (p. 100) for this week, and send it home with your children. Encourage parents to use the handout to plan meaningful family activities to reinforce this week's topic. Follow up the "Today I Learned..." activities next week by asking children what their families did.

Closing

Follow the Leader (up to 5 minutes)

● **The Point**

Have the children sit in a circle on the floor. Say: **Today we learned that ❶ Jesus helps us follow him when we don't understand. When we have questions, Jesus has the answers and he'll help us. Let's learn a new song about following Jesus.**

Lead the children in singing "Jesus Knows" (track 11) with the *CD* to the tune of "Frère Jacques."

Sing

When I ask why,
When I ask why,
Jesus knows.
Jesus knows.
When I have a question,
Jesus has the answer.
Jesus knows.
Jesus knows.

● **The Point**

Say: **In the Bible story, Cleopas and his friend went to tell others that Jesus is alive. They wanted to help their friends follow Jesus. We can encourage each other to follow Jesus, too. Go around the circle and encourage the friend sitting on your right by saying, ❶ "Jesus helps us follow him when we don't understand."** Have children take turns repeating the point to the friend on the right.

● **The Point**

Say: **Let's close with a prayer.** Pray: **Dear God, help us follow Jesus in everything we do. Help us also remember that ❶ Jesus helps us follow him when we don't understand. In Jesus' name, amen.**

If children chose Option 1, remind them to take their flowers home.

Jesus helps us follow him when we don't understand.

For Extra Time

If you have a long class time or want to add additional elements to your lesson, try one of the following activities.

LIVELY LEARNING: Friend in Disguise

Bring in jackets, hats, scarves, and sunglasses for children to wear as disguises. Point out that in the Bible story, Cleopas and his friend didn't recognize Jesus at first. Tell children they'll get to put on a disguise so their friends won't recognize them. Set the disguises in the hall or behind a large table or desk. Have children close their eyes. Choose two children to put on disguises by lightly tapping them on the shoulders. The rest of the class guesses who's wearing the disguises. Be sure each child has a turn dressing up. Explain that at dinner Jesus let his friends recognize him because ● Jesus helps us follow him when we don't understand.

● **The Point**

MAKE TO TAKE: Streamer Sticks

Set out ribbon or crepe paper, scissors, and tape. Hand each child a large stick, and explain that they'll make walking sticks much like the ones many people used in Jesus' time. Have children cut colorful streamers from ribbon then tape the streamers onto the tops of the sticks. As children work, explain that Jesus talked to his friends as they walked down the road to Emmaus. He explained why he had to die, then let them see that he was alive again. Remind children that ● Jesus helps us follow him even when we don't understand. Invite children to "hike" around the room using their walking sticks.

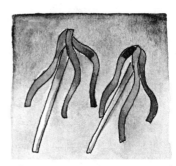

● **The Point**

TREAT TO EAT: Rocky Roads

You'll need graham crackers, peanut butter, chocolate chips, plastic knives, and paper towels. Have children make rocky roads in an assembly line. Form three groups: Breakers, Spreaders, and Sprinklers. The Breakers break large graham crackers into smaller squares and place each square on a paper towel. The Spreaders spread peanut butter on each cracker, and the Sprinklers add chocolate chip "bumps" to the road. As children work, make comments such as "Roads with bumps are hard to follow. I'm glad that ● Jesus helps us follow him even when we don't understand" and "Jesus helps us find the right road to take when we follow him." Eat and enjoy the Rocky Roads as children tell ways they can follow Jesus every day.

Tip:
Before preparing the snacks, make sure children are not allergic to the ingredients.

● **The Point**

STORY PICTURE: The Road to Emmaus

Give each child a photocopy of the "Today I Learned..." handout from page 100. Set out glue, cotton swabs, and a small bowl of sand or soil with plastic spoons. Have the children use cotton swabs to apply glue to the road in the picture. Then let them use the spoons to sprinkle sand or soil on the road.

TODAY I LEARNED . . .

The Point 🖊 Jesus helps us follow him when we don't understand.

Today your child learned that Jesus helps us follow him when we don't understand. Children learned that Jesus helped two friends on the road to Emmaus understand that he was alive. Children talked about the importance of following Jesus all the time.

Verse to Learn

"Believe in the Lord Jesus, and you will be saved—you and your household" (Acts 16:31).

Ask Me . . .

● What happened on the road to Emmaus?

● How does Jesus help you follow him when you don't understand?

● How can our family learn and understand more about Jesus?

Family Fun

● Make Emmaus Road toast for your family's breakfast. Let your child toast bread then spread a butter road down the center of the toast. Sprinkle the road with cinnamon sugar. As your family enjoys their breakfast treat, encourage your child to tell what happened on the road to Emmaus and how Jesus helps us follow him.

The Road to Emmaus (Luke 24:13-35)

Thomas Believes

The Point

🖉 Jesus helps us follow him when we have questions.

The Bible Basis

John 20:24-29. Jesus helped Thomas believe that he had risen from the dead.

Thomas was absent when Jesus first appeared in the room where his disciples were hiding behind locked doors. He didn't believe the other disciples' reports that Jesus was alive. Many questions troubled him: How could anyone rise from the dead? If Jesus had risen, where was he? And why hadn't Thomas seen Jesus if the other disciples had? Thomas steadfastly refused to believe what had eluded his eyes and hands. He demanded nothing less than physical proof. Then, as the disciples met together behind locked doors, Jesus came to them once again. Showing the wounds in his hands and side, Jesus commanded Thomas to stop doubting and believe. In one of the most moving passages of Scripture, Thomas acknowledged Jesus as "My Lord and my God."

Five- and six-year-olds are wonderfully inquisitive. They ask countless questions that range from the practical ("When's lunch?") to the profound ("Why did Jesus die?"). Use this lesson to teach children that their questions are important to Jesus and that Jesus is always ready and willing to help them find the right answers.

Getting The Point

🖉 **Jesus helps us follow him when we have questions.**

It's important to say The Point just as it's written in each activity. Repeating The Point again and again will help the children remember it and apply it to their lives.

Children will
- learn that their questions are important,
- know that Jesus helps us find the right answers,
- help Pockets learn that it's important to believe without always seeing, and
- realize that faith helps us follow Jesus.

🖉 **The Point**

This Lesson at a Glance

Before the lesson, collect the necessary items for the activities you plan to use. Refer to the Classroom Supplies and Learning Lab Supplies columns to determine what you'll need. Remember to make photocopies of the "Today I Learned..." handout (p. 112) to send home with your children.

Section	Minutes	What Children Will Do	Classroom Supplies	Learning Lab Supplies
Welcome Time	up to 5	**Welcome!**—Receive name tags and be greeted by the teacher.	"Cross Name Tags" handouts (p. 30), markers, pins or tape	
Let's Get Started Direct children to one or more of the Let's Get Started activities until everyone arrives.	up to 10	**Option 1: Seeing Is Believing**—Make special eyeglasses to wear during the Bible-Story Time.	"See With Your Heart" handout (p. 111), markers, scissors	Flame stamp and ink pad
	up to 10	**Option 2: Blind Touch**—Identify objects using their sense of touch.	Spoon, cotton ball, comb, rubber band, paper clip, crayon, paper bag	
	up to 10	**Option 3: Seeing Small**—Look at things in different ways.	Magnifying glass and small objects such as leaves, twigs, cloth, flowers	
Pick-Up Song	up to 5	**We Will Pick Up**—Sing a song as they pick up toys and gather for Bible-Story Time.	CD player	CD: "We Will Pick Up" (track 2)
Bible-Story Time	up to 5	**Setting the Stage**—Ask questions and guess what's in a box.	Box with lid, small boxes of raisins, string, scissors	
	up to 5	**Bible Song and Prayer Time**—Sing a song, bring out the Bible, and pray together.	Bible, construction paper, scissors, basket or box, CD player	CD: "God's Book" (track 3), flame stamp and ink pad
	up to 10	**Hear the Bible Story**—Add sensory items to the Learning Mat as they listen to a Bible Story from John 20:24-29.	Bible; blue, red, yellow, and green markers or crayons; glue stick; heart-shaped eyeglasses from Option 1	Learning Mat: Follow Jesus, sequins, gauze square
	up to 10	**Do the Bible Story**—Identify friends without seeing them.	CD player, scarf for a blindfold	CD: "Jesus Knows" (track 11)
Practicing The Point	up to 5	**Pockets' Problem**—Help Pockets learn about believing.	Pockets the Kangaroo, index card	Flame stamp and ink pad
Closing	up to 5	**String of Questions**—Ask Jesus to answer their questions and say a prayer.	Strings from "Setting the Stage"	
For Extra Time		For extra-time ideas and supplies, see page 110.		

Jesus helps us follow him when we have questions.

Welcome Time

Welcome! (up to 5 minutes)

- Bend down and make eye contact with children as they arrive.
- Greet each child individually with an enthusiastic smile.
- Thank each child for coming to class today.
- As children arrive, ask them about last week's "Today I Learned..." discussion. Ask questions such as "How did you follow Jesus last week?"
- Say: **Today we're going to learn that**  **Jesus helps us follow him when we have questions.**
- Hand out the cross name tags children made in Lesson 1, and help them attach the name tags to their clothing. If some of the name tags were damaged or if children weren't in class that week, have them make new name tags using the photocopiable patterns on page 30.
- Direct children to the Let's Get Started activities you've set up.

● The Point

Let's Get Started

Set up one or more of the following activities for children to do as they arrive. After you greet each child, invite him or her to choose an activity.

Circulate among the children to offer help as needed and to direct children's conversation toward today's lesson. Ask questions such as "Who helps you answer hard questions?" or "What can you do if you have questions?"

OPTION 1: Seeing Is Believing (up to 10 minutes)

Before class, photocopy the "See With Your Heart" pattern on page 111. Photocopy the patterns on medium-weight paper. Cut out eyeglasses for each child and adult in class. To save time, cut out two or three pairs at once.

Set out markers and the *flame stamp and ink pad* from the Learning Lab. Hand each child a pair of heart-shaped eyeglasses. Invite children to decorate their glasses using markers and the *flame stamp*. Then show children how to fold their glasses on the dotted lines and fit them over their ears.

Circulate and offer help as needed. As children work, ask questions such as "Do we need to see with our eyes to know something's real?" and "Besides using our eyes, how else do we learn about things?" Explain that today's Bible story is about a man who wanted to see and touch Jesus to know he was alive. Point out that  Jesus helps us follow him when we have questions and that sometimes we can't see answers with our eyes.

When children are finished, let them model their glasses and look at different items in the room. You'll use the eyeglasses with the Bible story later.

● The Point

✔ If not all children in class chose to do Option 1, ask volunteers to decorate extra pairs of eyeglasses to share.

☐ OPTION 2: **Blind Touch (up to 10 minutes)**

Before class, collect one each of the following items and place them in a paper bag: a spoon, a cotton ball, a comb, a rubber band, a paper clip, and a crayon.

As children arrive, ask them how they think a blind person "sees" things. Invite children to reach in the sack and identify the objects by touching them. Ask children questions such as "How can touching something help us 'see' it?" and "Can touching something help you know it's real?" Tell children that sometimes we have questions that can't be answered by what we see or touch.

● **The Point**
Explain that the Bible story is about a man who wanted to see and touch all the answers to his questions. Point out that ✎ Jesus helps us follow him when we have questions, and he'll help us find the right answers with or without seeing them.

☐ OPTION 3: **Seeing Small (up to 10 minutes)**

Set out a magnifying glass and small objects to view such as leaves, cloth, twigs, and flowers. Encourage children to explore each object without the magnifying glass, with the magnifying glass, and with their hands. Encourage children to ask questions about what they see. Point out that there are many ways to see things and discover that they're real. Tell children that today's Bible story is about a man who had a big question about what was real.

● **The Point**
Explain that ✎ Jesus helps us follow him when we have questions, and Jesus helped the man see the right answers to his questions.

When everyone has arrived and you're ready to move on to the Bible-Story Time, encourage the children to finish what they're doing and get ready to clean up.

Pick-Up Song

We Will Pick Up (up to 5 minutes)

Lead children in singing "We Will Pick Up" (track 2) with the *CD* to the tune of "London Bridge." Encourage children to sing along as they help clean up the room.

If you want to include the names of all the children in your class, sing the song without the *CD* and repeat the naming section. If you choose to use the *CD*, vary the names you use each week.

Sing 🎵

We will pick up all our toys,
All our toys, all our toys.
We will pick up all our toys
And put them all away.

I see (name) picking up,
Picking up, picking up.
I see (name) picking up
And putting toys away.

(Repeat)

Jesus helps us follow him when we have questions.

Bible-Story Time

Setting the Stage (up to 5 minutes)

Tell the children you'll clap your hands to get their attention. Explain that when you clap, the children are to stop what they're doing, raise their hands, and focus on you. Encourage children to respond quickly so you'll have time for all the fun activities you've planned.

Before the children arrive, put a treat-sized box of raisins for each child in a box with a lid. Loosely knot one piece of string around the box for each child.

Gather children in a circle on the floor. Say: **I have a mystery box. What's inside?** Pause to allow children to guess. **The only way to find the answer is to ask questions. We'll pass the box around the circle. When it's your turn, untie a string and ask a "yes" or "no" question about what's inside the box.**

After each child has asked a question and the strings are untied, hold up the box and ask:

● **How do you know there's something in the box?** (You said there was; I heard it rattle.)

Say: **You've asked good questions about the box. Now we'll see what's inside.** Open the box, and show children the treats. Pass the box, and let each child choose a small box of raisins. As children eat their treats, ask:

● **Why is it important to ask questions?** (It helps you learn things.)

● **Who helps when you have questions?** (Parents; teachers; Jesus; God.)

Say: **Asking questions helps us learn and understand. Our questions are important to Jesus, and he always helps us find answers. ◗ Jesus helps us follow him when we don't understand. Let's find out about a man who had some questions and how Jesus helped him find the right answers.** Have children throw their empty raisin boxes away. Set the strings aside until later.

◗ The Point

Bible Song and Prayer Time (up to 5 minutes)

Before class, make surprise cards for this activity by cutting construction paper into two-by-six-inch strips. Prepare a surprise card for each child plus a few extras for visitors. Fold the cards in half, then stamp the *flame stamp* inside one of the surprise cards. Mark John 20:24-29 in the Bible you'll be using.

Have children sit in a circle. Say: **Now it's time to choose a Bible person to bring me the Bible marked with today's Bible story. As we sing our Bible song, I'll pass out the surprise cards. Don't look inside your surprise card until the song is over.**

Lead children in singing "God's Book" (track 3) with the *CD* to the tune of "Old MacDonald Had a Farm." As you sing, pass out the folded surprise cards. If you want to include the names of all the children in your class, sing the song without the *CD* and repeat the naming section. If you choose to use the *CD*, vary the names you use each week.

Sing

Now it's time to read God's Book	Now it's time to read God's Book
And hear a Bible story.	And hear a Bible story.
It's fun to be here with my friends	It's fun to be here with my friends
And hear a Bible story.	And hear a Bible story.
(Name)'s **here.**	(Name)'s **here.**
(Name)'s **here.**	(Name)'s **here.**
Here is (name).	**Here is** (name).
Here is (name).	**Here is** (name).
Now it's time to read God's Book	Now it's time to read God's Book
And hear a Bible story.	And hear a Bible story.

After the song, say: **You may look inside your surprise cards. The person who has the flame stamped inside his or her card will be our Bible person for today.**

Identify the Bible person, then have the rest of the children clap for him or her. Ask the Bible person to bring you the Bible. Help the Bible person open the Bible to the marked place, and show children where your story comes from. Then have the Bible person sit down.

✏ The Point

Say: (Name) **was our special Bible person today. Each week, we'll have only one special Bible person, but each one of you is a special part of our class! Today we're all learning that** ⬤**Jesus helps us follow him when we have questions.**

Let's say a special prayer now and ask God to help us follow Jesus. I'll pass around this basket. When the basket comes to you, put your surprise card in it and say, "God, please help us follow Jesus."

Pass around the basket or box. When you've collected everyone's surprise card, set the basket aside and pick up the Bible. Lead children in this prayer:

✏ The Point

God, thank you for the Bible and all the stories in it. Teach us today that ⬤**Jesus helps us follow him when we have questions. In Jesus' name, amen.**

Hear the Bible Story (up to 10 minutes)

Set out the *gauze square* and *sequins* from the Learning Lab. Also set out a glue stick and blue, red, yellow, and green markers or crayons. Gather children around the *Learning Mat: Follow Jesus* on the floor. Have the children hold their heart-shaped eyeglasses from Option 1. If you chose not to do Option 1, have children use their hands and fingers as pretend eyeglasses.

Say: **Some people wear glasses to help them see. Let's use our heart glasses to help us see if we know the answers to some questions. I'll ask a question about our story. If you know the answer, put on your glasses. I'll call someone to tell the answer, then color a footprint on the *Learning Mat.*** Ask the following review questions. After each child answers, let him or her choose a marker or crayon and color a footprint on the *Learning Mat.* Point to the picture showing the road to Emmaus.

- **Who was walking on the road?** (Two friends; Jesus' friends.)
- **Why were the men sad and confused?** (They didn't know why Jesus

died; they didn't know if Jesus was alive.)

● **Who did they meet on the road to Emmaus?** (A man; Jesus.)

● **Did they know the man was Jesus?** (No.)

● **What did Jesus tell them?** (Jesus explained why he had to die.)

● **What happened when Jesus broke bread at dinner?** (The men knew it was Jesus; Jesus showed who he was.)

● **What did the men do then?** (They ran to tell others about Jesus.)

Say: **Good job! Did your glasses help you? I think you knew the answers because you learned so much last week!** Hold up the Bible. Say: **Our Bible story today comes from the book of John.** Point to the *Learning Mat.* **Our *Learning Mat* shows pictures of the story. Today we'll learn how Jesus helps us follow him. When you hear the word "Thomas," remove your glasses and say, "I doubt it." When I say the word "Jesus," put your glasses on and say, "I see!"**

Read: **All the disciples knew that Jesus** ("I see!") **is alive—all but one that is. Thomas** ("I doubt it") **wasn't sure that Jesus** ("I see!") **was alive. Do you know why? Thomas** ("I doubt it") **didn't think anything was real unless he saw it or touched it. Thomas** ("I doubt it") **was a doubter. "I won't believe until I see Jesus'** ("I see!") **hands and touch his side."**

The disciples and Thomas ("I doubt it") **were in a house with the doors locked. Guess who came in? Jesus!** ("I see!") **Thomas** ("I doubt it") **saw him but still didn't believe. Jesus** ("I see!") **said, "Look at my hands. Touch my side. Stop doubting and believe!" Do you think he believed?** Pause for children to respond.

Thomas ("I doubt it") **bowed before Jesus** ("I see!"). **"My Lord and my God!" he said. He finally believed that Jesus** ("I see!") **was alive. Then Jesus** ("I see!") **said, "You believe because you see me. People who believe without seeing are truly blessed and special."** Have children put their glasses on the floor behind them. Ask:

● **Why did Thomas want to see and touch Jesus?** (To know Jesus was alive.)

Say: **Thomas had to see with his eyes to believe, but Jesus wanted him to have faith and believe in his heart. Let's make a sequin heart on Thomas to remind us that Jesus wants us to believe without having to see.** Help children glue *sequins* in the shape of a small heart on the picture of Thomas on the *Learning Mat.* Ask:

● **Did the other disciples want to touch Jesus to believe he was alive? Explain.** (No, they saw him; no, they believed anyway.) **Let's add Jesus' robe to the picture.** Have children glue the *gauze square* to Jesus.

● **Why did Jesus say it was special for people to believe without seeing?** (Because we can't see Jesus with our eyes but we know he's alive.)

Say: **Jesus knows it's hard to follow him when we have questions. But Jesus wants us to have faith in him. He answers our questions so we can follow him better. Let's color a happy yellow glow around Jesus to remind us that ⬤ Jesus helps us follow him when we have questions.** Have children color yellow around Jesus. Set the *Learning Mat* aside.

The Point

Do the Bible Story (up to 10 minutes)

Gather children in a group. Say: **Jesus wanted to help Thomas believe, and Jesus wants us to believe in him even if we can't see him. Let's play**

a fun game to see if you can tell who a person is without seeing him or her. I'll choose someone to be Thomas and wear a blindfold. Then I'll tap one of you to stand beside Thomas. Thomas will try to guess who you are by touching your head and face and asking you questions such as "Do you have red hair?" or "Are you a boy or a girl?" Play until everyone's had a turn. Ask:

● **What are some ways to discover who a person is without seeing?** (By touching; by hearing someone's voice.)

● **How can you believe in Jesus without seeing him?** (Because the Bible tells me about him; because I feel his love.)

● **Why is it important to believe?** (So we can obey Jesus; so we can follow him; so we can tell others about Jesus.)

Say: **Jesus knows we have questions about God and about him. And Jesus helps us follow him when we have questions. Let's sing a song about how good it is to know that when we have questions Jesus has the answers!**

The Point

Lead the children in singing "Jesus Knows" (track 11) with the *CD* to the tune of "Frère Jacques."

Sing

When I ask why,
When I ask why,
Jesus knows.
Jesus knows.

When I have a question,
Jesus has the answer.
Jesus knows.
Jesus knows.

Practicing The Point

Pockets' Problem (up to 5 minutes)

Have children sit in a circle. Bring out Pockets the Kangaroo, the *flame stamp and ink pad,* and an index card. Go through the following script. When you finish, put Pockets out of sight.

Pockets' Problem

PUPPET SCRIPT

Teacher: Hi, Pockets! What's new?

Pockets: You won't believe what's happened! I can't believe it!

Teacher: Believe what, Pockets?

Pockets: Well, I have a really neat sticker collection. (*Looking at children*) Do you have sticker collections? (*Pause for response.*) I've got 581 stickers! Well, I told my friend Sarah about my collection, but she doesn't <u>believe</u> me. She said she won't believe it until she sees it!

Teacher: Sarah sounds like doubting Thomas, doesn't she?

(Continued)

Jesus helps us follow him when we have questions.

Pockets: Who?

Teacher: Thomas, the man in our Bible story who doubted that Jesus is alive. Children, let's tell Pockets about Thomas and how he found out that Jesus is alive. *(Have children retell the Bible story. Encourage them to point out how Jesus helped Thomas by letting Thomas see.)*  Jesus helps us follow him when we have questions. Jesus helped Thomas by letting him see the scars in his hands. Maybe it will help Sarah if she sees your collection. Then next time she'll be able to believe without seeing.

Pockets: Good idea. I'll invite Sarah over. Then she can see my collection and believe me. It's important to believe without seeing but when we do have questions, I'm glad that  Jesus helps us follow him when we have questions.

Teacher: Let's add to Pockets' collection. *(Let children make a new kind of sticker by stamping the card Pockets is holding with the flame stamp.)* Here, Pockets. This will remind you that  Jesus helps us follow him when we have questions.

Pockets: Thank you! Now I have 582 stickers! Can I stamp your hands so you'll remember, too? *(Have Pockets stamp each child's hand with the flame stamp.)* Goodbye everyone!

⬤ **The Point**

⬤ **The Point**

⬤ **The Point**

TODAY I LEARNED...

We believe that Christian education extends beyond the classroom into the home. Photocopy the "Today I Learned..." handout (p. 112) for this week, and send it home with your children. Encourage parents to use the handout to plan meaningful family activities to reinforce this week's topic. Follow up the "Today I Learned..." activities next week by asking children what their families did.

Closing

String of Questions (up to 5 minutes)

Seat children in a circle. Say: **We've been learning today that ⬤ Jesus helps us follow him when we have questions.**

Hand each child a piece of string from "Setting the Stage." Say: **Let's share some questions we can ask Jesus. We'll go around the circle. As you ask your question, I'll tie a string to your finger.** Ask:

● **How can we ask Jesus to help with those questions?** (Pray; just ask.)

Say: **The string around your finger will remind you that ⬤ Jesus helps us follow him when we have questions. Let's pray.** Pray: **Dear God, we thank you that Jesus helps us follow him better. Help us have faith to believe in Jesus even if we can't see him with our eyes. In Jesus' name, amen.**

⬤ **The Point**

⬤ **The Point**

For Extra Time

If you have a long class time or want to add additional elements to your lesson, try one of the following activities.

LIVELY LEARNING: Is It Really You?

Gather children in a group on the floor. Choose three children to be Tappers, and have them stand at the front of the room. Tell the rest of the children to hide their eyes. The Tappers tiptoe among the children, and each tap a child on the head. Then the Tappers return to the front of the room. Children who were tapped stand up. Each child gets one guess as to who tapped him or her. If the guess is correct, he or she trades places with that Tapper. Play until everyone has been tapped at least once. Tell children that Thomas didn't have to guess who Jesus was because ⬤ Jesus helps us follow him when we have questions, and Jesus helped Thomas know he was alive.

⬤ **The Point**

MAKE TO TAKE: Seeing Heart Pins

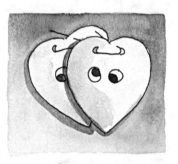

Before this activity, make a four-inch heart pattern for children to trace.

Set out red poster board, scissors, pencils, glue, and tape. Hand each child a pair of wiggly craft eyes and a safety pin. Tell children to use the heart pattern to trace a heart on red poster board then cut out the heart. Glue on the wiggly eyes. Then tape the safety pin to the back of the heart. Help children pin their seeing hearts on their clothing and model them. Explain that we can't see Jesus with our eyes, but we can believe in him with our hearts. Remind children that ⬤ Jesus helps us follow him when we have questions. Encourage children to touch their seeing hearts and tell one way they can follow Jesus this week.

⬤ **The Point**

TREAT TO EAT: Believe It Cookies

Make Believe It cookies for a special treat. Have children help slice refrigerator sugar-cookie dough into one-quarter-inch thick circles. Let each child press his or her thumb into the center then drop in a teaspoon of jam. Bake on a greased cookie sheet at 350 degrees until the cookies are golden brown. As you're preparing the cookies, talk about how Thomas wanted to see the marks in Jesus' hands to believe that Jesus was alive. Remind children that Jesus says we're special if we believe in him without seeing and that ⬤ Jesus helps us follow him when we have questions.

⬤ **The Point**

STORY PICTURE: Jesus Helps Thomas Believe

Hand each child a photocopy of the "Today I Learned..." handout from page 112. Set out crayons, white tissue paper, and a glue stick. Have children color the picture of Jesus talking with Thomas. Then let children glue white tissue paper to Jesus' robe. As children work, remind them that ⬤ Jesus helps us follow him when we have questions and that no question is too hard for Jesus—he wants to help us find the right answers.

⬤ **The Point**

Jesus helps us follow him when we have questions.

See With Your Heart

Photocopy this page. Cut out the eyeglasses and ear pieces. Tape the ear pieces to the hearts on the dotted lines, then fold back.

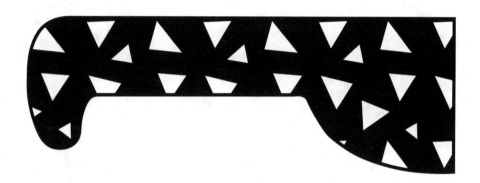

Jesus helps us follow him when we have questions.

TODAY I LEARNED . . .

The Point ✏ Jesus helps us follow him when we have questions.

Today your child learned that Jesus helps us follow him when we have questions. Children learned that Jesus helped Thomas believe when he questioned if Jesus was alive. They talked about asking Jesus' help to answer their questions.

Verse to Learn

"Believe in the Lord Jesus, and you will be saved—you and your household" (Acts 16:31).

Ask Me . . .

● How did Jesus help Thomas believe?
● Who can help when you have questions?
● What are some things we believe in even though we can't see them?

Family Fun

● Play a game of I Spy with your child. Take turns giving clues about an item in the room. Use clues such as "I spy something red. It gives light in a dark room. What do I spy?" The other person has three tries to guess the item. Remind your child that even though we can't "spy" Jesus with our eyes, we can believe in him with our hearts.

Jesus Helps Thomas Believe (John 20:24-29)

LESSON 7

Heaven Bound

The Point

✏ Jesus helps us follow him.

The Bible Basis

Matthew 28:16-20; Acts 1:6-11. Jesus rose to heaven.

Shortly before Jesus ascended to heaven, he commissioned his followers to make disciples of all nations; to baptize them in the name of the Father, the Son, and the Holy Spirit; and to teach them to obey all God commanded. Go. Make. Baptize. Teach. But *how?* Jesus knew the disciples needed help. So along with the Great Commission, Jesus gave his followers two promises: that he'd always be with them and that the Holy Spirit would come with enabling power. After giving these promises, Jesus ascended to heaven and left his followers to spread the good news throughout the world.

Kindergartners are eager to learn but are even more excited to share what they've learned. Whether it's a neat new way to tie their shoelaces or the latest playground pandemonium, five- and six-year-olds are ready and willing to tell exciting news. Children truly have a natural desire to witness. Use this lesson to help children learn that one way to follow Jesus is by telling others about his love.

Getting The Point

✏ **Jesus helps us follow him.**

It's important to say The Point just as it's written in each activity. Repeating The Point again and again will help the children remember it and apply it to their lives.

Children will
● realize that Jesus went to heaven to live with God,
● understand that Jesus wants us to tell others about him,
● teach Pockets to spread the good news about Jesus, and
● know that Jesus is always with us.

✏ **The Point**

This Lesson at a Glance

Before the lesson, collect the necessary items for the activities you plan to use. Refer to the Classroom Supplies and Learning Lab Supplies columns to determine what you'll need. Remember to make photocopies of the "Today I Learned..." handout (p. 125) to send home with your children.

Section	Minutes	What Children Will Do	Classroom Supplies	Learning Lab Supplies
Welcome Time	up to 5	**Welcome!**—Receive name tags and be greeted by the teacher.	"Cross Name Tags" handouts (p. 30), markers, pins or tape	
Let's Get Started Direct children to one or more of the Let's Get Started activities until everyone arrives.	up to 10	**Option 1: Going Up!**—Make a pop-up card to show Jesus on his way to heaven.	"Jesus Is With Us" handout (p. 124), glue sticks, scissors, crayons, cotton balls	
	up to 10	**Option 2: Walking on Clouds**—Have fun walking on feathery pillows.	Pillows	
	up to 10	**Option 3: Cloud Building**—Build whimsical cloud shapes.	Cotton balls	
Pick-Up Song	up to 5	**We Will Pick Up**—Sing a song as they pick up toys and gather for Bible-Story Time.	CD player	CD: "We Will Pick Up" (track 2)
Bible-Story Time	up to 5	**Setting the Stage**—Take an important message around the world.	Paper, tape, ribbon, paper bag, stickers, markers	
	up to 5	**Bible Song and Prayer Time**—Sing a song, bring out the Bible, and pray together.	Bible, construction paper, scissors, basket or box, CD player	CD "God's Book" (track 3), flame stamp and ink pad
	up to 10	**Hear the Bible Story**—Learn that Jesus rose to heaven in Matthew 28:16-20 and Acts 1:6-11.	Bible, glue stick, crayons	Learning Mat: Follow Jesus, batting, gauze square
	up to 10	**Do the Bible Story**—Follow fun directions using clouds.	Newspapers, CD player	CD: "Spread the Good News" (track 12)
Practicing The Point	up to 5	**Spread Out**—Help Pockets understand what spreading the good news about Jesus means.	Pockets the Kangaroo, plastic knife, rubber band, CD player	CD: "Spread the Good News" (track 12)
Closing	up to 5	**Friends Follow**—Say the names of people they can tell about Jesus then pray.		
For Extra Time		For extra-time ideas and supplies, see page 123.		

Jesus helps us follow him.

Welcome Time

Welcome! (up to 5 minutes)

- Bend down and make eye contact with children as they arrive.
- Greet each child individually with an enthusiastic smile.
- Thank each child for coming to class today.
- As children arrive, ask them about last week's "Today I Learned..." discussion. Ask questions such as "In what ways did you follow Jesus last week?" and "What did you discover that you believe in even if you can't see it?"
- Say: **Today we're going to learn that 🖊 Jesus helps us follow him.**
- Hand out the cross name tags children made in Lesson 1, and help them attach the name tags to their clothing. If some of the name tags were damaged or if children weren't in class that week, have them make new name tags using the photocopiable patterns on page 30.
- Direct children to the Let's Get Started activities you've set up.

🖊 **The Point**

Let's Get Started

Set up one or more of the following activities for children to do as they arrive. After you greet each child, invite him or her to choose an activity.

Circulate among the children to offer help as needed and to direct children's conversation toward today's lesson. Ask questions such as "Why is it important to follow Jesus?" or "What's the best thing about following Jesus?"

☐ Option 1: Going Up! (up to 10 minutes)

Before class, make photocopies of the "Jesus Is With Us" handout from page 124. Be sure to make a copy for each child plus a few extras for visitors.

Set out crayons, scissors, glue sticks, and cotton balls. Give each child a handout. Direct each child to color the picture then carefully cut out the card along the bold lines. Help children fold their cards on the center line, then pinch the top center of the card and fold the sides together, tucking the center portion inside the card. Crease the folds. Now the card will open and close and the figure of Jesus will pop up through the clouds. Have children glue pieces of cotton on the clouds around Jesus. As children work, remind them that 🖊 Jesus helps us follow him. Tell them that today's Bible story is about the time that God lifted Jesus to heaven.

🖊 **The Point**

☐ Option 2: Walking on Clouds (up to 10 minutes)

Scatter three or four old pillows in one corner of the room. Invite children to take a walk on "heavenly clouds." Let children step from cloud to cloud or crawl over the clouds.

As children play on the clouds, ask questions such as "Where do you think heaven is?" and "Where do clouds go?" Tell children they'll hear a story about how God lifted Jesus up through the clouds to live in heaven. Explain that since Jesus went back to heaven, now it's our job to go everywhere and tell

The Point people about him. Remind children that  Jesus helps us follow him and that we can follow Jesus by telling others about him.

☐ OPTION 3: Cloud Building (up to 10 minutes)

Set out a large bag of cotton balls, and invite children to build interesting things out of "clouds" such as feathery buildings, fluffy flowers, and cloud towers. Stimulate children's imagination by asking questions such as "What do you think heaven might look like?" and "What do you think a choir of angels sounds like?" Mention that they'll hear a story about how Jesus went to live in

The Point heaven. Point out that Jesus helps us follow him and we want to tell others about the place Jesus is making for us in heaven.

When everyone has arrived and you're ready to move on to the Bible-Story Time, encourage the children to finish what they're doing and get ready to clean up.

Pick-Up Song

We Will Pick Up (up to 5 minutes)

Lead children in singing "We Will Pick Up" (track 2) with the *CD* to the tune of "London Bridge." Encourage children to sing along as they help clean up the room.

If you want to include the names of all the children in your class, sing the song without the *CD* and repeat the naming section. If you choose to use the *CD*, vary the names you use each week.

Sing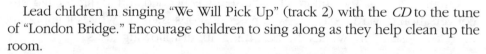

We will pick up all our toys,
All our toys, all our toys.
We will pick up all our toys
And put them all away.

I see (name) picking up,
Picking up, picking up.
I see (name) picking up
And putting toys away.

(Repeat)

Bible-Story Time

Setting the Stage (up to 5 minutes)

Tell the children you'll clap your hands to get their attention. Explain that when you clap, the children are to stop what they're doing, raise their hands, and focus on you. Encourage children to respond quickly so you'll have time for all the fun activities you've planned.

Before class, write the letters N, E, W, and S on separate sheets of paper.

Tape the appropriate letters to the north, south, east, and west corners of the room. On another sheet of paper, write: "Look under the table." Then roll the paper and tie it with yarn or ribbon. Place a sticker for each child in a paper bag, and set it under a table in the room. Leave the backing on the stickers.

Say: **Let's play a game. See the letters on the walls? They stand for north or east, south or west. When I point to you, call out any direction, then go to the letter on the wall that stands for the direction you chose.**

When everyone is standing by a letter, hold up the roll of paper tied with the ribbon. Say: **There's an important message on this paper. I'll hand it to a messenger and whisper what it says. The messenger will run to someone else and hand him or her the paper and whisper the message. Then the first messenger will sit down and the new messenger will travel to another person to spread the message. We'll play until everyone has heard the message and is sitting down.**

When you're finished, ask:

● **How did the message get to everyone?** (We told the message; we spread the message.)

● **Would a message make it to everyone if even ONE person hadn't been a messenger? Explain.** (No, the message would've stopped; yes, someone would have to tell the message again.)

● **Where did we carry our message?** (To everyone; to every corner of the room.)

Say: **We carried our message to the north, south, east, and west—all around our room! When a message is important, people want to be told. And if everyone tells someone else, the message goes all around the world. Today, we'll hear about the special message Jesus wants us to tell all around the world.** ● **Jesus helps us follow him, and one way to follow Jesus is to tell others about him. Now let's read the message.** Have a child untie the ribbon around the paper. Read the message aloud, and have children find the sack. Open the sack, and hand each child a sticker. Say: **Don't take the backing off your stickers, because in just a minute we'll use these stickers as we listen to the Bible story.**

● **The Point**

Bible Song and Prayer Time (up to 5 minutes)

Before class, make surprise cards for this activity by cutting construction paper into two-by-six-inch strips. Prepare a surprise card for each child plus a few extras for visitors. Fold the cards in half, then stamp the *flame stamp* inside one of the surprise cards. Mark Acts 1:6-11 in the Bible you'll be using.

Have children sit in a circle. Say: **Now it's time to choose a Bible person to bring me the Bible marked with today's Bible story. As we sing our Bible song, I'll pass out the surprise cards. Don't look inside your surprise card until the song is over.**

Lead children in singing "God's Book" (track 3) with the *CD* to the tune of "Old MacDonald Had a Farm." As you sing, pass out the folded surprise cards. If you want to include the names of all the children in your class, sing the song without the *CD* and repeat the naming section. If you choose to use the *CD*, vary the names you use each week.

Sing

Now it's time to read God's Book
And hear a Bible story.
It's fun to be here with my
  friends
And hear a Bible story.
	Now it's time to read God's Book
	And hear a Bible story.
	It's fun to be here with my
	  friends
	And hear a Bible story.

(Name)**'s here.** (Name)**'s here.** **Here is** (name). **Here is** (name). Now it's time to read God's Book And hear a Bible story.	(Name)**'s here.** (Name)**'s here.** **Here is** (name). **Here is** (name). Now it's time to read God's Book And hear a Bible story.

After the song, say: **You may look inside your surprise cards. The person who has the flame stamped inside his or her card will be our Bible person for today.**

Identify the Bible person, then have the rest of the children clap for him or her. Ask the Bible person to bring you the Bible. Help the Bible person open the Bible to the marked place, and show children where your story comes from. Then have the Bible person sit down.

Say: (Name) **was our special Bible person today. Each week, we'll have only one special Bible person, but each one of you is a special part of our class! Today we're all learning that**  **Jesus helps us follow him.**

The Point

Let's say a special prayer now and ask God to help us follow Jesus. I'll pass around this basket. When the basket comes to you, put your surprise card in it and say, "God, please help us follow Jesus."

Pass around the basket or box. When you've collected everyone's surprise card, set the basket aside, and pick up the Bible. Lead children in this prayer: **God, thank you for the Bible and all the stories in it. Teach us today that** Jesus **helps us follow him. In Jesus' name, amen.**

The Point

Hear the Bible Story (up to 10 minutes)

Set out crayons, a glue stick, and the *batting* and *gauze square* from the Learning Lab. Spread the *Learning Mat: Follow Jesus* on the floor. Say: **Let's play a story game. Leave the backing on your stickers, and lay your sticker on a footprint on the mat. I'll ask a story question. If the answer is "yes," move your sticker forward two footprints. If the answer is "no," move it back one footprint. We'll follow the footprints and see where they lead.** Ask the following yes and no story questions.

- **Did Cleopas and his friend know who Jesus was at first?** (No.)
- **Were Cleopas and his friend glad that Jesus was alive?** (Yes.)
- **Will Jesus help us follow him?** (Yes.)
- **Did Thomas believe without seeing?** (No.)
- **Does Jesus answer our questions?** (Yes.)
- **Did Thomas finally believe that Jesus is alive?** (Yes.)

Say: **You've traveled quite a way on the mat. Where did the path lead?** Have children take turns telling about the pictures their stickers are beside. Point out the fact that everyone's sticker is on a path leading to Jesus. Say:

The path on the *Learning Mat* always leads to Jesus. We want to follow Jesus every day. It's good that ⬤Jesus helps us follow him. Hold up the Bible. **Our story today comes from the books of Matthew and Acts in the Bible.** Point to the *Learning Mat*. **The *Learning Mat* shows us pictures of the Bible story.** Point to the picture of Jesus ascending to heaven. Ask:

● **What's happening in this picture?** (Jesus is going up to heaven; he's leaving to go be with God.)

Say: **Sometime after Jesus visited Thomas, Jesus and eleven disciples went to a mountain. Let's have two volunteers color the mountains in the picture. Jesus said to his disciples, "All power is given to me and this is what I want you to do. Go all over the world and tell people about me. Baptize them in my name and God's name and the name of the Holy Spirit. Teach the people to obey the things I've taught. And remember, I'll always be with you."** Ask:

● **What did Jesus want us to do?** (Teach others about Jesus; go all over the world to tell people about Jesus; baptize people; remember that Jesus is always with us.)

Say: **It sounds as if Jesus is going somewhere. Where do you think he's going? Let's find out.** Continue with the story. **Jesus wanted to cover us with his love so he sent us the Holy Spirit. Let's put a robe on Jesus to remind us how his love is all around us like a warm coat.** Let one child be the gluer and another child stick the *gauze* on Jesus' robe.

As Jesus said these things, he began to rise into the air. Up and up he went, until a cloud hid him from their sight. Who can add the clouds to our picture? Have two children attach the *batting* for the clouds. **The disciples were amazed!**

Suddenly two men in white stood beside the followers. "Why are you looking into the sky?" they asked. "Jesus went to heaven but he'll come back just as you saw him go." Ask:

● **Who did Jesus say would come to help us?** (The Holy Spirit.)

● **Why did Jesus promise to send the Holy Spirit?** (To help us; so we can follow him better; because Jesus loves us.)

Say: **Jesus went to live with God in heaven. Someday we'll live in heaven with Jesus, too, but we can follow Jesus today. Let's play a game to help us remember that ⬤Jesus helps us follow him.**

Do the Bible Story (up to 10 minutes)

Hand each child a sheet of newspaper. Tell children to crumple the newspapers to make "fluffy clouds." Have the children stand with their clouds around the room in a large circle.

Say: **I'll be Captain Cloud and give you directions to follow using your clouds. We'll see how many good cloud followers we have in our room. If you need help, use your hands to balance the clouds.** Give the following commands to the children:

● **Skip around the room with your cloud under your chin.**

● **Walk with your cloud between your knees.**

● **Put your cloud on your head, and tiptoe around the room. You may use your hands if you need help.**

● **Balance your cloud on your nose, and hop up and down. You may use your hands.**

⬤ **The Point**

⬤ **The Point**

● Sit quietly on your clouds.

Say: **We'll go around the circle and take turns telling which directions were easy or hard for you to follow and why.** Allow time for children to tell their ideas. Ask:

● **Why was it easier when you used your hands?** (It helped balance the cloud; hands kept the clouds from falling.)

● **How was using your hands in this game like Jesus helping us follow him?** (Jesus helps us just like our hands helped us; it's easier to follow when we have help.)

● **What are some ways to follow Jesus?** (Reading the Bible; praying; telling others about Jesus.)

● **The Point**

Say: ●**Jesus helps us follow him in all we do. We learned today that Jesus wants us to follow him by telling other people about him. And Jesus promised to send the Holy Spirit to help us. Let's sing an exciting new song about following Jesus and telling others about him!**

Lead children in singing "Spread the Good News" (track 12) with the *CD* to the tune of "Old MacDonald Had a Farm." Do the accompanying actions for a lively touch. Sing the song through twice.

Sing

Spread the good news everywhere (*clap in rhythm*),
Jesus is alive! (*Pat alternating knees.*)
Take the good news here and there (*clap in rhythm*),
Jesus is alive! (*Pat alternating knees.*)
Step-step-hop (*step, step, hop*),
Don't be slow. (*Turn around in place.*)
Right foot, left foot (*step with your right foot, then left foot*),
Do-si-do! (*Fold arms and step in a backward circle.*)
Spread the good news everywhere (*clap in rhythm*),
Jesus is alive! (*Pat alternating knees.*)

● **The Point**

Say: **I'm so glad that we can follow Jesus' directions and tell others about him. And isn't it great that ●Jesus helps us follow him? Now let's quietly do-si-do and find a place to sit. We'll see what Pockets is up to today.**

Practicing The Point

Spread Out (up to 5 minutes)

Before class, fasten a plastic knife in Pockets' paw with a rubber band.

Bring out Pockets the Kangaroo. Go through the following script. When you finish the script, put Pockets out of sight.

Spread Out

PUPPET SCRIPT

Pockets: *(Comes in singing mixed-up words to the song children just sang.)* "Spread the good food everywhere, Jesus is alive!" Hi, everyone! I'm ready to spread the good food! Are we having peanut butter or strawberry jam?

Teacher: What's the plastic knife for, Pockets? What's going on?

Pockets: I'm ready to spread the good food all around. I heard you singing earlier, and I'm ready to... *(sings)* "spread the good food everywhere, Jesus is alive!"

Teacher: *(Laughing)* No, Pockets, we're not spreading good food, we're spreading the good <u>news</u>! We've been learning that ✏ Jesus helps us follow him, and he wants us to follow by telling people the good news. Children, let's tell Pockets about our Bible story and the good news Jesus wants us to tell. *(Encourage children to retell how Jesus wants us to follow him by telling others about his love.)*

● **The Point**

Pockets: Oh, I get it now. Jesus wants us to follow him and one way is to tell others about his love.

Teacher: Right! Would you like to sing that song with us, Pockets?

Pockets: I sure would! It makes me glad to know that ✏ Jesus helps us follow him. Thanks, boys and girls! *(Have Pockets help you lead children in singing "Spread the Good News" (track 12) with the CD to the tune of "Old MacDonald Had a Farm." Let Pockets wave her plastic knife like a baton, and have her do-si-do with the children.)*

● **The Point**

Sing

Spread the good news everywhere *(clap in rhythm),*
Jesus is alive! *(Pat alternating knees.)*
Take the good news here and there *(clap in rhythm),*
Jesus is alive! *(Pat alternating knees.)*
Step-step-hop *(step, step, hop),*
Don't be slow. *(Turn around in place.)*
Right foot, left foot *(step with your right foot, then left foot),*
Do-si-do! *(Fold arms and step in a backward circle.)*
Spread the good news everywhere *(clap in rhythm),*
Jesus is alive! *(Pat alternating knees.)*

(Repeat)

Jesus helps us follow him.

TODAY I LEARNED . . .

We believe that Christian education extends beyond the classroom into the home. Photocopy the "Today I Learned..." handout (p. 125) for this week, and send it home with your children. Encourage parents to use the handout to plan meaningful family activities to reinforce this week's topic. Follow up the "Today I Learned..." activities next week by asking children what their families did.

Closing

Friends Follow (up to 5 minutes)

Have children form groups of two to four. Hand each group a cotton ball. Say: **Jesus rose to heaven to live with God. But we know that Jesus is always with us, too. How do we know that? The Bible tells us.** Read Matthew 28:19-20 from an easy-to-understand Bible such as the New International Version. Ask:

● **How long will Jesus be with us?** (Forever; always.)

● **What does Jesus want us to do?** (Teach other people what Jesus taught; tell people about Jesus.)

Say: **The cotton ball you have is like a little cloud. It will remind you that even though Jesus lives in heaven, he's with us always. And Jesus wants us to follow by telling others about him. When I clap my hands, the person holding the cotton-ball cloud will say who he or she can tell about Jesus this week. When I clap again, hand the cotton-ball cloud to someone else in your group.**

Continue until all the children have had a turn. Say: **Let's join hands and pray.** Pray: **Dear God, thank you that Jesus is always with us. Help us follow Jesus by telling others about him. In Jesus' name, amen.**

● **The Point**

Hand a cotton ball to each child. Say: **You may take this little cloud home as a reminder that Jesus is always with us and that ● Jesus helps us follow him.**

Jesus helps us follow him.

For Extra Time

If you have a long class time or want to add additional elements to your lesson, try one of the following activities.

LIVELY LEARNING: Bubble Up!

Before this activity, make a cloud blower for each child by taping a group of three or four drinking straws together, side by side. Then mix 1 cup of water, ⅓ cup liquid dish soap, and 1 teaspoon sugar in a bowl or jar. Stir the mixture until the sugar is dissolved.

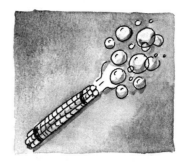

Spread newspapers on the floor or take the children outside, and invite them to blow bubble clouds as you review the Bible story together. Fill paper cups half full of bubble soap for each child, and hand them each a cloud blower. Show children how to dip the ends of their straws into the liquid then blow bubbles into the air. Challenge the children to follow their bubble clouds as you remind them that ● Jesus helps us follow him.

● **The Point**

MAKE TO TAKE: Take Jesus to the World

Before class, inflate and tie a blue balloon for each child. Set out green construction paper, markers, scissors, and tape. Distribute blue balloons and invite children to cut or tear the shapes of pretend countries to tape on the "world" like a globe. As children work, point out that Jesus wants us to go into all the world to make followers of people. Remind them that ● Jesus helps us follow him. When the balloon globes are done, let children bop them back and forth with a partner and call out the names of places where they could tell about Jesus.

● **The Point**

TREAT TO EAT: Edible Clouds

Make yummy clouds to eat and enjoy! Hand each child a ten-by-ten-inch piece of wax paper and a plastic spoon. Place a large dollop of whipped cream in the center of the wax paper, and encourage children to use their spoons to shape and mold cloud formations such as billowing thunderheads, fluffy cumulus, and wispy cirrus clouds. Remind children that ● Jesus helps us follow him, and even though he rose to heaven through the clouds, he's ready to help us follow him here on earth, too. Let children enjoy eating their clouds with their spoons.

● **The Point**

STORY PICTURE: Jesus Rises to Heaven

Hand each child a photocopy of the "Today I Learned..." handout from page 125. Set out cotton balls, glue, and a yellow highlighter pen. Allow children to stretch cotton balls then glue them as clouds in the picture. Let children trace the sunbeams with a yellow highlighter pen.

Jesus Is With Us

Photocopy this page and cut along the solid lines. Fold on the dotted lines.

"I am with you always."
Matthew 28:20b

"Jesus is with _____ ."

Jesus helps us follow him.

TODAY I LEARNED . . .

The Point ✏ Jesus helps us follow him.

LESSON 8

Today your child learned that Jesus helps us follow him. Children learned that Jesus rose to heaven but said he'd always be with us. Children talked about telling others about Jesus.

Verse to Learn

"Believe in the Lord Jesus, and you will be saved—you and your household" (Acts 16:31).

Ask Me . . .

● What did Jesus tell the disciples as he rose to heaven?

● Who can you tell about Jesus?

● What are some ways our family can follow Jesus?

Family Fun

● Make Crazy Clouds with your child for a fun family treat. Beat 3 egg whites, 1 teaspoon vanilla, and ¼ teaspoon cream of tartar. Slowly add 1 cup of white sugar and beat until stiff, glossy peaks form. Cover a cookie sheet with a brown paper sack. Let your child mound cloud shapes on the paper. Bake at 275 degrees for 1 hour. Cool in the *closed* oven for 2 hours. Enjoy the crazy clouds while your child tells how Jesus rose to heaven and wants us to tell others about him.

Jesus Rises to Heaven (Matthew 28:16-20; Acts 1:6-11)

Pentecost Praise

The Point

✏ Jesus helps us follow him by giving us the Holy Spirit.

The Bible Basis

Acts 2:1-13, 38-41. At Pentecost, Jesus sent us a helper and friend called the Holy Spirit.

As Jesus ascended to heaven, he told his disciples to wait in Jerusalem for the Holy Spirit—the gift promised by God. The disciples waited and prayed while the rest of Jerusalem prepared for the Feast of Pentecost, a celebration of the grain harvest. On the day of Pentecost, suddenly a sound like the rushing of wind filled the house where Jesus' friends were gathered, and tongues of fire descended and stood above the head of each person. The Holy Spirit had descended! And with the Spirit came the enabling power God promised, which transformed Jesus' followers into bold witnesses who spread the good news about Jesus in the face of incredible opposition.

Kindergartners are often confused about the concept of the Holy Spirit. Experiencing their world in concrete terms, young children may be afraid of the word "spirit" which conjures up images of ghosts. Assure your five- and six-year-olds that the Holy Spirit is a gift from God and that God sent the Holy Spirit to help us follow Jesus. Use this lesson to help your children focus on how exciting it is that the Holy Spirit helps us do God's work and that they can be like Peter and boldly tell people about Jesus.

✔ To prepare for possible questions about the Holy Spirit, you may wish to study the following Scriptures: Luke 11:13; John 14:15-17, 26; 15:26; 16:13; Acts 2:33; and Ephesians 1:13-14.

Getting The Point

✏ **Jesus helps us follow him by giving us the Holy Spirit.**

It's important to say The Point just as it's written in each activity. Repeating The Point again and again will help the children remember it and apply it to their lives.

Children will
● understand that Jesus gave us the Holy Spirit to help us,
● share ways the Holy Spirit can help them follow Jesus,
● help Pockets learn who the Holy Spirit is, and
● experience how the Holy Spirit gives them power to help others.

✏ **The Point**

This Lesson at a Glance

Before the lesson, collect the necessary items for the activities you plan to use. Refer to the Classroom Supplies and Learning Lab Supplies columns to determine what you'll need. Remember to make photocopies of the "Today I Learned..." handout (p. 140) to send home with your children.

Section	Minutes	What Children Will Do	Classroom Supplies	Learning Lab Supplies
Welcome Time	up to 5	**Welcome!**—Receive name tags and be greeted by the teacher.	"Cross Name Tags" handouts (p. 30), markers, pins or tape	
Let's Get Started Direct children to one or more of the Let's Get Started activities until everyone arrives.	up to 10	**Option 1: Rushing of Windsocks**—Make a rustling tissue paper windsock.	Tape, scissors, paper towel tubes, yarn	Red and yellow tissue paper
	up to 10	**Option 2: Holy Spirit Bakery**—Decorate a giant treat together.	Large prepared sugar cookie, canned icing, tiny cinnamon candies, plastic knives	
	up to 10	**Option 3: Power Puppets**—Create puppet friends, then help them move and talk.	Paper lunch sacks, tape, construction paper scraps, markers, glue	Sequins
Pick-Up Song	up to 5	**We Will Pick Up**—Sing a song as they pick up toys and gather for Bible-Story Time.	CD player	CD: "We Will Pick Up" (track 2)
Bible-Story Time	up to 5	**Setting the Stage**—Blow paper wads and learn that the Holy Spirit gives us power to follow Jesus.	Paper, straws	
	up to 5	**Bible Song and Prayer Time**—Sing a song, bring out the Bible, and pray together.	Bible, construction paper, scissors, basket or box, CD player	CD: "God's Book" (track 3), flame stamp and ink pad
	up to 10	**Hear the Bible Story**—Help tell the story of Pentecost from Acts 2:1-13, 38-41 and add flames to the Learning Mat.	Bible, glue stick, scissors, markers or crayons	Learning Mat: Follow Jesus, red and yellow tissue paper, color cube, sequins
	up to 10	**Do the Bible Story**—Play a game and sing a song to review the story of Pentecost.	CD player, crayons	Color cube, CD: "Spread the Good News" (track 12)
Practicing The Point	up to 5	**Power Up!**—Help Pockets learn about the Holy Spirit and how he helps us follow Jesus.	Pockets the Kangaroo, flashlight with batteries	
Closing	up to 5	**One for All**—Learn that God loves everyone and pray.	Cookie from Option 2 or other snack	
For Extra Time		For extra-time ideas and supplies, see pages 137-138.		

Jesus helps us follow him by giving us the Holy Spirit.

Welcome Time

Welcome! (up to 5 minutes)

- Bend down and make eye contact with children as they arrive.
- Greet each child individually with an enthusiastic smile.
- Thank each child for coming to class today.
- As children arrive, ask them about last week's "Today I Learned..." discussion. Ask questions such as "What does Jesus want us to tell others?" and "Who did you tell about Jesus last week?"
- Say: **Today we're going to learn that ◐ Jesus helps us follow him by giving us the Holy Spirit.**
- Hand out the cross name tags children made in Lesson 1, and help them attach the name tags to their clothing. If some of the name tags were damaged or if children weren't in class that week, have them make new name tags using the photocopiable patterns on page 30.
- Direct children to the Let's Get Started activities you've set up.

◐ **The Point**

Let's Get Started

Set up one or more of the following activities for children to do as they arrive. After you greet each child, invite him or her to choose an activity.

Circulate among the children to offer help as needed and to direct children's conversation toward today's lesson. Ask questions such as "What's the neatest gift you've received?" or "Who helps you do things when you need help?"

OPTION 1: Rushing of Windsocks (up to 10 minutes)

Before class, cut four strips each of red and yellow *tissue paper* from the Learning Lab for each child. Be sure to save enough *tissue paper* for the flames in "Hear the Bible Story." Cut paper towel or bathroom tissue tubes into half-inch segments. You'll need one segment for each child.

Set out *tissue paper* strips, tape, yarn, and scissors. Hand each child a segment of cardboard tube. Demonstrate how to tape *tissue paper* strips around the tube. Direct children to use two strips of each color. Roughly measure and cut a ten-inch piece of yarn for each child. Help them tape the yarn on opposite sides of their tubes for handles.

While children work, ask questions such as "What makes paper move and rustle?" and "What kinds of power can we use to make the paper move?" Let children have fun twirling their windsocks around and exploring different ways to move the paper. Explain that just as wind power moves the windsock, the Holy Spirit helps give us power to follow Jesus.

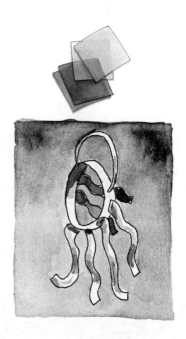

OPTION 2: Holy Spirit Bakery (up to 10 minutes)

Before this activity, prepare a large cookie using refrigerator sugar cookie dough and pressing it into the shape of a large circle on a greased pizza pan or cookie sheet. Bake as directed on the tube of dough.

Set out the big cookie, canned icing, plastic knives, and tiny cinnamon candies. Invite children to be bakery chefs and decorate a very large cookie. Have some of the children help spread the icing and other children add decorations on top. As they work together, explain that they'll hear a story about how Jesus helps us follow him by giving us the Holy Spirit. Explain that God gave us the Holy Spirit because he loves us and wanted to help us follow Jesus.

 The Point

Set the cookie aside for the Closing.

> ✔ If you choose not to do Option 2, provide another snack such as two oranges, a pineapple, or a small loaf of cinnamon bread. You'll use the snack item for the Closing.

☐ **OPTION 3: Power Puppets (up to 10 minutes)**

Set out markers or crayons, construction paper scraps, glue, and tape. Hand each child a paper lunch sack. Have children create puppets using torn pieces of construction paper and *sequins* from the Learning Lab to decorate their puppets. Save a few *sequins* for later.

 The Point

While the children work, tell them they'll hear a Bible story about a special friend called the Holy Spirit who gives us power to follow Jesus especially when we're shy or afraid. Tell children that Jesus helps us follow him by giving us the Holy Spirit. Invite children to move their power puppets and make them talk. Point out that just as they help their puppets to have the power to move and talk, the Holy Spirit helps us follow Jesus. Encourage children to use their puppets to tell ways to follow Jesus.

> ✔ Hold back a few red *sequins* and some *tissue paper* for the "Hear the Bible Story" activity. Then let children use any leftover sensory items and the *flame stamp* from the Learning Lab to decorate their puppets.

When everyone has arrived and you're ready to move on to the Bible-Story Time, encourage the children to finish what they're doing and get ready to clean up.

Pick-Up Song

We Will Pick Up (up to 5 minutes)

Lead children in singing "We Will Pick Up" (track 2) with the *CD* to the tune of "London Bridge." Encourage children to sing along as they help clean up the room.

Jesus helps us follow him by giving us the Holy Spirit.

If you want to include the names of all the children in your class, sing the song without the *CD* and repeat the naming section. If you choose to use the *CD*, vary the names you use each week.

Sing

We will pick up all our toys,
All our toys, all our toys.
We will pick up all our toys
And put them all away.

I see (name) picking up,
Picking up, picking up.
I see (name) picking up
And putting toys away.

(Repeat)

Bible-Story Time

Setting the Stage (up to 5 minutes)

Before class, crumple two sheets of paper into balls.

Tell the children you'll clap your hands to get their attention. Explain that when you clap, the children are to stop what they're doing, raise their hands, and focus on you. Encourage children to respond quickly so you'll have time for all the fun activities you've planned.

Gather children in two lines facing each other at opposite ends of the room. Say: **Let's play an exciting game to get things moving!** Give each child a drinking straw. Hand the first person in each line a paper wad. **When I clap my hands, the first person in each line will use the straws to blow the paper wads across the room to the next people in line. Then those people will blow the paper wads back across the room. Let's see how fast we can get these paper wads moving!**

When everyone's had a turn, ask:

● **What kind of power did we use to move the paper wads?** (Our breath; wind power.)

● **What would've happened if we set them on the floor but didn't blow them?** (They wouldn't move; they'd still be in the same place.)

Say: **Just like the paper wads needed power to move, we need special power to follow Jesus. Jesus wants us to follow him, and ◐ Jesus helps us follow him by giving us the Holy Spirit. In our Bible story, we'll learn about the day God sent the Holy Spirit to Jesus' friends in Jerusalem. Right now, let's see if you can use your muscle power to gather in a circle around the *Learning Mat.***

◐ The Point

Bible Song and Prayer Time (up to 5 minutes)

Before class, make surprise cards for this activity by cutting construction paper in two-by-six-inch slips. Prepare a surprise card for each child plus a few extras for visitors. Fold the cards in half, then stamp the *flame stamp* inside one of the surprise cards. Mark Acts 2:1-13, 38-41 in the Bible you'll be using.

Have the children sit in a circle. Say: **Now it's time to choose a Bible person to bring me the Bible marked with today's Bible story. As we sing**

Jesus helps us follow him by giving us the Holy Spirit.

our Bible song, I'll pass out the surprise cards. Don't look inside your card until the song is over.

Lead children in singing "God's Book" (track 3) with the *CD* to the tune of "Old MacDonald Had a Farm." As you sing, pass out the folded surprise cards. If you want to include the names of all the children in your class, sing the song without the *CD* and repeat the naming section. If you choose to use the *CD*, vary the names you use each week.

Sing

Now it's time to read God's Book
And hear a Bible story.
It's fun to be here with my
  friends
And hear a Bible story.

(Name)'s here.
(Name)'s here.
Here is (name).
Here is (name).
Now it's time to read God's Book
And hear a Bible story.

Now it's time to read God's Book
And hear a Bible story.
It's fun to be here with my
  friends
And hear a Bible story.

(Name)'s here.
(Name)'s here.
Here is (name).
Here is (name).
Now it's time to read God's Book
And hear a Bible story.

After the song, say: **You may look inside your surprise cards. The person who has the flame stamped inside his or her card will be our Bible person for today.**

Identify the Bible person, then have the rest of the children clap for him or her. Ask the Bible person to bring you the Bible. Help the Bible person open the Bible to the marked place, and show children where your story comes from. Then have the Bible person sit down.

Say: (Name) **was our special Bible person today. Each week, we'll have only one special Bible person, but each one of you is a special part of our class! Today we're all learning that 🖉 Jesus helps us follow him by giving us the Holy Spirit.**

🖉 The Point

Let's say a special prayer now and ask God to help us follow Jesus. I'll pass around this basket. When the basket comes to you, put your surprise card in it and say, "God, please help us follow Jesus."

Pass around the basket or box. When you've collected everyone's surprise card, set the basket aside and pick up the Bible. Lead children in this prayer: **God, thank you for the Bible and all the stories in it. Teach us today that 🖉 Jesus helps us follow him by giving us the Holy Spirit. In Jesus' name, amen.**

🖉 The Point

Hear the Bible Story (up to 10 minutes)

Before class, cut five three-inch flames from the *tissue paper* in the Learning Lab. Use markers to color the sides of the *color cube* found in the Learning Lab. Color each side of the cube one of the following colors: red, blue, green, or yellow. You may repeat the colors.

Lay the *Learning Mat: Follow Jesus* on the floor. Set the *tissue paper* flames and glue stick beside the mat. Hand each child a red, blue, yellow, or green crayon or marker. Set the *color cube* in the center of the mat. Say: **Let's** review our Bible story and how Jesus helps us follow him. We'll take turns rolling the *color cube*. The color it lands on means I'll choose someone holding that color crayon to answer a story question. Then everyone with that color crayon may color a footprint on the *Learning Mat*. Use the following questions. Be sure each child has a chance to either roll the cube or answer a story question.

● **Who wouldn't believe Jesus was alive until he saw Jesus?** (Thomas.)

● **Name one way Jesus helps us follow him.** (By answering our questions; by helping us believe; by listening to our prayers.)

● **What did Jesus explain to the two friends on the road to Emmaus?** (Why he had to die; he explained the Scriptures about Jesus.)

● **Just before Jesus went back to heaven, what did he tell his disciples to do?** (Tell others about him; go into the world and baptize people; bring people to him.)

● **Where did Jesus go when he rose through the clouds?** (To heaven; to live with God.)

If there are still footprints to color, allow children time to finish coloring all the footprints. Say: **We've been learning about how Jesus helps us follow him. Today we'll learn that** ⬤ **Jesus helps us follow him by giving us the Holy Spirit.** Hold up the Bible. **Our Bible story comes from the book of Acts, and the *Learning Mat* shows a picture of the story.**

Remember when Jesus rose to heaven? He promised to send someone to help us know how to follow Jesus. That special friend is the Holy Spirit. Let's hear how Jesus sent us the Holy Spirit. You can help me tell the story. Whenever you hear the word "fire," rub your hands together quickly. Rubbing your hands together makes them toasty and warm like when you're near a fire. Whenever you hear the word "wind," make a whooshing sound. And when I say the word "power," make a muscle with your arm. Let's practice once. Say the cue words and allow children to respond with the accompanying actions.

Say: **Jerusalem was full of people who'd come to celebrate the grain harvest called Pentecost. Many of Jesus' followers were gathered together in a house. Let's color the group of people on the *Learning Mat*.**

Jesus' followers had been waiting for God to send them the Holy Spirit. They knew that Jesus keeps his promises, and they were excited about the new friend who would help them follow Jesus.

Suddenly a noise came from heaven! It sounded like a mighty <u>wind</u> blowing. The sound of the mighty <u>wind</u> filled the whole house where they were sitting. Then they saw something like flames of <u>fire</u> that broke apart and stood over each person there. But no one got burned. Imagine what that must've been like!

Say: **Let's glue *tissue paper* flames and sparkles above the followers' heads in the picture.** Allow each child to glue a flame or *sequins* above the heads of the followers.

Continue the story. **After the <u>wind</u> and the <u>fire</u>, the people were filled with the Holy Spirit. They began talking in different languages. The Holy Spirit gave them the <u>power</u> to speak in languages they'd never spoken before!**

People from many different countries crowded into Jerusalem to celebrate a special feast. When they heard the noise of the <u>wind</u>, they

⬤ **The Point**

gaped in astonishment! All the visitors heard Jesus' disciples speaking in their own languages. "How can this be?" they wondered. "These men live around here. How can they speak our different languages?" The disciples told everyone how wonderful God is and how much <u>power</u> he has!

The Holy Spirit helped Peter tell a huge crowd of people about Jesus. Peter warned people about sin and invited them to believe in Jesus. Because Peter spoke with the <u>power</u> of the Holy Spirit, about 3,000 people believed in Jesus that day!

Ask:

● **Who helped Peter tell the crowds about Jesus?** (The Holy Spirit.)

● **What did Peter tell the crowds?** (That Peter would forgive them; that they should believe in Jesus.)

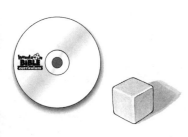

● The Point

Say: **Jesus knew that after he went back to heaven, his disciples would need help. That's why ● Jesus helps us follow him by giving us the Holy Spirit. One way the Holy Spirit helps is by giving us the power to tell others about Jesus, just like Peter did. When we tell others about Jesus, then they can love him, too. The Holy Spirit gives us power to do what Jesus wants us to do. Let's play a game to remind us of Pentecost when God sent the Holy Spirit.** Return the *Learning Mat* to the Learning Lab. You'll need the *color cube* and crayons for the next game.

Do the Bible Story (up to 10 minutes)

Say: **To play this game, you'll each need a crayon.** Be sure children have their crayons. **We'll take turns rolling the *color cube*. If the color called matches your crayon, stand and tell one thing about Jesus.**

Continue playing until each child has had a turn to stand and tell about Jesus.

● The Point

Say: **Just like the Holy Spirit helped Peter stand and tell about Jesus, the Holy Spirit gives us power to follow him, too. It's important to remember that ● Jesus helps us follow him by giving us the Holy Spirit. And the Holy Spirit helps give us the power to tell others about Jesus just like Peter told the crowds.**

Let's sing a song about following Jesus and telling everyone about him. Lead children in singing "Spread the Good News" (track 12) with the *CD* to the tune of "Old MacDonald Had a Farm." Do the accompanying actions for a lively touch. Sing the song through twice.

Sing

Spread the good news everywhere (clap in rhythm),
Jesus is alive! (Pat alternating knees.)
Take the good news here and there (clap in rhythm),
Jesus is alive! (Pat alternating knees.)
Step-step-hop (step, step, hop),
Don't be slow. (Turn around in place.)
Right foot, left foot (step with your right foot, then left foot),
Do-si-do! (Fold arms and step in a backward circle.)
Spread the good news everywhere (clap in rhythm),
Jesus is alive! (Pat alternating knees.)

Jesus helps us follow him by giving us the Holy Spirit.

Practicing The Point

Power Up! (up to 5 minutes)

Before class, remove the batteries from a flashlight. Keep the batteries with you to replace during the activity. Place the flashlight in Pockets' pouch.

Bring out Pockets the Kangaroo. When you finish the script, put Pockets out of sight.

Power Up!

PUPPET SCRIPT

Teacher: Hello, Pockets. What do you have?

Pockets: *(Looking sad and shaking her head)* I was cleaning out my closet, and I found this flashlight, but I can't get it to work.

Teacher: Let's see, maybe it's not turned on. *(Flip the switch a few times.)*

Pockets: See? It won't work. There's no power.

Teacher: Do you know that there is someone who never runs out of power, Pockets? It's a special friend we have.

Pockets: Really? Never runs out of power? Oh, who is it? Can I be friends, too? Can I?

Teacher: *(Laughing)* Yes, Pockets, this friend is a gift from God. Children, let's tell Pockets who we've been learning about today and how our special friend helps us follow Jesus. *(Encourage children to tell Pockets the story of Pentecost. Be sure to have them bring out how the Holy Spirit helped Peter by giving him the power to tell about Jesus. Lead children in repeating the point to Pockets.)* You see, Pockets, the Holy Spirit gives us the power to follow Jesus. Here, let's try some new batteries in your flashlight. *(Replace the batteries and turn on the flashlight.)* See? Just like the batteries give power to your flashlight, the Holy Spirit gives us power to follow Jesus!

Pockets: That's a <u>lot</u> of power! I want to be like Peter and tell everyone about Jesus. *(Shines the flashlight under her face.)* "Jesus is Lord!" Now you can have a turn! *(Hands the flashlight to a child.)*

   (Invite each child to shine the flashlight and say, "Jesus is Lord" or ● Jesus helps us follow him by giving us the Holy Spirit.) Thanks for helping me learn about the Holy Spirit, boys and girls. And thanks for helping me with my flashlight, too. 'Bye!

● **The Point**

Jesus helps us follow him by giving us the Holy Spirit.

TODAY I LEARNED . . .

We believe that Christian education extends beyond the classroom into the home. Photocopy the "Today I Learned..." handout (p. 140) for this week, and send it home with your children. Encourage parents to use the handout to plan meaningful family activities to reinforce this week's topic. Follow up the "Today I Learned..." activities next week by asking children what their families did.

Closing

One for All (up to 5 minutes)

As children are finding seats at the table, break apart the big cookie from Option 2 so each child receives a piece. If you use another snack such as two oranges, have them peeled before beginning this activity.

● **The Point**

Say: ● **Jesus helps us follow him by giving us the Holy Spirit. The Holy Spirit gives us power to be brave and helps us think of the right things to say. But who is the Holy Spirit for? Let's use our big cookie to help us find out. When I call your name, come get a napkin and a piece of cookie.** When each child has a portion of the snack, ask:

- ● **How many cookies did we start with?** (One.)
- ● **Was there enough to go around?** (Yes.)

Say: **Just like our one cookie was big enough to serve everyone, the Holy Spirit is big enough and powerful enough to help everyone who believes in Jesus! Before we eat our treats, we'll go around the circle. Tell the person on your right: "The Holy Spirit can help *you!*"**

● **The Point**

After each child has been affirmed, say: **Let's pray.** Pray: **Dear God, thank you for the Holy Spirit. Thank you that ● Jesus helps us follow him by giving us the Holy Spirit. In Jesus' name, amen.**

Let children enjoy eating their snacks. Remind them to take home any projects they made in the Let's Get Started activities.

Jesus helps us follow him by giving us the Holy Spirit.

For Extra Time

If you have a long class time or want to add additional elements to your lesson, try one of the following activities.

LIVELY LEARNING: Group Review

Let children review this lesson with an exciting "board" game. First have children get into groups of three and divide the following roles among their group members: the Marker, the Roller, and the Speaker. Spread the *Learning Mat* on the floor, and give each group four dry beans.

To play the game, ask each group a different story review question. After a group decides on an answer, the Speaker will share the group's answer with the class. Then the Roller will toss the *color cube* like a die, and the Marker will place a bean on the first footprint of the same color. For example, if the *color cube* lands with a red square facing up, the Marker will place a bean on the closest red footprint.

Then ask another story review question to continue the game. Each time a group comes to a story picture on the *Learning Mat,* have the Marker leave a bean on the picture. Play until each group has placed a bean on the picture of Pentecost. You can use the story review questions below, repeating or adding as you need to.

- **Who were Cleopas and Peter?** (Two of Jesus' followers.)
- **Where were they walking?** (Emmaus.)
- **Who came to walk with them?** (Jesus.)
- **What good news did the two friends tell Jesus' followers in Jerusalem?** (Jesus is alive.)
- **What did Thomas want to do before he believed Jesus was alive?** (Touch him.)
- **What helped Thomas believe?** (Jesus showed his hands.)
- **Before Jesus went to heaven, what did he tell the disciples to do?** (Go into all the world and tell people about him.)
- **Who did Jesus promise to send?** (The Holy Spirit.)
- **What happened at Pentecost?** (The Holy Spirit came; there was a sound of wind and flames; Peter told people about Jesus.)
- **How did the Holy Spirit help Peter?** (He helped Peter preach to a big crowd; the Holy Spirit helped Peter be brave.)
- **What did the Holy Spirit help the disciples do?** (Tell about Jesus; speak in different languages.)

As children play, remind them that ✏ Jesus helps us follow him by giving us the Holy Spirit.

✏ The Point

MAKE TO TAKE: Holy Spirit Spirals

Make photocopies of the "Holy Spirit Spiral" handout (p. 139) for each child. Use yellow or orange construction paper to make the photocopies.

Set out scissors. Give each child a handout. Have them cut on the solid lines around and around to the center. When the center of the circle is lifted, the spiral will twirl downward. As children work, have them retell the story of Pentecost. Then as children unfurl their spirals, point out that the flame drops

Jesus helps us follow him by giving us the Holy Spirit.

● The Point

down and reminds us of the flames of fire that descended on Jesus' followers at Pentecost. Remind children that the Holy Spirit is our friend and that ● Jesus helps us follow him by giving us the Holy Spirit.

TREAT TO EAT: No-Bake Story Dough

Before class, mix the following no-bake cookie dough:
4 ½ c. graham cracker crumbs
1 c. powdered sugar
⅓ c. thawed frozen orange juice concentrate
¼ c. light corn syrup
¼ c. softened margarine

Hand each child a square of wax paper and a palm-size ball of cookie dough. Invite children to create one of the following items from the Bible story: a flame, Peter, or a house. After they've made their shapes, have children use their shapes to retell the story of Pentecost. As children eat their dough shapes,

● The Point

tell them that ● Jesus helps us follow him by giving us the Holy Spirit and that we can be like Peter and tell others about Jesus.

STORY PICTURE: The Holy Spirit Comes at Pentecost.

Hand each child a photocopy of the "Today I Learned..." handout from page 140. Set out glitter glue and markers. Let children color their pictures. Then invite them to use glitter glue to highlight the flames of fire. As they work, ask children to tell how the Holy Spirit helps us follow Jesus.

Jesus helps us follow him by giving us the Holy Spirit.

Holy Spirit Spiral

Photocopy this page on orange or yellow paper. Have children cut on the solid lines.

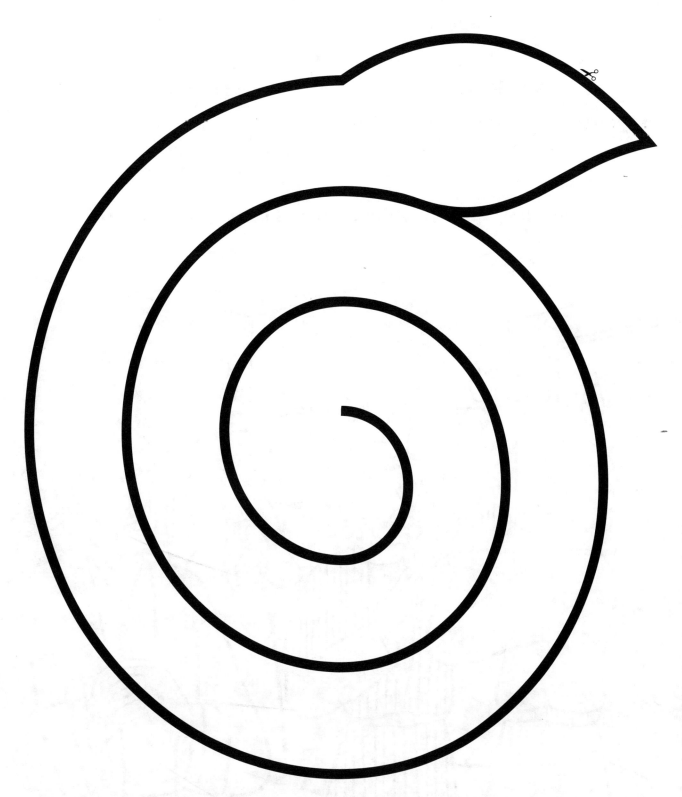

Jesus helps us follow him by giving us the Holy Spirit.

TODAY I LEARNED . . .

The Point Jesus helps us follow him by giving us the Holy Spirit.

Today your child learned that Jesus helps us follow him by giving us the Holy Spirit. Children learned about Pentecost when God sent the Holy Spirit to Jesus' followers. They talked about how the Holy Spirit helps us follow Jesus today.

Verse to Learn

"Believe in the Lord Jesus, and you will be saved—you and your household" (Acts 16:31).

Ask Me . . .

- What happened at the first Pentecost?
- How does the Holy Spirit help you follow Jesus?
- Who can our family tell about Jesus?

Family Fun

● Let your child make a window banner. Grate old red, orange, and yellow crayons. Spread a sixteen-inch piece of wax paper on an ironing board, and heat the iron on low. Sprinkle the grated crayons on half of the wax paper. Fold the wax paper in half. Iron over the wax paper, allowing the crayons to melt and mix. Cool the picture for ten minutes, then tape it in a window. Have your child tell about Pentecost when flames of fire and the sound of rushing wind marked the coming of the Holy Spirit.

The Holy Spirit Comes at Pentecost (Acts 2:1-13, 38-41)

Peter Serves

Stories of Peter and John leap from the pages of Acts, providing us with powerful examples of servanthood. In the name of Jesus, Peter and John healed the man who couldn't walk. With the help of the Holy Spirit, they boldly witnessed in the face of threats and opposition. Answering the pleas of her grieving friends, Peter raised Tabitha from the dead. In another demonstration of divine power, an angel miraculously helped Peter escape from prison. These stories assure us that although as Jesus' followers we will face challenges, we never have to face them alone. When we dedicate our lives to God's service, we can trust God to empower us.

Kindergartners are eager helpers and are ready to serve in a snap. Mention that the classroom is dusty, and children swing into a dusting frenzy. Or ask for one crayon, and young helpers will hand you a dozen. Eager and sincere, most five- and six-year-olds are willing to serve in any way possible. Use these lessons on Peter to help young children learn that we can serve Jesus in different ways and that he's always ready to help us.

Four Lessons on Peter

	Page	Point	Bible Basis
Lesson 10 **A Leap of Praise**	145	Jesus helps us serve him.	Acts 3:1-10
Lesson 11 **Speak Up for Jesus**	157	Jesus helps us serve him.	Acts 4:1-21
Lesson 12 **Dead—Then Alive!**	169	Jesus helps us serve him.	Acts 9:36-42
Lesson 13 **Peter's Set Free**	181	Jesus helps us serve him.	Acts 12:4-17

Time Stretchers

Who Can You Serve?

Explain to children that serving means helping and doing things for others. Tell them that we can serve Jesus just as we serve other people. Suggest ways to serve Jesus, such as telling other people about him, praying for others, and helping people when they're sick. Point out that when we serve Jesus, we're spreading his love to everyone.

Tape one less paper plate than there are children to the floor. Explain that you'll call out a Who, When, Where, or How question about serving. The children will run to stand on a paper plate. The child left without a plate will answer the question. For example, if you say, "Who can you serve?" the child will tell the name of someone he or she can serve. Use the following questions:

● **Who can you serve?** (Friend; family member; someone at church or school.)
● **When can you serve?** (Any time; at dinner; when I'm with my family.)
● **Where can you serve?** (At home; at school; at church; anywhere.)
● **How can you serve?** (Help around the house; bake cookies for a sick friend; rake grandma's yard.)

Story Rhyme Review

Review this module's Bible stories with a fun rhyming game. Make three photocopies each of the "Today I Learned..." handouts from pages 156, 168, 179, and 192. Cut out the story pictures, and tape them to the floor. As children say this rhyme, lead them in the accompanying motions, then have them hop to the correct story picture.

One, two, take the lead *(hold up one finger, then two);*
Jesus helps us serve indeed! *(Clap in rhythm with the words.)*
Help a lame man jump and hop. *(Go to the picture of the lame man.)*
Talk of Jesus—never stop! *(Go to the picture of Peter and the Temple leaders.)*
Heal the sick and help the poor *(go to the picture of Tabitha),*
And God will open any door! *(Go to the picture of Peter and the angel.)*
Jesus / helps us / serve him! *(Clap in rhythm with the words.)*

Remembering God's Word

Each four- or five-week module focuses on a key Bible verse. The key verse for this module is "You are serving the Lord Christ" (Colossians 3:24b, New Century Version).

This module's key verse will teach children that we can serve Jesus in many ways. Have fun using these ideas any time during the module.

Servants and Masters

Read aloud Colossians 3:24b from an easy-to-understand Bible translation. Ask:
● **What does it mean to serve someone?** (To help him; to give her something; to be kind and sharing.)

● **How can we serve God?** (By telling other people about him; by helping others.)

Say: **We can serve God by serving others. This game will help us practice fun ways to serve.**

Form pairs, and have partners decide who will be the Servant and who will be the Master. Assure children that they'll switch roles shortly. Explain that you're the Head Master and that you'll tell a way to serve each other. For example, you may say, "Servants, clap for your Masters" or "Masters, help your Servants sit down." After the command is carried out, have children repeat the key verse. Then switch roles for the next round.

For extra fun, choose a child to act as the Head Master while you take that child's place as Servant or Master. Use the following suggestions for ways to serve.

● Servants, polish your Masters' shoes.
● Masters, brush off your Servants' clothes.
● Masters, pat your Servants' heads.
● Servants, fan your Masters.
● Masters, hum a tune for your Servants.

When you're done playing, discuss how both servants and masters serve each other and how we can all serve Jesus in different ways.

Verse Jumping

Read aloud the key verse, and then ask:

● **Why does Jesus want us to serve him?** (To show that we love him; to show that he's special.)

Say: **We serve Jesus when we serve and help others.** Ask:

● **How can you serve someone this week?** (By helping my mom make dinner; I can set the table for my sister; I'll help my brother rake the lawn.)

Say: **It's important to remember to serve each other. Let's play a game to help us remember our key verse.**

Form six groups. Groups may be as small as one child. Seat the groups in a line across the floor. Assign each group a word in the key verse. Explain that when you point to a group, that group will jump up and call out their word. Go slowly at first, pointing to each group from left to right. Add an element of excitement by pointing to the groups more quickly each time. When you're finished, allow each child to stamp his or her hand with the *serving stamp*. Take a breather between games, and ask questions such as "Who in our church serves Jesus?" and "How can you serve Jesus?" Explain that we serve Jesus in many ways including helping and praying for others.

Note:
If the ink pad is dry, moisten it with three to five drops of water.

Story Enhancements

Make Bible stories come alive in your classroom by bringing in Bible costumes, by setting out sensory items that fit with the stories, or by creating exciting bulletin boards. When children learn with their five senses as well as with their hearts and minds, lessons come alive, and children remember them. Each week, bring in one or more of the following items to help motivate and involve children in the Bible lessons they'll be learning. These ideas will get you started.

Module Bulletin Board

Create a bulletin board that children can interact with during this module. Cover the bulletin board or wall space with black or dark blue paper. In the center, tape the words "We Serve Jesus Hand in Hand." Let each child trace a hand on construction paper and carefully cut out the hand shape. Help children write their names on the palms. Tape the hands under the words on the bulletin board. Each time children tell a way they've served Jesus that week, have them draw a small heart on a finger of their hand. Challenge students to collect five hearts on their hands.

Lesson 10

● Bring in a small woven mat or area rug. Explain that in Jesus' day, people who couldn't walk had to lie on mats and beg for money. Let children take turns sitting on the mat and thinking about what it would be like to beg. Before they leave the mat, encourage children to name five things they're thankful that they don't have to beg for.

● Bring in coins from around the world. Point out that in Jesus' day, a "lepta" was worth only a little more than a penny, but even that small amount could help buy food. Tell them they'll hear a story about a man who couldn't walk and begged money from people to help buy food.

Lesson 11

● Bring in a variety of tools for communicating, such as a telephone, a radio, paper and pencil, and drawing paper and crayons. Ask children what these items have in common. Explain that we can serve Jesus by telling others about him in many ways.

● Make a mock "witness stand" in your classroom by placing a small table or TV tray beside a chair. Invite children to sit in the chair and hold a Bible. Encourage them to tell one thing about Jesus. Explain that a witness chair is used when people are telling the truth in court. Point out that each of us can be a witness for Jesus because we can tell others about him. Tell children they'll hear a story about how Peter and John were witnesses for Jesus.

Lesson 12

● Bring in afghans, cross-stitch samplers, or other handmade items from members of your congregation. (Or invite the members to personally display their creations.) Explain that the woman in today's Bible story made beautiful clothes for people to wear, and she made them with love. Point out that the woman's friends showed Peter all the beautiful things she'd made just as you're showing beautiful items made by people in your church.

Lesson 13

● Bring a padlock and key. Let children take turns locking and unlocking the padlock. Talk about the fact that locks may keep people out of things but that locks aren't strong enough for Jesus. Tell children they'll hear a story about how Jesus sent an angel to help Peter in prison.

● Bring in a variety of chains such as small necklace chains, dog-leash chains, and large chains from swing sets. Compare and contrast the chains. Then invite children to try pulling the large chains apart. Explain that Peter was locked in chains, but that didn't stop Jesus from sending an angel to rescue Peter.

A Leap of Praise

The Point

🖊 Jesus helps us serve him.

The Bible Basis

Acts 3:1-10. Peter and John heal a lame man.

Though many people could be seen in the Temple area at any time, devout Jews in Jesus' day faithfully attended morning and evening prayer hours. Three p.m. in Jerusalem heralded the hour of evening prayer at the Temple, and Peter and John worshiped there daily, frequently meeting the same man sitting near the Temple gate. The man had been unable to walk since birth and was carried every day to the Temple to beg money from people entering through the east gate. When he begged Peter and John for coins, they gave him a much greater treasure—they healed him in the name of Jesus Christ. As the man leapt about and praised God, crowds witnessed the healing power of Jesus. The miracle cleared the way for Peter to preach the gospel.

The man in the Bible story received an amazing gift of healing. Ask most kindergartners what's the best gift they've ever received, and you'll hear everything from super walkie-talkies to dolls that grow their own hair. Children typically understand gift giving and receiving in material terms. It's important for us to communicate Jesus' teachings—that giving and serving don't require money but a loving heart. Use this lesson to teach children that they can serve Jesus as Peter and John did: by helping others.

Getting The Point

🖊 **Jesus helps us serve him.**

It's important to say The Point just as it's written in each activity. Repeating The Point again and again will help the children remember it and apply it to their lives.

Children will
● realize that it's Jesus' power which helps us,
● understand that helping others is a way to serve Jesus,
● help Pockets understand that we're all servants, and
● find ways to serve.

🖊 **The Point**

This Lesson at a Glance

Before the lesson, collect the necessary items for the activities you plan to use. Refer to the Class-room Supplies and Learning Lab Supplies columns to determine what you'll need. Remember to make photocopies of the "Today I Learned..." handout (p. 156) to send home with your children.

Section	Minutes	What Children Will Do	Classroom Supplies	Learning Lab Supplies
Welcome Time	up to 5	**Welcome!**—Receive name tags and be greeted by the teacher.	"Cross Name Tags" hand-outs (p. 30), markers, pins or tape	
Let's Get Started — Direct children to one or more of the Let's Get Started activities until everyone arrives.	up to 10	**Option 1: Great Gate**—Help each other build an archway gate.	Building blocks, cardboard	
	up to 10	**Option 2: Leg Lifts**—Use their legs and feet to balance pillows.	Pillows or cushions, blanket	
	up to 10	**Option 3: Praise Raisers**—Create musical instruments and praise Jesus.	Crepe paper, scissors, tape, plastic drinking straws, jingle bells	
Pick-Up Song	up to 5	**We Will Pick Up**—Sing a song as they pick up toys and gather for Bible-Story Time.	CD player	CD: "We Will Pick Up" (track 2)
Bible-Story Time	up to 5	**Setting the Stage**—Run an unusual race and learn what it's like to be helped.	Paper grocery sacks	
	up to 5	**Bible Song and Prayer Time**—Sing a song, bring out the Bible, and pray together.	Bible, construction paper, scissors, basket or box, CD player	CD: "God's Book" (track 3), serving stamp and ink pad
	up to 10	**Hear the Bible Story**—Help tell a Bible story from Acts 3:1-10 and wave their praise streamers.	Bible, CD player, praise rais-ers from Option 3	Bible Big Book: How Peter Served Jesus, CD: "How Peter Served Jesus, Part I" (track 13)
	up to 10	**Do the Bible Story**—Play a game and sing an action song.		
Practicing The Point	up to 5	**Unhappy Hopper**—Encourage Pock-ets to serve Jesus in her own special way.	Pockets the Kangaroo, tennis shoes	
Closing	up to 5	**Servant Song**—Pray and sing about serving Jesus.		Serving stamp and ink pad
For Extra Time		For extra-time ideas and supplies, see page 154.		

Jesus helps us serve him.

Welcome Time

Welcome! (up to 5 minutes)

- Bend down to make eye contact with children as they arrive.
- Greet each child individually with an enthusiastic smile.
- Thank each child for coming to class today.
- As children arrive, ask them about last week's "Today I Learned..." discussion. Use questions such as "Who did you help last week?" or "How did you thank God?"
- Say: **Today we're going to learn that**  **Jesus helps us serve him.**
- Hand out the cross name tags children made during Lesson 1, and help them attach the name tags to their clothing. If some of the name tags were damaged or if some of the children weren't in class that week, have them make new name tags using the photocopiable handout on page 30.
- Direct the children to the Let's Get Started activities you've set up.

Let's Get Started

Set up one or more of the following activities for children to do as they arrive. After you greet each child, invite him or her to choose an activity.

Circulate among the children to offer help as needed and to direct their conversation toward today's lesson. Ask questions such as "How has someone helped you?" and "What's it like to get a surprise gift?"

☐ OPTION 1: Great Gate (up to 10 minutes)

Set out building blocks, and encourage children to build an archway gate by making two stacks of blocks, by placing a piece of cardboard across the top, and then by placing a row of blocks on top of the cardboard. As children build, explain that they'll hear a story today about something amazing that happened at the Temple gate. Point out that the Temple gate was similar to the gate they're making, only much bigger. Tell children that ⬤ Jesus helps us serve him, and in today's story, Jesus helps Peter serve someone at the Temple.

✔ For extra fun, provide cardboard boxes and duct tape, and let children create a giant gate. Use the structure for the "Hear the Bible Story" activity.

☐ OPTION 2: Leg Lifts (up to 10 minutes)

Spread an old blanket in one corner of the room. Set a variety of pillows or small cushions on the blanket. As children arrive, invite them to remove their shoes and lie on their backs with their feet in the air. Let children practice balancing the pillows on their feet and doing tricks such as flipping and catching

● The Point

● The Point

the pillows with their toes. Or have them use their feet and legs to pass pillows to their friends. As children play, make comments such as "Look at all the fun you can have with your feet and legs. Imagine what it would be like not to be able to move them." Explain that you'll hear a Bible story about a man who couldn't use his legs and how Peter and John, Jesus' followers, helped the man. Tell children that helping others is a way to serve Jesus and that Jesus helps us serve him.

● **The Point**

> ✔ If girls are wearing dresses, encourage them to do pillow tricks while standing up. Have them pick up pillows with their toes, pass pillows to their friends with their feet, and flip pillows upside down.

OPTION 3: Praise Raisers (up to 10 minutes)

Set out crepe paper, tape, scissors, and jingle bells. Hand out drinking straws, and invite children to create colorful musical instruments. Let children cut and tape two paper streamers to their straws and then tie two jingle bells to the ends of each streamer. As children work, tell them that they'll hear a story about a time Peter and John served Jesus by healing a man who couldn't walk. Explain that the man was so happy that he praised God again and again. Tell children that we can praise God just as the man in the story did. Allow children to wave their musical streamers; then put them aside to use during the Bible story.

> ✔ If some children didn't choose to do Option 3, ask volunteers to make enough for everyone in the class. You'll be using the praise raisers in the "Hear the Bible Story" activity.

After everyone has arrived and you're ready to move on to the Bible-Story Time, encourage the children to finish what they're doing and get ready to clean up.

Pick-Up Song

We Will Pick Up (up to 5 minutes)

Lead children in singing "We Will Pick Up" (track 2) with the *CD* to the tune of "London Bridge." Encourage the children to sing along as they help clean up the room.

If you want to include the names of all the children in your class, sing the song without the *CD,* and repeat the naming section. If you choose to use the *CD,* vary the names you use each week.

Jesus helps us serve him.

Sing

We will pick up all our toys,
All our toys, all our toys.
We will pick up all our toys
And put them all away.

I see (name) picking up,
Picking up, picking up.
I see (name) picking up
And putting toys away.
(Repeat)

Bible-Story Time

Setting the Stage (up to 5 minutes)

Tell the children you'll clap your hands to get their attention. Explain that when you clap, children are to stop what they're doing, raise their hands, and focus on you. Encourage children to respond quickly so you'll have time for all the fun activities you've planned.

Have children choose partners and line up at one end of the room. Hand each pair of children a brown paper grocery sack. Say: **Let's have an unusual race. Stand next to your partner and lock arms. Then each partner will put one foot in the grocery sack.** Pause for children to each put a foot in the bag. **When I say "go," walk with your partner to the other end of the room, tap the wall, then return to the starting place.**

After children have returned to their places, ask:

● **Why was this race difficult?** (Our legs were in the bag; we had to walk together; we had to help each other.)

● **How did you help each other get to the wall and back?** (We held each other's arms; we stepped at the same time.)

● **What would it be like to have people help you walk?** (It would be hard; I wouldn't like it.)

Say: **Not being able to use your legs would be hard, and you might need people to help you. Our Bible story today is about a man who had never taken a step in his whole life. He needed help from his friends just as you helped each other in our race. 🖊Jesus helps us serve him, and today we'll see how Peter served Jesus by helping the man who couldn't walk.**

● The Point

Bible Song and Prayer Time (up to 5 minutes)

Before class, make surprise cards for this activity by cutting construction paper into two-by-six-inch slips. Prepare a surprise card for each child plus a few extras for visitors. Fold the cards in half, then stamp the *serving stamp* inside one of the surprise cards. Mark Acts 3:1-10 in the Bible you'll be using.

Have the children sit in a circle. Say: **Now it's time to choose a Bible person to bring me the Bible marked with today's Bible story. As we sing our Bible song, I'll pass out the surprise cards. Don't look inside your card until the song is over.**

Lead children in singing "God's Book" (track 3) with the *CD* to the tune of

"Old MacDonald Had a Farm." As you sing, pass out the surprise cards. If you want to include the names of all the children in your class, sing the song without the *CD,* and repeat the naming section. If you choose to use the *CD,* vary the names you use each week.

Sing

Now it's time to read God's Book	Now it's time to read God's Book
And hear a Bible story.	And hear a Bible story.
It's fun to be here with my friends	It's fun to be here with my friends
And hear a Bible story.	And hear a Bible story.
(Name)'s here.	(Name)'s here.
(Name)'s here.	(Name)'s here.
Here is (name).	Here is (name).
Here is (name).	Here is (name).
Now it's time to read God's Book	Now it's time to read God's Book
And hear a Bible story.	And hear a Bible story.

After the song, say: **You may look inside your surprise cards. The person who has the serving hand stamped inside his or her card will be our Bible person for today.**

Identify the Bible person, then have the rest of the children clap for him or her. Ask the Bible person to bring you the Bible. Help the Bible person open the Bible to the marked place and show the children where your story comes from. Then have the Bible person sit down.

Say: (Name) **was our special Bible person today. Each week, we'll have only one Bible person, but each of you is a special part of our class! Today we'll be learning that** ⬛ **Jesus helps us serve him.**

✏ The Point

Let's say a special prayer now and ask Jesus to help us serve him. I'll pass around this basket. When the basket comes to you, put your surprise card in it and say, "Jesus, please help me serve you."

Pass around the basket or box. When you've collected everyone's surprise card, set the basket aside, and pick up the Bible. Lead children in this prayer: **God, thank you for the Bible and for all the stories in it. Teach us today that** ⬛ **Jesus helps us serve him. In Jesus' name, amen.**

✏ The Point

Hear the Bible Story (up to 10 minutes)

Bring out the *Bible Big Book: How Peter Served Jesus,* and gather children in a circle on the floor. Have them hold their praise raisers from Option 3. Say: **What's the most amazing thing you've ever seen?** Pause to allow children to tell their ideas. Hold up the Bible and say: **The Bible tells us about many amazing things. Our story today is about how Peter served Jesus in a way that amazed a crowd of people and changed a beggar's life.**

Our Bible story comes from the book of Acts, and the *Bible Big Book* **shows us pictures of the story. You can help me tell the story. Each time you hear the name "Peter," wave your praise raisers to celebrate how Peter served Jesus.**

Cue the *CD* to track 13, and open the book to page 1. Play the *CD* and follow along with the back cover text, turning the page when you hear the chime. At the end of page 3, turn off the CD player.

Close the book, and have children sit on their streamers. Ask:

● **What did Peter give the man that was better than money?** (He helped heal the man; he wanted the man to know Jesus.)

● **How did healing the man serve Jesus?** (People knew that Jesus healed him; Peter got to tell a crowd of people about Jesus; Peter showed Jesus' love to the man who couldn't walk.)

Say: **Jesus gave Peter the power to heal the man's legs.** Ask:

● **What did the man do after he was healed?** (He jumped and walked; he thanked God; he praised God.)

● **What did Peter do after the man was healed?** (He told people about Jesus.)

Say: **Peter served Jesus by healing the man. He also served Jesus by telling the people in the crowd who Jesus was and that Jesus died to save them from their sins. We can serve Jesus in many ways, too. We can serve by praying and by helping others and by telling people about Jesus. Let's wave our praise raisers once more to show how glad we are that ⬤ Jesus helps us serve him.** Pause while children wave their streamers.

● The Point

Set the Big Book aside.

Do the Bible Story (up to 10 minutes)

Say: **We'll play a game that's like our Bible story. Get into groups of three.** Pause while children form their groups. **Choose one person in your group to be the man who couldn't walk. That person will lie at the far end of the room. The other two will be Peter and John and will stand at this end of the room. When I clap my hands, Peter and John may hop to the lame man and help him or her up. Then all three of you may lock arms and leap and jump back to the starting place.**

After the game is over, say: **That was fun. You served the lame person and were good at hopping and leaping!** Ask:

● **What good things happened because Peter and John served Jesus?** (The man walked and jumped and praised God; other people got to hear about Jesus.)

Say: **Just as Peter and John served Jesus by helping the man at the Temple, we can serve Jesus, too. Let's sing a song about Peter and John and how ⬤ Jesus helps us serve him. Let's form a standing circle.**

● The Point

Lead children in singing the following song (without the *CD*) to the tune of "This Old Man." Do the accompanying motions for added fun.

Sing

Peter and John went to pray *(walk in a circle)*
At the Temple every day. *(Kneel and fold hands.)*
On their way, they met a crippled man *(sit in place)*;
Healed his legs, and away he ran. *(Leap up and jog around in a circle.)*

He praised God on that day. *(Hands over your heart.)*
Ev-ry-body heard him say *(cup hands around mouth)*,
"Thank you, God, that I can jump and run. *(Leap and jog around in a circle.)*
I'll praise your name to ev'ryone!" *(Jog with hands in the air.)*

Say: **Isn't it fun to sing and tell others about Jesus? Let's serve Jesus by telling Pockets about him.**

Practicing The Point

Unhappy Hopper (up to 5 minutes)

Before class, put a pair of tennis shoes on Pockets.

Bring out Pockets the Kangaroo. Go through the following script. When you finish the script, put Pockets out of sight.

Unhappy Hopper

PUPPET SCRIPT

Teacher: Hi, Pockets. Do you have new shoes? I didn't know kangaroos wore tennis shoes. Did you, children?

Pockets: I thought my shoes could help me serve Jesus, but they don't work.

Teacher: Your shoes don't work?

Pockets: No. They don't help me walk at all—all I can do is hop, hop, HOP! *(Hops higher and higher.)*

Teacher: But kangaroos are <u>supposed</u> to hop, Pockets.

Pockets: But if I don't <u>walk</u>, I'll never be able to serve Jesus! The man in the story today walked, didn't he?

Teacher: Oh, Pockets. I think you misunderstood. Children, let's tell Pockets about the story we heard today and how we can all serve Jesus. *(Encourage children to tell Pockets the Bible story. Lead them to repeat The Point and tell Pockets different ways to serve Jesus. Help children point out that after the man was healed, he began <u>leaping</u> and praising God.)*

Pockets: I can leap! Watch me! *(Leaps very high in the air.)*

Teacher: *(Laughing)* That's a real joy-jump, Pockets. You see, 🖤 Jesus helps us serve him. It doesn't matter if you walk or hop or sit quietly. You can serve Jesus in lots of ways.

Pockets: Wow! *(Hops up and down.)* Thanks for helping me understand that 🖤 Jesus helps us serve him. Guess I don't need silly ol' tennis shoes now! *(Tosses the shoes aside.)* I'm so happy, I feel like <u>jumping</u> for joy!

(Have Pockets hop away and out of sight of the children.)

🖤 **The Point**

🖤 **The Point**

Jesus helps us serve him.

TODAY I LEARNED...

We believe that Christian education extends beyond the classroom into the home. Photocopy the "Today I Learned..." handout (p. 156) for this week, and send it home with your children. Encourage parents to use the handout to plan meaningful family activities to reinforce this week's topic. Follow up the "Today I Learned..." activities next week by asking children what their families did.

Closing

Servant Song (up to 5 minutes)

Have children sit in a circle. Say: **Let's end our time with a special song. As we sing, we'll pass the *serving stamp and ink pad*. When we stop singing, the person with the stamp may tell one way he or she can serve Jesus this week, such as helping with a job at home or telling someone about Jesus. Then stamp your hand, and we'll sing again.**

Lead children in singing "I Can Serve the Lord" (without the *CD*) to the tune of "London Bridge." Continue singing and passing the stamp until each child has had a turn to stamp his or her hand.

Sing

I can help and serve the Lord,
Every day, every way.
I can help and serve the Lord
Because I love him.

When you're finished singing, have children join hands. Pray: **Dear God, thank you for helping us serve Jesus in all we do. In Jesus' name, amen.**

For Extra Time

If you have a long class time or want to add additional elements to your lesson, try one of the following activities.

LIVELY LEARNING: Sing Song

Sing the song (without the *CD*) that children learned in the "Do the Bible Story" activity.

Sing

Peter and John went to pray (*walk in a circle*)
At the Temple every day. (*Kneel and fold hands.*)
On their way, they met a crippled man (*sit in place*);
Healed his legs, and away he ran. (*Leap up and jog around in a circle.*)

He praised God on that day. (*Hands over your heart.*)
Ev-ry-body heard him say (*cup hands around mouth*),
"Thank you, God, that I can jump and run. (*Leap and jog around in a circle.*)
I'll praise your name to ev'ryone!" (*Jog with hands in the air.*)

● The Point

Remind children that ● Jesus helps us serve him just as he helped Peter and John heal the man who couldn't walk.

MAKE TO TAKE: Happy Hoppers

Before this activity, photocopy the "Happy Hopper" pattern from page 155 on green paper.

Set out scissors and crayons. Hand out the hopper papers, and let children cut out the frog shapes. Show children how to accordion-fold the legs. Draw googly eyes on the frogs with crayons. Allow children to have fun helping their hoppers "leap" around the room. Point out that we help puppets move just as Jesus helps us serve him.

TREAT TO EAT: Jump-for-Joy Corn

● The Point

Bring a hot-air corn popper or electric corn popper to class. Spread a clean sheet on the floor, and gather children around the edge of the sheet. Let the class watch as the popcorn pops onto the sheet. Point out that the popcorn jumps up and down just like the man whose legs were healed. Hand each child a paper cup filled with popcorn. Remind children that ● Jesus helps us serve him, and when we serve Jesus, we feel like jumping for joy, too. As children eat their snacks, encourage them to retell the Bible story.

STORY PICTURE: Peter and John Heal a Lame Man

● The Point

Hand each child a photocopy of the "Today I Learned . . ." handout from page 156. Set out glue sticks and small ½-by-3-inch paper strips. Invite children to color the picture. Then help them accordion-fold the paper strips into bouncy legs. Glue the legs onto the picture of the man jumping for joy. As children work, ask what they think the man did after he could walk. Since ● Jesus helps us serve him, how do they think the man served Jesus?

Happy Hopper

Photocopy this handout and cut out the frog. Accordion-fold the legs. Use crayons to add googly eyes.

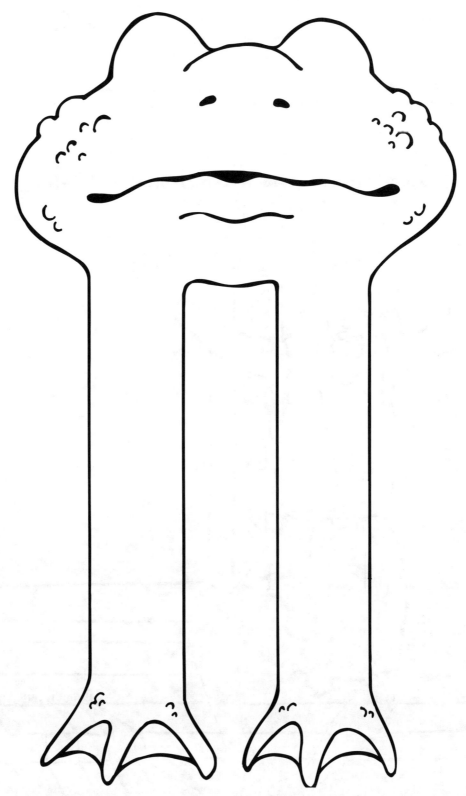

Jesus helps us serve him.   **Lesson 10 ● 155**

TODAY I LEARNED...

The Point ✏ Jesus helps us serve him.

Today your child learned that Jesus helps us serve him. Children learned that a lame man asked for help, and Peter and John healed him in Jesus' name. They talked about the importance of serving Jesus.

Verse to Learn

"You are serving the Lord Christ" (Colossians 3:24b, NCV).

Ask Me...

● How did Peter and John help the man who couldn't walk?
● How can you serve Jesus?
● What are ways our family can serve each other?

Family Fun

● Help your child make pretend crutches or a cane from wood scraps or old broom handles. As your child tries out the crutches, talk about how the lame man in the story felt before and after he was healed. Talk about the fact that anyone can serve Jesus because he helps us find ways to serve him.

Peter and John Heal a Lame Man (Acts 3:1-10)

LESSON 10

Speak Up for Jesus

LESSON 11

The Bible Basis

Acts 4:1-21. Peter and John preach boldly.

Chapter 4 of Acts reveals the first serious clash between Jesus' followers and the Jewish leaders who were determined to stamp out all memory of Jesus and deny his resurrection. Peter and John stood before the Sanhedrin in the same place Jesus had stood—as the accused. Their crime was healing, in the name of Jesus, a man the Temple leaders had just put to death for blasphemy. Peter and John boldly proclaimed the truth of Jesus' resurrection. The rulers and elders of the Sanhedrin were astounded at the boldness and courage of Peter and John and noted that these ordinary, unschooled men had been with Jesus.

Most kindergartners love being the center of attention. But teaching children to be bold about their faith can be challenging. Five- and six-year-olds may feel shy and unsure of what to say when someone asks them about Jesus. Use this lesson to teach children the importance of telling others about Jesus and to reassure them that Jesus helps us speak boldly when we're shy and unsure of what to say.

Getting The Point

✏ **Jesus helps us serve him.**

It's important to say The Point just as it's written in each activity. Repeating The Point again and again will help the children remember it and apply it to their lives.

Children will
- learn that Jesus helped Peter tell others about him,
- experience telling someone about Jesus,
- help Pockets learn to speak loud and clear, and
- discover things to tell about Jesus.

● **The Point**

This Lesson at a Glance

Before the lesson, collect the necessary items for the activities you plan to use. Refer to the Classroom Supplies and Learning Lab Supplies columns to determine what you'll need. Remember to make photocopies of the "Today I Learned..." handout (p. 168) to send home with your children.

Section	Minutes	What Children Will Do	Classroom Supplies	Learning Lab Supplies
Welcome Time	up to 5	**Welcome!**—Receive name tags and be greeted by the teacher.	"Cross Name Tags" handouts (p. 30), markers, pins or tape	
Let's Get Started Direct children to one or more of the Let's Get Started activities until everyone arrives.	up to 10	**Option 1: Put On Peter and John**—Dress up like story characters and act out last week's story.	Bath robes, sandals, towels, large scarves, rope for belts, a throw rug, a basket	
	up to 10	**Option 2: Chalk It Up**—Draw colorful pictures and learn that it's important to talk boldly about Jesus.	Colored chalk, white paper, water, paper cups	
	up to 10	**Option 3: Mega Message**—Make megaphones and tell an important message about Jesus.	Construction paper, tape, markers or crayons	
Pick-Up Song	up to 5	**We Will Pick Up**—Sing a song as they pick up toys and gather for Bible-Story Time.	CD player	CD: "We Will Pick Up" (track 2)
Bible-Story Time	up to 5	**Setting the Stage**—Teach a crowd to blow bubbles.	Wrapped pieces of bubble gum	
	up to 5	**Bible Song and Prayer Time**—Sing a song, bring out the Bible, and pray together.	Bible, construction paper, scissors, basket or box, CD player	CD: "God's Book" (track 3), serving stamp and ink pad
	up to 10	**Hear the Bible Story**—Respond to cue words in a Bible story from Acts 4:1-21.	Bible, megaphones from Option 3, CD player	Bible Big Book: How Peter Served Jesus, CD: "Peter's Free" (track 14)
	up to 10	**Do the Bible Story**—Use their megaphones or hands for an action rhyme.	Megaphones from Option 3	
Practicing The Point	up to 5	**Psst, Pockets!**—Teach Pockets that important news needs to come through loud and clear.	Pockets the Kangaroo, lollipops	
Closing	up to 5	**Sweet Messages**—Use lollipop microphones to tell about Jesus.	Lollipops from Practicing The Point	
For Extra Time		For extra-time ideas and supplies, see page 167.		

Jesus helps us serve him.

Welcome Time

Welcome! (up to 5 minutes)

- Bend down to make eye contact with children as they arrive.
- Greet each child individually with an enthusiastic smile.
- Thank each child for coming to class today.
- As children arrive, ask them about last week's "Today I Learned…" discussion. Use questions such as "Who did you serve last week?" or "How did Jesus help you serve him?"
- Say: **Today we're going to learn that ⬤ Jesus helps us serve him.**
- Hand out the cross name tags children made during Lesson 1, and help them attach the name tags to their clothing. If some of the name tags were damaged or if some of the children weren't in class that week, have them make new name tags using the photocopiable handout on page 30.
- Direct the children to the Let's Get Started activities you've set up.

⬤ **The Point**

Let's Get Started

Set up one or more of the following activities for children to do as they arrive. After you greet each child, invite him or her to choose an activity.

Circulate among the children to offer help as needed and to direct children's conversation toward today's lesson. Ask questions such as "What's it like to tell good news?" and "Were you ever afraid to talk in front of a group of people?"

▢ OPTION 1: Put On Peter and John (up to 10 minutes)

Provide a box of dress-up items and props, including bath robes, sandals, towels, large scarves, rope for belts, a throw rug, and a basket. Invite children to dress up like their favorite characters from the story of Peter and John and the man who couldn't walk. Encourage children to act out last week's story. Have the children playing the beggar sit on the throw rug and hold the basket as they beg for coins. "Peter and John" can tell others about Jesus. Remind children that ⬤ Jesus helps us serve him. Point out that today children will learn about what happened when Peter told others about Jesus.

⬤ **The Point**

▢ OPTION 2: Chalk It Up (up to 10 minutes)

Set out colored chalk, paper, and cups of water. Hand each child two sheets of paper, and invite children to make "loud and soft" pictures. On one paper, have them use the chalk to draw a picture of something that's quiet, such as a butterfly or a kitten. On the second paper, have children draw a picture of something they can hear clearly, such as a lion or a train whistle. For the loud picture, direct children to dip their chalk in water to get brighter colors.

As children compare their loud and soft pictures, explain that today's Bible story is about someone who spoke up loud and clear for Jesus. Point out that when we tell others about Jesus, we want to be like the bright chalk colors so

● The Point

people hear us loud and clear. Remind children that ●Jesus helps us serve him and that Peter served Jesus by boldly telling people about him.

☐ OPTION 3: Mega Message (up to 10 minutes)

Set out tape and markers or crayons. Hand out construction paper, and have children decorate one side of the paper using markers. Then show children how to roll their papers into cone shapes with the colored side facing out and tape the edges to make megaphones. As children work, explain that megaphones help people talk loud and clear so everyone can hear what they're saying. Tell children they'll hear a story about how Peter spoke loud and clear. Remind children that ●Jesus helps us serve him and that telling others about him is one way to serve. Let children repeat The Point using their megaphones.

● The Point

✔ If some children don't choose Option 3, have volunteers make extra megaphones. Children will use the megaphones later in the lesson.

When everyone has arrived and you're ready to move on to the Bible-Story Time, encourage the children to finish what they're doing and get ready to clean up.

Pick-Up Song

We Will Pick Up (up to 5 minutes)

Lead children in singing "We Will Pick Up" (track 2) with the *CD* to the tune of "London Bridge." Encourage the children to sing along as they help clean up the room.

If you want to include the names of all the children in your class, sing the song without the *CD,* and repeat the naming section. If you choose to use the *CD,* vary the names you use each week.

Sing

We will pick up all our toys,	I see (name) picking up,
All our toys, all our toys.	Picking up, picking up.
We will pick up all our toys	I see (name) picking up
And put them all away.	And putting toys away.
	(Repeat)

Jesus helps us serve him.

Bible-Story Time

Setting the Stage (up to 5 minutes)

Tell the children you'll clap your hands to get their attention. Explain that when you clap, children are to stop what they're doing, raise their hands, and focus on you. Encourage children to respond quickly so you'll have time for all the fun activities you've planned.

Hand each child a piece of wrapped, sugar-free bubble gum. Say: **You may unwrap and chew your gum. Today we'll take turns being unusual teachers. This is bubble gum school, and I'm looking for someone to be the teacher and tell us how to blow bubbles.** Choose two volunteers to stand in front of the class and tell how to blow bubbles with their gum. After thirty seconds, choose two new teachers.

Continue until everyone who cares to has had a turn to be teacher. Ask:
● **What was it like to stand in front of others and talk?** (I was a little scared; I thought it was fun.)
● **Was it easy or hard to teach others? Explain.** (It was hard because I couldn't explain it; it was easy because some people knew how to blow bubbles already; it was hard because not everyone listened.)

Say: **Sometimes it's hard to talk to lots of people. Today we'll hear about a time when Peter spoke in front of a lot of people and taught them about Jesus. Do you think Peter and John might have been a little nervous? Maybe, but ✏Jesus helps us serve him, and he helped Peter say the right words and speak loud and clear. Before we hear our Bible story, shake two people's hands and tell them what a good job they did teaching or blowing bubbles this morning.**

● The Point

Bible Song and Prayer Time (up to 5 minutes)

Before class, make surprise cards for this activity by cutting construction paper in two-by-six-inch slips. Prepare a surprise card for each child plus a few extras for visitors. Fold the cards in half, then stamp the *serving stamp* inside one of the surprise cards. Mark Acts 4:1-21 in the Bible you'll be using.

Have the children sit in a circle. Say: **Now it's time to choose a Bible person to bring me the Bible marked with today's Bible story. As we sing our Bible song, I'll pass out the surprise cards. Don't look inside your card until the song is over.**

Lead children in singing "God's Book" (track 3) with the *CD* to the tune of "Old MacDonald Had a Farm." As you sing, pass out the surprise cards. If you want to include the names of all the children in your class, sing the song without the *CD*, and repeat the naming section. If you choose to use the *CD*, vary the names you use each week.

Sing 🎵

Now it's time to read God's Book
And hear a Bible story.
It's fun to be here with my
    friends
And hear a Bible story.

(Name)'s here.
(Name)'s here.
Here is (name).
Here is (name).
Now it's time to read God's Book
And hear a Bible story.

Jesus helps us serve him.

Now it's time to read God's Book	(Name)'s here.
And hear a Bible story.	(Name)'s here.
It's fun to be here with my	Here is (name).
friends	Here is (name).
And hear a Bible story.	Now it's time to read God's Book
	And hear a Bible story.

After the song, say: **You may look inside your surprise cards. The person who has the serving hand stamped inside his or her card will be our Bible person for today.**

Identify the Bible person, then have the rest of the children clap for him or her. Ask the Bible person to bring you the Bible. Help the Bible person open the Bible to the marked place and show the children where your story comes from. Then have the Bible person sit down.

Say: **(Name) was our special Bible person today. Each week, we'll have only one Bible person, but each of you is a special part of our class! Today we'll be learning that Jesus helps us serve him.**

Let's say a special prayer now and ask Jesus to help us serve him. I'll pass around this basket. When the basket comes to you, put your surprise card in it and say, "Jesus, please help me serve you."

Pass around the basket or box. When you've collected everyone's surprise card, set the basket aside, and pick up the Bible. Lead children in this prayer: **God, thank you for the Bible and for all the stories in it. Teach us today that Jesus helps us serve him. In Jesus' name, amen.**

Hear the Bible Story (up to 10 minutes)

Hold the *Bible Big Book: How Peter Served Jesus,* and say: **Let's play a review game. The girls can answer a question about last week's story, and the boys will point to the story picture that tells about that part of the story. Then we'll switch, and the boys will answer while the girls point.** Open the Big Book to page 1. Use the following review questions.

● **Who was going to the Temple to pray?** (Peter and John.)
● **Who did they meet at the Temple?** (The man who couldn't walk; a beggar.)
● **What did the man ask Peter and John to give him?** (Money.)
● **Whose power healed the man so he could walk and jump?** (Jesus' power healed the man.)
● **What did the man do when he was healed?** (He jumped and praised God; he thanked God.)
● **Who looked angry when Peter and John talked about Jesus?** (The Temple leaders; the priests.)

Say: **You remembered our story well! Give yourselves a hand.** Have children clap for one another. Say: **Last week we learned that Peter served Jesus by healing the man who couldn't walk. Today we'll learn another way that Jesus helps us serve him.**

Open the Big Book so children see page 4. Hand children their megaphones. If you chose not to do Option 3, have children cup their hands around their mouths. Hold up the Bible and say: **Our story comes from the book of Acts in the Bible.** Hold up the Big Book. **The *Bible Big Book* shows us pictures of the story. Listen carefully, and whenever you hear**

The Point

The Point

The Point

Jesus helps us serve him.

the name "Peter," jump up and use your megaphones or hands to cheer, "Yay! Yay! That's the way!"

Read the following story as children look at page 4.

The Temple priests and leaders didn't love Jesus, and they didn't want <u>Peter</u> and John telling people about him. The Temple leaders got madder and madder as <u>Peter</u> told how Jesus' power could raise people from the dead. The leaders grabbed <u>Peter</u> and John and threw them in jail.

The next day, the High Priest questioned <u>Peter.</u> "By whose power did you heal the lame man?" he asked. <u>Peter</u> said, "It was Jesus' power that did this wonderful thing. Jesus is the only one who can save people."

The priests realized that <u>Peter</u> and John weren't afraid. They heard <u>Peter's</u> amazing words and saw that many people believed and praised God. The priests couldn't find a reason to punish <u>Peter</u> and John, so they let the two disciples go. "Stop telling others about Jesus," the priests commanded. But <u>Peter</u> continued to tell people everywhere about Jesus.

Close the Big Book. Have children set their megaphones beside them. Ask:

● **What did Peter and John do after the man was healed?** (They told people about Jesus.)

● **Why were the Temple leaders so angry?** (They didn't like Peter and John; they were jealous; they didn't want people to know Jesus; they thought they were the bosses.)

● **Why didn't Peter and John stop talking about Jesus?** (They wanted people to know about Jesus; Jesus wanted them to keep telling.)

Say: **Peter and John wanted to tell everyone about Jesus. They wouldn't stop because they knew Jesus wanted them to tell others about him. Let's sing a song to remind us that even chains and jail cells didn't stop Peter from serving Jesus.**

Lead children in singing "Peter's Free" (track 14) with the *CD* to the tune of "Here We Go 'Round the Mulberry Bush." For extra fun, have two children hold "Peter" (another child) as you sing the first verse. Then have children set Peter free on the second verse.

Sing

Lock Peter up and hold him tight,
Hold him tight,
Hold him tight.
Lock Peter up and hold him tight.
Don't let him out of jail.

These chains will never stay on him,
Stay on him,
Stay on him.
These chains will never stay on him,
'Cause God will set him free!

Say: **Just like Peter and John, we can speak out loud and clear and tell others about Jesus. Let's use our megaphones and hands once more to say,** ● **"Jesus helps us serve him!"** Pause for children to say The Point. Then say: **Let's form a circle and use our megaphones to play a game.**

Put the Big Book away.

● **The Point**

Do the Bible Story (up to 10 minutes)

When children have formed a standing circle, say: **We'll play a game called Loud and Clear. It will help us be like Peter and John when they spoke boldly to the people about Jesus. I'll give you directions. Listen closely because sometimes you'll answer loud and clear with your megaphones, and sometimes you'll put your megaphones down and whisper.** Use the following responses for the class.

Loud and clear, say your name. *(Call out your names.)*
Whisper and repeat the same. *(Whisper your names.)*
Loud and clear—you can shout—
Who did Peter tell about? *(Call out the name "Jesus.")*
Whisper now and tell us true
What Jesus wants us all to do. *(Whisper the words "serve him.")*
Three more times, loud and clearly,
Who's the one we love so dearly? *(Call out, "Jesus! Jesus! Jesus!")*
Repeat the rhyme a second time. When you're finished, ask:
● **Why does Jesus want us to tell others about him?** (So everyone gets to know Jesus; so more people can love Jesus and serve him.)
● **Who can you tell about Jesus?** (My friends; family; kids at school; my neighbors; people who are sad or hurt; everyone.)

Say: **Peter and John spoke boldly about Jesus. And they didn't stop telling people because they knew that** **Jesus helps us serve him. I'm glad that we can be like Peter and John and tell others about Jesus. I'm also glad that** ●**Jesus helps us serve him. Let's visit Pockets. We can tell her more about Jesus.** Have children set their megaphones against a wall until they go home.

● **The Point**
● **The Point**

Practicing The Point

Psst, Pockets! (up to 5 minutes)

Bring out Pockets the Kangaroo. Go through the following script. When you finish the script, put Pockets out of sight.

Psst, Pockets!

PUPPET SCRIPT

Teacher: Hello, Pockets. How are you this fine day?

Pockets: *(Whispers and mumbles, but no one can understand what she's saying.)*

Teacher: What was that? We didn't hear you, Pockets.

Pockets: *(Whispers and mumbles.)*

Teacher: I'm having a hard time hearing you. Is it something important?

(Continued)

Jesus helps us serve him.

Pockets: Yes, it's really important! *(Whispers and mumbles once more.)*

Teacher: We've been learning that when something is important to say, we want to say it loud and clear so people hear.

Pockets: But if I speak out, you may be angry.

Teacher: We heard a story of how Peter and John spoke about Jesus even when the Temple leaders were angry. Children, let's tell Pockets the story. Maybe it'll help her understand that we can tell important messages loud and clear. *(Have children take turns telling the story. Encourage them to tell Pockets that Jesus helps us to be brave and speak out. Lead children to tell Pockets The Point.)* Peter and John knew it was important to tell others about Jesus, so they spoke boldly. Even though they knew the Temple leaders would be upset, it was more important to serve Jesus. Can you tell us your important message, Pockets?

Pockets: Well, my message isn't as important as telling others about Jesus. <u>That's</u> really important! But I guess I can tell you loud and clear—I ATE THE SNACKS!

Teacher: *(Shake head and laugh.)* Well, that message was certainly loud and clear, wasn't it, children? I bet you didn't find these treats! *(Hold up a bag of small wrapped lollipops.)* Would you like to help hand them out?

Pockets: Oh, yes! I'm happy that you're not upset with me. But I'm happier that 🖊 Jesus helps us serve him. Now I can help by serving the snacks.

    (Have Pockets hand each child a lollipop. Tell children to hold their treats until everyone's been served. Then put Pockets out of sight.)

 **The Point**

TODAY I LEARNED . . .

    We believe that Christian education extends beyond the classroom into the home. Photocopy the "Today I Learned..." handout (p. 168) for this week, and send it home with your children. Encourage parents to use the handout to plan meaningful family activities to reinforce this week's topic. Follow up the "Today I Learned..." activities next week by asking children what their families did.

Closing

Sweet Messages (up to 5 minutes)

    Say: **We've been learning today that** 🖊 **Jesus helps us serve him. We learned that Peter and John told others about Jesus and kept telling**

🖊 **The Point**

Jesus helps us serve him.

them even when the leaders warned them to stop. It's important to serve Jesus by telling others about him no matter what. Let's pretend that our lollipops are microphones. Who'd like to use his or her microphone to tell something about Jesus such as "Jesus loves us" or "Jesus is always with us"? Allow children time to stand and tell their ideas about Jesus using their lollipops as microphones.

✔ If children are shy or have a difficult time thinking of something to say, encourage them by whispering The Point and helping them repeat it. You may want to use a lollipop of your own and repeat The Point with them.

When everyone's had a turn to speak into their "microphones," say: **Join hands, and let's serve with a prayer.** Pray: **Dear God, it's fun to tell others about Jesus. Please help us to be brave like Peter and John. In Jesus' name, amen.** Let children take their lollipop microphones home to enjoy.

Jesus helps us serve him.

For Extra Time

If you have a long class time or want to add additional elements to your lesson, try one of the following activities.

LIVELY LEARNING: Loud and Clear Cheer

Repeat the action rhyme children learned in the "Do the Bible Story" activity.
Loud and clear, say your name. (*Call out your names.*)
Whisper and repeat the same. (*Whisper your names.*)
Loud and clear—you can shout—
Who did Peter tell about? (*Call out the name "Jesus."*)
Whisper now and tell us true
What Jesus wants us all to do. (*Whisper the words "serve him."*)
Three more times, loud and clearly,
Who's the one we love so dearly? (*Call out, "Jesus! Jesus! Jesus!"*)
Remind children that if we speak loudly and clearly, others hear what we say. Tell them that 🖊Jesus helps us serve him and will help us tell others about him.

MAKE TO TAKE: Message Makers

Before this activity, cut a ½-by-3-inch strip of paper for each child.
Set out markers, paper strips, tape, and red construction paper. Hand out index cards, and tell children to fold their cards in half. Let children decorate the outside of the cards using markers. Show children how to accordion-fold a strip of paper. Tape the folded paper to the center of the open card. Have children cut out small hearts and tape them to the other end of the accordion-folded paper. Help each child write "Jesus" above the heart and "you" below the heart. Read the message aloud to the children. Point out that because Jesus loves us, 🖊Jesus helps us serve him. Encourage children to serve Jesus by giving their cards to someone outside of class.

TREAT TO EAT: Crunch 'n' Quiet Snacks

Provide quiet snacks and crunchy snacks. Crackers and raw carrot slices make loud crunching sounds, while banana slices or grapes and raisins make quiet noises. Point out that Peter and John spoke out loudly and clearly to the people. Remind children that 🖊Jesus helps us serve him by helping them tell people about him loudly and clearly.

STORY PICTURE: Peter and John Speak Boldly About Jesus

Hand each child a photocopy of the "Today I Learned..." handout from page 168. Set out craft glue and a box of alphabet cereal. Help children pick out letters to spell the name "Jesus." Then let children glue the letters beside Peter to show how Peter spoke boldly about Jesus. As children work, ask questions such as "Why did Peter keep telling people about Jesus?" and "Why does Jesus want us to tell others about him?" Explain that we can speak boldly about Jesus because 🖊Jesus helps us serve him.

● **The Point**

● **The Point**

● **The Point**

● **The Point**

Jesus helps us serve him.

TODAY I LEARNED...

The Point 🖊 Jesus helps us serve him.

Today your child learned that Jesus helps us serve him. Children learned that Peter and John spoke boldly about Jesus even when they were warned to stop. They talked about the importance of telling others about Jesus.

Verse to Learn

"You are serving the Lord Christ" (Colossians 3:24b, NCV).

Ask Me...

● Why did Peter and John tell people about Jesus?
● Who can you tell about Jesus?
● How can our family help others learn about Jesus?

Family Fun

● Invite your child to make a plate of Tell-It Treats to share with someone in the neighborhood. Let your child decorate a plate of graham crackers with canned icing and colorful sprinkles or raisins. Then cut out a paper heart, and help your child write, "Jesus loves you" on it. Set the plate on someone's doorstep to remind them of Jesus' love.

Peter and John Speak Boldly About Jesus (Acts 4:1-21)

Permission to photocopy this handout from Group's Hands-On Bible Curriculum™ for Pre-K & K granted for local church use. Copyright © Group Publishing, Inc., P.O. Box 481, Loveland, CO 80539.

Dead– Then Alive!

The Point

✎ Jesus helps us serve him.

The Bible Basis

Acts 9:36-42. Peter brings Tabitha back to life.

The people of Joppa loved and respected Tabitha (whose Greek name was Dorcas) for creating clothing for the poor. Tabitha loved Jesus and served him faithfully. When she died, the community of believers felt a great loss. Her friends grieved and summoned Peter to help. As Jesus did when he healed Jairus' daughter, Peter sent the others out of the room. He knelt by Tabitha's bed and prayed. Then Peter turned and commanded, "Tabitha, get up." And through Jesus' awesome power came the miracle of new life!

Five- and six-year-olds have a simple concept of death. They know that when someone dies, they don't get up again. Yet Tabitha did. This is a wonderful time to review the Easter story and how Jesus rose from the dead to help us serve him. This lesson will help young children learn that they can be like Peter and help those who are sick and that it's important to keep our bodies healthy so we can serve Jesus.

Getting The Point

✎ **Jesus helps us serve him.**

It's important to say The Point just as it's written in each activity. Repeating The Point again and again will help the children remember it and apply it to their lives.

Children will
- understand that Jesus helps us find ways to serve him,
- hear that Peter served in Jesus' name and with his power,
- learn to serve Jesus by helping Pockets feel better, and
- share healthy snacks.

✎ **The Point**

This Lesson at a Glance

Before the lesson, collect the necessary items for the activities you plan to use. Refer to the Classroom Supplies and Learning Lab Supplies columns to determine what you'll need. Remember to make photocopies of the "Today I Learned..." handout (p. 179) to send home with your children.

Section	Minutes	What Children Will Do	Classroom Supplies	Learning Lab Supplies
Welcome Time	up to 5	**Welcome!**—Receive name tags and be greeted by the teacher.	"Cross Name Tags" handouts (p. 30), markers, pins or tape	
Let's Get Started Direct children to one or more of the Let's Get Started activities until everyone arrives.	up to 10	**Option 1: Serve the Sick**—Be pretend doctors and nurses in their classroom "hospital."	Toy doctor's kit, blankets, pillows, stuffed animals or dolls	
	up to 10	**Option 2: Care Cards**—Create cheerful get-well cards for someone who's sick.	Tape, scissors, markers, construction paper	
	up to 10	**Option 3: Healthy Hearts**—Make heart-shaped sandwiches.	Bread, cheese and bologna slices, heart-shaped cookie cutters, paper plate, plastic tablecloth	
Pick-Up Song	up to 5	**We Will Pick Up**—Sing a song as they pick up toys and gather for Bible-Story Time.	CD player	CD: "We Will Pick Up" (track 2)
Bible-Story Time	up to 5	**Setting the Stage**—Play an unusual game of Tag.	Round stickers	
	up to 5	**Bible Song and Prayer Time**—Sing a song, bring out the Bible, and pray together.	Bible, construction paper, scissors, basket or box, CD player	CD: "God's Book" (track 3), serving stamp and ink pad
	up to 10	**Hear the Bible Story**—Participate in a Bible story from Acts 9:36-42 using their chickenpox spots.	Bible, stickers from "Setting the Stage"	Bible Big Book: How Peter Served Jesus
	up to 10	**Do the Bible Story**—Act out a fun action rhyme and review the Bible story.		
Practicing The Point	up to 5	**Kerchoo, Kangaroo!**—Serve by helping Pockets feel better.	Pockets the Kangaroo, facial tissue, small blanket	Bible Big Book: How Peter Served Jesus
Closing	up to 5	**Hearts Share**—Have a healthy picnic and pray.	Tablecloth and sandwiches from Option 3 (or other snack), napkins	
For Extra Time		For extra-time ideas and supplies, see page 178.		

Jesus helps us serve him.

Welcome Time

Welcome! (up to 5 minutes)

- Bend down to make eye contact with children as they arrive.
- Greet each child individually with an enthusiastic smile.
- Thank each child for coming to class today.
- As children arrive, ask them about last week's "Today I Learned..." discussion. Use questions such as "Who did you tell about Jesus last week?" or "What's a way that Jesus helped you serve him?"
- Say: **Today we're going to learn that ⬤ Jesus helps us serve him.**

⬤ **The Point**

- Hand out the cross name tags children made during Lesson 1, and help them attach the name tags to their clothing. If some of the name tags were damaged or if some of the children weren't in class that week, have them make new name tags using the photocopiable handout on page 30.
- Direct the children to the Let's Get Started activities you've set up.

Let's Get Started

Set up one or more of the following activities for children to do as they arrive. After you greet each child, invite him or her to choose an activity.

Circulate among the children to offer help as needed and to direct children's conversation toward today's lesson. Ask questions such as "What can you do to help someone in your family who gets sick?" and "How do you feel when someone you love gets sick?"

OPTION 1: Serve the Sick (up to 10 minutes)

Create a pretend hospital in one corner of the room. Provide small blankets and pillows for stuffed-animal or doll patients. Set out a toy doctor's kit or other props such as spoons and bowls to feed the "patients," a stethoscope, bandages, and flowers to cheer them up. As children care for their patients, ask questions such as "Why do we want to help people feel better?" and "When's a time someone helped you feel better?"

Encourage children to take turns being the doctors and nurses. Point out that boys and girls can be both doctors and nurses. Explain that ⬤ Jesus helps us serve him and that today's Bible story is about a time Jesus helped Peter make someone better.

⬤ **The Point**

✔ You may want to ask members of your congregation who work in health-related fields to visit and demonstrate real stethoscopes and blood pressure cuffs.

Jesus helps us serve him.

☐ OPTION 2: Care Cards (up to 10 minutes)

Before class, cut sheets of construction paper in half for children.

Set out scissors, tape, and markers. Hand out construction paper, and have children fold their papers in half. Invite them to create colorful cards to give to someone who's sick. Encourage children to use unusual decorating techniques such as curling strips of paper around a marker, making fringe, and accordion-folding paper decorations to tape to their cards.

As children work, make comments such as "It's so nice to make someone feel better when they're sick" and "You can save this card and use it to cheer up someone who's sick." Tell children that today they'll hear a story about how Peter helped a woman who had been very sick and died. Remind children that Jesus helps us serve him and that we can serve by helping people when they're ill.

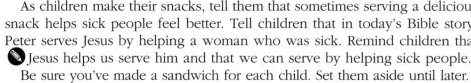

● The Point

☐ OPTION 3: Healthy Hearts (up to 10 minutes)

Cover a table with a clean plastic tablecloth. Set out bread, a paper plate, cheese and bologna slices, and heart-shaped cookie cutters. Invite children to make heart-shaped sandwiches. Have a few children be the Cutters and cut heart-shaped pieces of bread, meat, and cheese. Other children can be the Stackers and place one slice each of cheese and meat on the bread. The Toppers may place tops on the sandwiches and then place them on the paper plate.

As children make their snacks, tell them that sometimes serving a delicious snack helps sick people feel better. Tell children that in today's Bible story, Peter serves Jesus by helping a woman who was sick. Remind children that ●Jesus helps us serve him and that we can serve by helping sick people.

Be sure you've made a sandwich for each child. Set them aside until later.

When everyone has arrived and you're ready to move on to the Bible-Story Time, encourage the children to finish what they're doing and get ready to clean up.

● The Point

Pick-Up Song

We Will Pick Up (up to 5 minutes)

Lead children in singing "We Will Pick Up" (track 2) with the *CD* to the tune of "London Bridge." Encourage the children to sing along as they help clean up the room.

If you want to include the names of all the children in your class, sing the song without the *CD,* and repeat the naming section. If you choose to use the *CD,* vary the names you use each week.

Jesus helps us serve him.

Sing

We will pick up all our toys,
All our toys, all our toys.
We will pick up all our toys
And put them all away.

I see (name) picking up,
Picking up, picking up.
I see (name) picking up
And putting toys away.
(Repeat)

Bible-Story Time

Setting the Stage (up to 5 minutes)

Tell the children you'll clap your hands to get their attention. Explain that when you clap, children are to stop what they're doing, raise their hands, and focus on you. Encourage children to respond quickly so you'll have time for all the fun activities you've planned.

Ask children to help you clear an area in the center of the room. Hand each child four round stickers.

✔ Round stickers from the office-supply section of most stores work well for this game; however, any stickers will do.

Say: **We're going to play a fun game called Chickenpox Spots. When I flip the lights off and on, you'll have thirty seconds to tag people with spots. You must walk and put spots on four different people's arms. Try to keep from catching the chickenpox spots!**

After thirty seconds, clap to get children's attention. When children's hands are raised and they're looking at you, have them sit in a circle. Ask:

● **Who can tell about a time they were sick or had the chickenpox?** Allow children time to share their experiences.

● **Who took care of you, and what did they do?** (My mom and dad read to me; my friends came to visit; Grandma made me soup.)

Say: **It's no fun to feel sick. Today we'll hear a story about a woman who was so sick that she died. But Jesus gave Peter the power to make her well. ◐ Jesus helps us serve him just as he helped Peter. Keep your chickenpox spots on because you'll need them to help tell our Bible story later.**

◐ The Point

Bible Song and Prayer Time (up to 5 minutes)

Before class, make surprise cards for this activity by cutting construction paper in two-by-six-inch slips. Prepare a surprise card for each child plus a few extras for visitors. Fold the cards in half, then stamp the *serving stamp* inside one of the surprise cards. Mark Acts 9:36-42 in the Bible you'll be using.

Have the children sit in a circle. Say: **Now it's time to choose a Bible person**

to bring me the Bible marked with today's Bible story. As we sing our Bible song, I'll pass out the surprise cards. Don't look inside your card until the song is over.

Lead children in singing "God's Book" (track 3) with the *CD* to the tune of "Old MacDonald Had a Farm." As you sing, pass out the surprise cards. If you want to include the names of all the children in your class, sing "God's Book" without the *CD,* and repeat the naming section. If you choose to use the *CD,* vary the names you use each week.

Sing

Now it's time to read God's Book	Now it's time to read God's Book
And hear a Bible story.	And hear a Bible story.
It's fun to be here with my friends	It's fun to be here with my friends
And hear a Bible story.	And hear a Bible story.
(Name)'s here.	(Name)'s here.
(Name)'s here.	(Name)'s here.
Here is (name).	Here is (name).
Here is (name).	Here is (name).
Now it's time to read God's Book	Now it's time to read God's Book
And hear a Bible story.	And hear a Bible story.

After the song, say: **You may look inside your surprise cards. The person who has the serving hand stamped inside his or her card will be our Bible person for today.**

Identify the Bible person, then have the rest of the children clap for him or her. Ask the Bible person to bring you the Bible. Help the Bible person open the Bible to the marked place and show the children where your story comes from. Then have the Bible person sit down.

Say: (Name) **was our special Bible person today. Each week, we'll have only one Bible person, but each of you is a special part of our class! Today we'll all be learning that** ● **Jesus helps us serve him.**

● The Point

Let's say a special prayer now and ask Jesus to help us serve him. I'll pass around this basket. When the basket comes to you, put your surprise card in it and say, "Jesus, please help us serve you."

Pass around the basket or box. When you've collected everyone's surprise card, set the basket aside, and pick up the Bible. Lead children in this prayer: **Jesus, thank you for the Bible and for all the stories in it. Teach us today that** ● **Jesus helps us serve him. In Jesus' name, amen.**

● The Point

Hear the Bible Story (up to 10 minutes)

Bring out the *Bible Big Book: How Peter Served Jesus.* Say: **Before we hear our Bible story, lets play a story-review game. I'll ask a story question. If you know the answer, stand on one leg. Then I'll choose someone to answer.** Use the following story questions to review the two previous Bible stories.

● **Why were Peter and John going to the Temple?** (To pray; to talk about Jesus.)

● **Why was the man at the gate begging for money?** (He couldn't walk; he couldn't work and needed money.)

Jesus helps us serve him.

- **How did Peter help the man?** (He healed him; he made him walk again.)
- **How did Peter heal the man?** (In Jesus' name; it was Jesus' power.)
- **What did the man do after he could walk?** (He jumped up; he praised God; he thanked God.)
- **Why did Peter tell people about Jesus?** (He wanted them to know that Jesus loves them; Jesus wanted him to.)
- **Who helps us serve Jesus?** (Jesus does.)

Say: **You did a wonderful job of remembering! I'm proud of you.** Give each child a quick hug or pat on the back. Say: **We've been learning that ✎Jesus helps us serve him, and today we'll learn how Peter helped a woman named Tabitha. Some people called her Dorcas.** Hold up the Bible. **Our story comes from the book of Acts in the Bible.** Hold up the *Bible Big Book*. **The Big Book shows us pictures of the story. You can use your chickenpox spots to help tell our story. You'll need four spots. If you need a spot or two, ask a friend to share.** Be sure each child has four spot stickers.

Put your spots on your fingers. Then listen carefully as I read the story. I'll tell you when and where to stick a chickenpox spot. Read the story below while showing children page 5 of the *Bible Big Book.*

Peter traveled to Joppa where a woman named Tabitha lived. Tabitha loved Jesus. She made beautiful shirts and coats for people who didn't have enough money for clothes. When Tabitha got sick and died, her friends begged Peter to help.

Peter sent everyone out of Tabitha's room. He knelt by her bed and prayed. Stick a chickenpox spot to your knee to show how Peter got on his knees to pray. Pause. **Then he said, "Tabitha, stand up!" Tabitha opened her eyes and saw Peter. Put a chickenpox spot on your eyebrow to show that Tabitha saw Peter.** Pause. **Then she sat up. She was alive! Peter offered Tabitha his hand and helped her get up. Stick a chickenpox spot on your hand.** Pause. **Then he called her friends into the room. They were amazed at the miracle. Soon people everywhere in Joppa had heard about Tabitha. Place a spot on your ear to show how people heard about Tabitha. They believed in Jesus. And Peter kept serving Jesus everywhere he went.**

Close the Big Book. Ask:
- **How did Jesus help Peter serve him?** (He helped Peter make Tabitha alive.)
- **What did Tabitha's friends do when they saw she was alive?** (They told other people about what had happened; they were glad and amazed.)
- **Why do you think it was good that her friends told people?** (It helped others learn about Jesus; they could serve Jesus.)

Say: **Peter served Jesus by praying in his name and by asking that Tabitha be made well again. Peter did three things for Tabitha. He cared for her, prayed for her, and helped her. We can do those things, too. It's good to know that ✎Jesus helps us serve him. Stick your chickenpox spots on your hearts to show how much we love Jesus and want to serve him. Then we'll act out a fun rhyme to review our story.**

● **The Point**

● **The Point**

Do the Bible Story (up to 10 minutes)

Say: **I have a story rhyme for you. Follow along with the actions as I tell you the story.**

Tabitha loved and helped the poor *(hands on your hearts)*
And sewed the clothes that they wore. *(Make sewing motions.)*
Then Tabitha got sick and died. *(Fall gently to the floor.)*
All her friends just cried and cried. *(Pretend to cry.)*
They called for Peter right away *(cup hands around mouth)*—
Peter served Jesus, and he would pray. *(Drop to your knees.)*
He told her friends, "Please go away. *(Motion to leave.)*
In Jesus' name I will pray." *(Make prayer hands.)*
"Tabitha, stand up!" Peter said. *(Lift arms in the air.)*
She opened her eyes and sat up in bed! *(Sit up straight on the floor.)*

◐ The Point

Say: **We know that ◖Jesus helps us serve him, and we can serve others when they're sick, too. I heard Pockets sneezing earlier today. Maybe we can serve Jesus by helping our friend Pockets.**

Practicing The Point

Kerchoo, Kangaroo! (up to 5 minutes)

Before class, tape a facial tissue in Pockets' paw.

Bring out Pockets the Kangaroo. Go through the following script. When you finish the script, put Pockets out of sight.

◐ The Point

Kerchoo, Kangaroo!

PUPPET SCRIPT

Pockets: *(Sneezing)* Ahh...ahhhh...ahhhchooOOOOY! Hi, ebrybody.

Teacher: It sounds like you have a cold, Pockets.

Pockets: Yes, I hab a code. By nose itches and by eyes are watery and ...(sniffles)...I keep snee...snee...sneeeeaahhhchoo! *(Wipes her nose.)* S'cuse be.

Teacher: Oh, we're sorry you don't feel well today. *(Leans and whispers to children.)* I think we can serve Pockets and help her feel better. Let's wrap her in a blanket and read her a story. That helps me feel better. *(Speaking aloud to Pockets)* Pockets, we've been learning that ◖Jesus helps us serve him and that Peter helped someone get better. We'd like to help you feel better. *(Hand a small blanket to one of the children and let him or her tuck it around Pockets.)*

Pockets: Thank you so buch. That feels nice.

Teacher: Would you like us to tell you a story? *(Hold up the Bible Big Book: How Peter Served Jesus.)* Children, let's tell

(Continued)

Jesus helps us serve him.

Pockets about our Bible story and how Jesus helped Peter serve him. Two of you can help hold the Big Book, and the rest of us will point to pictures and retell the story. *(Have children tell Pockets The Point and that helping sick people is a good way to serve Jesus.)*

Pockets: *(Sniffles and wipes nose.)* Thanks for telling be such a good story. I feel better already. I'm so glad that  Jesus helps us serve him. And I'm glad that you love be and want to help be.

Teacher: We have something else that will help you feel better—a hug! Children, let's give Pockets a warm hug to show we care. *(Let each child hug Pockets and tell her goodbye.)*

● **The Point**

TODAY I LEARNED . . .

We believe that Christian education extends beyond the classroom into the home. Photocopy the "Today I Learned . . ." handout (p. 179) for this week, and send it home with your children. Encourage parents to use the handout to plan meaningful family activities to reinforce this week's topic. Follow up the "Today I Learned . . ." activities next week by asking children what their families did.

Closing

Hearts Share (up to 5 minutes)

Spread the tablecloth from Option 3 on the floor. Set the plate of heart-shaped sandwiches in the center of the tablecloth. Say: **Find a place to sit on the picnic cloth.** Pause for children to be seated. Hand each child a napkin. **We're going to enjoy the snacks we made. One good way to serve Jesus is to make a nice snack for a sick person and take it to that sick person on a tray. Isn't it nice to know that ● Jesus helps us serve him? I'll pass out our picnic sandwiches. As you take one, tell a way you can serve Jesus this week, such as helping a sick friend or praying for someone or telling others about Jesus. Don't eat your treats until everyone has a sandwich.**

● **The Point**

After everyone's told a way to serve Jesus, say: **Let's join hands and pray.** Pray: **Dear Jesus, thank you for your love and for helping us serve you. Please help those who are sick get better so they can serve you, too. In Jesus' name, amen.**

As children leave, have them throw their napkins away.

Jesus helps us serve him.

For Extra Time

If you have a long class time or want to add additional elements to your lesson, try one of the following activities.

LIVELY LEARNING: Grug Hug

Form two lines facing each other at opposite ends of the room. Help children in each line number off by threes. Say: **One way to serve Jesus is to spread his love. This game is called Grug, and it will remind us to spread Jesus' love to others. I'll call a number. The people with that number can walk heel to toe to the center of the room and give each other a hug. Then return to your places, and I'll call another number.**

● The Point

End by calling all three numbers at once so all children receive hugs at once. Remind children that ● Jesus helps us serve him and that it's important to spread Jesus' love to others.

MAKE TO TAKE: Patch-Me-Ups

Before this activity, cut a brown grocery sack into three-by-six-inch strips. Cut one strip for each child. Draw a large square in the center of each strip to make it look like a plastic bandage.

Set out markers, glue sticks, sequins, the ink pad, and all three rubber stamps from the Learning Lab. Hand each child a paper strip. Explain that these bandages are to remind them that ● Jesus helps us serve him and that we can be like Peter and help those who are sick. Invite children to decorate their paper bandages with the items you set out. As they work, encourage them to retell the story of Tabitha and how Peter helped raise her from the dead. Tell children to use their bandages as Bible bookmarks.

TREAT TO EAT: Smile Snacks

Set out small bowls of applesauce, plastic spoons, and hot cinnamon candies. Let children make a cheery smile with cinnamon candies on their applesauce. Explain that cheering someone up when they're sick helps them feel better. Let children enjoy their treats and tell about a time they were sick and someone helped them feel better.

STORY PICTURE: Peter Helps Tabitha

Before class cut out one-half-inch squares of colored felt. Cut three or four squares for each child.

Hand each child a photocopy of the "Today I Learned..." handout from page 179. Set out glue sticks and the felt squares. Invite children to make Tabitha a colorful mat by gluing felt in patchwork designs on the mat in the picture. As children work, remind them how Tabitha helped poor people by making them blankets, mats, and clothes to keep them warm. Point out that ● Jesus helps us serve him and that Tabitha served Jesus by helping others.

● The Point

TODAY I LEARNED...

The Point ✏ Jesus helps us serve him.

LESSON 12

Today your child learned that Jesus helps us serve him. Children learned that Peter brought Tabitha back to life. They talked about ways to serve Jesus and help sick people.

Verse to Learn

"You are serving the Lord Christ" (Colossians 3:24b, NCV).

Ask Me...

● How did Peter serve Jesus when he helped Tabitha?

● What's one way you can help someone who's sick?

● How can our family stay healthy to serve Jesus?

Family Fun

● Let your child help make Tabitha biscuits for a family treat. Have your child put refrigerator biscuits on a cookie-sheet "bed." Then spread a "blanket" of butter on biscuits and sprinkle them with cinnamon sugar. Add a few chocolate chip "pillows." Bake at 350 degrees for eight minutes. Peek at the biscuits while they bake, and point out that biscuits rise up just as Tabitha rose when Peter prayed to Jesus.

Peter Helps Tabitha (Acts 9:36-42)

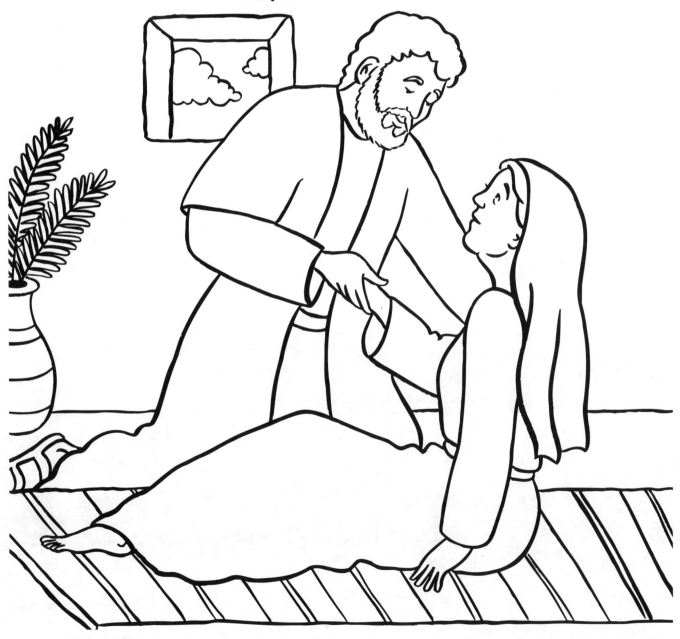

Peter's Set Free

The Point

🖉 Jesus helps us serve him.

The Bible Basis

Acts 12:4-17. Peter is freed from prison.

Arrested for serving Jesus, Peter was chained between two guards while fourteen more kept watch outside his cell. An impossible situation? Not for our Lord! He'd heard the prayers of Peter's friends, and his answer appeared in the form of a heavenly rescue mission. Peter's chains fell free, and an angel led Peter past the guards and into the streets of Jerusalem. Peter quickly ran to Mary's house to tell his friends he was free. Not even chains and a jail cell could stop Peter from serving the Lord!

Five and six-year-olds have wonderful imaginations that can capture the excitement of this Bible story. An angel, chains dropping away, and a gate opening by itself make it easy for kindergartners to grasp the excitement of Peter's miraculous midnight rescue. It gives children confidence to know that Jesus helps them overcome obstacles. Use this lesson to help children understand that nothing can stand in the way of serving Jesus.

Getting The Point

🖉 **Jesus helps us serve him.**

It's important to say The Point just as it's written in each activity. Repeating The Point again and again will help the children remember it and apply it to their lives.

Children will
- learn that serving Jesus can be exciting,
- realize that Peter chose to keep serving Jesus,
- help Pockets learn that Jesus keeps us safe, and
- know that Jesus always helps us.

🖉 **The Point**

This Lesson at a Glance

Before the lesson, collect the necessary items for the activities you plan to use. Refer to the Classroom Supplies and Learning Lab Supplies columns to determine what you'll need. Remember to make photocopies of the "Today I Learned..." handout (p. 192) to send home with your children.

Section	Minutes	What Children Will Do	Classroom Supplies	Learning Lab Supplies
Welcome Time	up to 5	**Welcome!**—Receive name tags and be greeted by the teacher.	"Cross Name Tags" handouts (p. 30), markers, pins or tape	
Let's Get Started Direct children to one or more of the Let's Get Started activities until everyone arrives.	up to 10	**Option 1: Peter-in-the Box**—Pretend to be Peter and have angels set them free.	Large boxes	
	up to 10	**Option 2: In Jail**—Build a pretend jail cell.	Crepe paper, building blocks, scissors, tape	
	up to 10	**Option 3: Chain Gang**—Make paper chains.	Newspaper or grocery sacks, markers, scissors, tape	
Pick-Up Song	up to 5	**We Will Pick Up**—Sing a song as they pick up toys and gather for Bible-Story Time.	CD player	CD: "We Will Pick Up" (track 2)
Bible-Story Time	up to 5	**Setting the Stage**—Sing an action song and escape paper chains.	Chains made in Option 3 or crepe paper, CD player	CD: "Peter's Free" (track 14)
	up to 5	**Bible Song and Prayer Time**—Sing a song, bring out the Bible, and pray together.	Bible, construction paper, scissors, basket or box, CD player	CD: "God's Book" (track 3), serving stamp and ink pad
	up to 10	**Hear the Bible Story**—Listen to a story from Acts 12:4-17 and learn how an angel saved Peter.	Bible, CD player, photocopies of "Today I Learned..." from Lessons 10-12, tape	Bible Big Book: How Peter Served Jesus, CD: "How Peter Served Jesus, Part II" (track 15)
	up to 10	**Do the Bible Story**—Act out Peter's miraculous rescue.		
Practicing The Point	up to 5	**All Tied Up**—Help untangle Pockets and teach her there are different ways to serve Jesus.	Pockets the Kangaroo, long shoelace	
Closing	up to 5	**Link Up to Serve**—Form a human chain and tell ways to serve Jesus this week.		
For Extra Time	For extra-time ideas and supplies, see page 191.			

Jesus helps us serve him.

Welcome Time

Welcome! (up to 5 minutes)

- Bend down to make eye contact with children as they arrive.
- Greet each child individually with an enthusiastic smile.
- Thank each child for coming to class today.
- As children arrive, ask them about last week's "Today I Learned..." discussion. Use questions such as "How did you help someone who wasn't feeling well last week?" or "How did you serve Jesus at home?"
- Say: **Today we're going to learn that ✏ Jesus helps us serve him.**
- Hand out the cross name tags children made during Lesson 1, and help them attach the name tags to their clothing. If some of the name tags were damaged or if some of the children weren't in class that week, have them make new name tags using the photocopiable handout on page 30.
- Direct the children to the Let's Get Started activities you've set up.

● **The Point**

Let's Get Started

Set up one or more of the following activities for children to do as they arrive. After you greet each child, invite him or her to choose an activity.

Circulate among the children to offer help as needed and to direct children's conversation toward today's lesson. Ask questions such as "What would it be like to be in jail?" and "What would you say if an angel rescued you from danger?"

OPTION 1: Peter-in-the-Box (up to 10 minutes)

Set out two or three large boxes. As children arrive, invite them to find a partner. Decide who will be Peter and who will be the Angel. Have Peter sit in the box like a jack-in-the-box. Direct the Angel to tap the box, and have Peter jump up and say, "I'm free to serve Jesus!" Then have the children switch places.

As children are playing, make comments such as "It wouldn't be fun to be stuck in jail" and "My, you look happy as you leap to freedom!" Tell children that they'll hear an amazing story about a time Peter was in jail and how he got free. Remind children that ● Jesus helps us serve him and that he helped Peter when Peter was in danger.

● **The Point**

OPTION 2: In Jail (up to 10 minutes)

Before class cut eighteen-inch strips of crepe paper or newspaper to use as jail bars. Cut at least twelve strips.

Place a table in the center of the room. Tape strips of crepe paper around the edges to create a jail cell. Encourage children to use building blocks to build a wall surrounding the jail. Let children crawl in and out of the jail cell and around the block walls. As they play, ask children questions such as "How would it feel to be put in jail for telling others about Jesus?" and "What

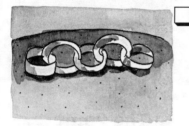

The Point

do you think it would be like in jail?" Tell children that they'll hear a story about a time Peter was put in jail for talking about Jesus. Explain that Jesus helped Peter get free in an amazing way and that 🖊 Jesus helps us serve him.

OPTION 3: Chain Gang (up to 10 minutes)

Before class cut two-by-six-inch strips from grocery sacks or newspaper. Cut five strips for each child.

Set out markers, paper strips, and tape. Invite children to draw on each link one way they can serve Jesus such as praying, helping someone who's sick, or telling people about Jesus. Then have them work together to make two long paper chains. Explain that the chains will be used in a later activity. As you work, ask the children if they've ever held big chains. Point out that in Jesus' time, chains were used to hold prisoners. The chains were heavy and impossible to break through. Mention that in today's Bible story they'll hear how Peter was miraculously freed from two chains. Tell children that 🖊 Jesus helps us serve him and that even strong chains didn't stop Peter from serving Jesus.

The Point

✔ To really motivate children for today's exciting Bible story, bring in an assortment of real chains and locks. Let children touch them and work the locks if you have keys.

When everyone has arrived and you're ready to move on to the Bible-Story Time, encourage the children to finish what they're doing and get ready to clean up.

Pick-Up Song

We Will Pick Up (up to 5 minutes)

Lead children in singing "We Will Pick Up" (track 2) with the *CD* to the tune of "London Bridge." Encourage the children to sing along as they help clean up the room.

If you want to include the names of all the children in your class, sing the song without the *CD*, and repeat the naming section. If you choose to use the *CD*, vary the names you use each week.

Sing

We will pick up all our toys,
All our toys, all our toys.
We will pick up all our toys
And put them all away.

I see (name) picking up,
Picking up, picking up.
I see (name) picking up
And putting toys away.
(Repeat)

Jesus helps us serve him.

Bible-Story Time

Setting the Stage (up to 5 minutes)

Tell the children you'll clap your hands to get their attention. Explain that when you clap, children are to stop what they're doing, raise their hands, and focus on you. Encourage children to respond quickly so you'll have time for all the fun activities you've planned.

Hold the paper chains made in Option 3. If you chose not to do Option 3, use two four-foot lengths of crepe paper as the chains. Say: **We'll sing an action song to help us get ready for the Bible story. But first we need two groups.** Help children get into two groups. **I'll choose a pretend Prisoner in each group. The rest of you are the Chain Gang. As we sing the first verse of our song, each Chain Gang will wrap a paper chain around the Prisoner in their group. While we sing the second verse, the Prisoners will wiggle to get free.**

Lead children in singing "Peter's Free" (track 14) with the *CD* to the tune of "Here We Go 'Round the Mulberry Bush."

Sing

Lock Peter up and hold him tight,
Hold him tight,
Hold him tight.
Lock Peter up and hold him tight.
Don't let him out of jail.

These chains will never stay on him,
Stay on him,
Stay on him.
These chains will never stay on him,
'Cause God will set him free.

Sing the song a second time without the *CD,* and choose two new Prisoners. Use transparent tape if the chains need a quick repair. Continue until each child has been in "chains." Then set the paper chains aside and ask:

● **What would it be like to be wrapped up in heavy chains?** (I wouldn't like it; you couldn't walk; I'd want to break them.)

● **What if you'd been put in jail for no reason?** (I'd be mad; it wouldn't be fair.)

Say: **Peter was arrested and put in jail because he talked about Jesus. Imagine! Peter was locked in chains and put in jail because he wanted others to know Jesus. But we'll see how Jesus helped Peter get free so Peter could keep on serving Jesus. ◗ Jesus helps us serve him wherever we are. Let's listen to our exciting story and see how Peter gets free.**

Bible Song and Prayer Time (up to 5 minutes)

Before class, make surprise cards for this activity by cutting construction paper in two-by-six-inch slips. Prepare a surprise card for each child plus a few extras for visitors. Fold the cards in half, then stamp the *serving stamp*

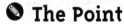

◗ **The Point**

Jesus helps us serve him.

inside one of the surprise cards. Mark Acts 12:4-17 in the Bible you'll be using.

Have the children sit in a circle. Say: **Now it's time to choose a Bible person to bring me the Bible marked with today's Bible story. As we sing our Bible song, I'll pass out the surprise cards. Don't look inside your card until the song is over.**

Lead children in singing "God's Book" (track 3) with the *CD* to the tune of "Old MacDonald Had a Farm." As you sing, pass out the surprise cards. If you want to include the names of all the children in your class, sing "God's Book" without the *CD,* and repeat the naming section. If you choose to use the *CD,* vary the names you use each week.

Sing

Now it's time to read God's Book
And hear a Bible story.
It's fun to be here with my
    friends
And hear a Bible story.
	Now it's time to read God's Book
	And hear a Bible story.
	It's fun to be here with my
	    friends
	And hear a Bible story.

(Name)'s here. (Name)'s here. Here is (name). Here is (name). Now it's time to read God's Book And hear a Bible story.	(Name)'s here. (Name)'s here. Here is (name). Here is (name). Now it's time to read God's Book And hear a Bible story.

After the song, say: **You may look inside your surprise cards. The person who has the serving hand stamped inside his or her card will be our Bible person for today.**

Identify the Bible person, then have the rest of the children clap for him or her. Ask the Bible person to bring you the Bible. Help the Bible person open the Bible to the marked place and show the children where your story comes from. Then have the Bible person sit down.

● **The Point**

Say: (Name) **was our special Bible person today. Each week, we'll have only one Bible person, but each of you is a special part of our class! Today we'll all be learning that ● Jesus helps us serve him.**

Let's say a special prayer now and ask Jesus to help us serve him. I'll pass around this basket. When the basket comes to you, put your surprise card in it and say, "Jesus, please help me serve you."

● **The Point**

Pass around the basket or box. When you've collected everyone's surprise card, set the basket aside, and pick up the Bible. Lead children in this prayer: **God, thank you for the Bible and for all the stories in it. Teach us today that ● Jesus helps us serve him. In Jesus' name, amen.**

Hear the Bible Story (up to 10 minutes)

● **The Point**

Before class, make a photocopy of the story pictures from Lessons 10, 11, and 12 found on the "Today I Learned…" handouts on pages 156, 168, and 179. Tape each picture to a different wall.

Say: **We've been learning that ● Jesus helps us serve him. Let's review the ways Peter served Jesus from the Bible stories we've heard. I'll read a sentence. Hop to the story picture that tells about the story I**

Jesus helps us serve him.

mention. Read the following sentences.

- **Jesus helped Peter raise Tabitha from the dead.**
- **Peter and John preached at the Temple.**
- **Peter and John met a man who couldn't walk.**
- **Tabitha was a woman who served Jesus by helping others.**
- **The man was healed and jumped and praised God.**
- **The Temple leaders warned Peter and John to stop telling others about Jesus.**

Say: **Good job! You can hop to the *Bible Big Book*, and let's hear the exciting story of how Jesus helped Peter keep serving him.** When children are seated, hold up the Bible and say: **Our Bible story comes from the book of Acts in the Bible.** Hold up the Big Book. **Our Big Book shows us pictures of the story. Our story today is amazing and exciting. Listen carefully to the story tape. When you hear how Peter was set free from jail, put one hand on your knee. When you hear where Peter went afterward, put your other hand on your other knee.**

Open the *Bible Big Book: How Peter Served Jesus* to the double illustration on pages 6 and 7. Turn on the *CD*, and listen to "How Peter Served Jesus, Part II" (track 15), turning the page at the chime. After page 8, close the Big Book and turn off the CD player.

Ask:

- **Why was Peter put in jail?** (For teaching about Jesus; for telling others about Jesus.)
- **What did Peter's friends do while Peter was in jail?** (They prayed for him.)
- **How do you know that God heard their prayers?** (Because an angel came; Peter was set free.)

Say: **When Peter was in jail and things looked impossible, Peter's friends didn't stop serving Jesus. They prayed for Peter. We can serve through our prayers, too, just as Peter's friends did.** Ask:

- **Why did Jesus send an angel to free Peter?** (So Peter could keep serving him; so Peter could tell more people about Jesus.)

Say: **Jesus wanted Peter to keep serving him. So he sent an angel to set Peter free. It's important to remember that we're never alone, and Jesus is always ready to help us just as he helped Peter.** Ask:

- **Why did Peter go see his friends after the angel freed him?** (He wanted his friends to know he was OK; he wanted to let them know Jesus had helped him.)

Say: **Peter ran to tell his friends that he was free so they'd know the great miracle Jesus performed. Then Peter left to tell even more people about Jesus. We can tell others about Jesus just as Peter did. And we can also be sure that 🌑 Jesus helps us serve him. What an exciting story! Let's play a game to help us remember how Jesus helped Peter serve and how 🌑 Jesus helps us serve him.**

🌑 **The Point**

🌑 **The Point**

Do the Bible Story (up to 10 minutes)

Say: **Think back to the Bible story we just heard, and let's see if you remember who was in the story.** Help children recall the following characters: Peter, the guards, the angel, Rhoda, and Peter's friends. Use *Bible Big Book* pages 6-8 if children need clues.

Say: **Let's act out the exciting story of Peter's release from jail. Follow along as I retell the story, and do what I do.**

Peter had been put in jail for teaching others about Jesus. He was chained between two strong guards.	*(Put your hands at your sides as if bound by chains.)*
He fell asleep with the chains on him.	*(Lie on the floor with your hands at your sides.)*
Suddenly, Peter felt someone touch his side.	*(Sit up and look surprised.)*
It was an angel of the Lord! The angel said, "Get dressed quickly. Then follow me." The chains fell off of Peter, and he was free!	*(Wiggle your arms.)*
Peter put on his coat.	*(Act as if you're getting dressed.)*
He thought he must be dreaming, but Peter quietly followed the angel.	*(Tiptoe around the room, leading children past chairs and around tables.)*
They went past the guards, and the guards never saw them! But wait. Peter looked up ahead.	*(Point in front of you.)*
There was a gate! How would it ever open?	*(Shake your head.)*
Then an amazing thing happened. The gate opened by itself, and Peter and the angel went through.	*(Step through the "gate.")*
When they were on the street, the angel suddenly left Peter.	*(Wave goodbye.)*
Peter ran to Mary's house, where his friends were staying.	*(Jog around the room, and stop by a closet door or wall.)*
Peter knocked at Mary's door.	*(Knock on the door or wall.)*
Rhoda, the servant girl, came to the door and heard Peter's voice. She was so happy to hear him that she forgot to open the door. As Rhoda ran to get Peter's friends, Peter knocked again.	*(Knock on the door.)*
When Peter's friends opened the door, they were so happy to see Peter. But Peter hushed them.	*(Put your finger to your lips.)*
Peter told them how Jesus had sent an angel to free him. And now Peter could continue to serve Jesus because he was free!	*(Jump up and down and cheer.)*

Jesus helps us serve him.

Sit with children on the floor. Ask:

● **Do you think Peter stopped telling people about Jesus? Why or why not?** (No, he wanted to serve Jesus; no, because he knew that Jesus would help him.)

Say: **Peter never stopped serving Jesus. Peter wanted everyone to know Jesus and to know that Jesus is Lord. He knew that Jesus helps us serve him, and Peter wanted to serve Jesus more than anything else. We want to serve Jesus more than anything, too. Telling others about Jesus and helping people are good ways to serve. Let's see if Pockets knows any other ways.**

● **The Point**

Practicing The Point

All Tied Up (up to 5 minutes)

Before class, tangle a long shoelace around Pockets.

Bring out Pockets the Kangaroo. Go through the following script. When you finish the script, put Pockets out of sight.

All Tied Up

PUPPET SCRIPT

Pockets: *(Wiggling and tangled in the shoelace)* Ummph... uhh...mmph...

Teacher: Hello, Pockets. Do you need some help?

Pockets: Well...umphh...sort of. I'm a little tied up at the moment.

Teacher: We can see that. What happened?

Pockets: Well, you know how we've been talking about serving Jesus by helping others?

Teacher: Yes. That's very important.

Pockets: I was trying to serve my friend Sarah by tying her new shoes...but...well, I kinda got tangled up.

Teacher: Children, let's help Pockets get free. *(Choose a few children to untie Pockets.)* There. Is that better?

Pockets: Oh, much better! I feel free! Wheee! *(Leaps around.)* I was beginning to feel like I was in jail.

Teacher: We learned about a time Peter was put in jail when he served Jesus. Children, let's tell Pockets about that exciting story and how Peter was set free. *(Have children retell the Bible story. Encourage them to point out that Jesus helped Peter get free because he wanted Peter to go on serving him. Have children tell Pockets The Point.)* So Peter was

(Continued)

Jesus helps us serve him.

The Point

free to continue serving Jesus. And now you're free to keep serving, too, Pockets.

Pockets: But how? I'm not much good at tying shoes.

Teacher: 🖉 Jesus helps us serve him. And we can serve Jesus in many ways. Children, maybe we can help Pockets think of other ways to serve. *(Let children tell their ideas.)*

Pockets: I know! Sarah's new shoes had scuff marks. I can polish them. I'm good at polishing things with my fuzzy tail. *(Turns around and wags her tail.)*

The Point

The Point

Teacher: That's the idea, Pockets. We never want to stop serving, and 🖉 Jesus helps us serve him in lots of ways.

Pockets: Thanks for telling me that exciting story, kids. And thanks for helping me learn that 🖉 Jesus helps us serve him. 'Bye!

TODAY I LEARNED...

We believe that Christian education extends beyond the classroom into the home. Photocopy the "Today I Learned..." handout (p. 192) for this week, and send it home with your children. Encourage parents to use the handout to plan meaningful family activities to reinforce this week's topic. Follow up the "Today I Learned..." activities next week by asking children what their families did.

Closing

Link Up to Serve (up to 5 minutes)

The Point

Say: **We've been learning that 🖉 Jesus helps us serve him. We heard today how chains and jail couldn't keep Peter from serving Jesus. Let's make a human chain to remind us that we can serve in many ways. I'll start by telling one way I can serve Jesus this week, such as helping a friend or caring for someone who's sick or by praying. Then another person can tell a way to serve and link his or her arm through my arm. We'll continue until we have a long human chain.**

When you've made a chain, lead children once around the room. Then form a circle with arms still linked. Say: **While our arms are linked together, let's link our hearts and say a prayer.** Pray: **Dear God, thank you for helping us learn about serving Jesus. We want to serve him forever. In Jesus' name, amen.**

Jesus helps us serve him.

For Extra Time

If you have a long class time or want to add additional elements to your lesson, try one of the following activities.

LIVELY LEARNING: Listening Center

For a fun review of this module's Bible stories, invite children to listen to the entire *Bible Big Book: How Peter Served Jesus* with the *CD*. Choose two children to hold the Big Book, and turn the pages at the chimes. Help children begin at page 1, and listen along to help them turn the pages at the appropriate times. The entire story is track 16 on the *CD*.

MAKE TO TAKE: Chain Links

Invite children to make chains from aluminum foil. Set out a roll of aluminum foil, and tear off narrow strips. Let children crumple each piece lengthwise. Then show them how to twist the ends together to form a circle. Loop the next piece through the circle, and twist the ends to make a link in a chain. Have children each make five or six links in their chains. As they work, point out how we can have faith as strong as a chain that no one can break. Explain that serving is one way to strengthen our faith and that 🖊 Jesus helps us serve him. Encourage children to hang their chains on their walls at home.

🖊 **The Point**

TREAT TO EAT: Jailhouse Crackers

Form an assembly line to make jailhouse crackers. Set out graham crackers, canned icing, plastic knives, and thin strips of licorice. Some of the children can be Jailbreakers and break the crackers in half. Other children can be the Spreaders and spread icing on each cracker. The rest of the children can be the Jailers and lay licorice-strip bars on the crackers. As you enjoy eating your treats, talk about how Jesus helped Peter when he was in jail. Remind children that 🖊 Jesus helps us serve him.

🖊 **The Point**

STORY PICTURE: Peter's Set Free

Hand each child a photocopy of the "Today I Learned..." handout from page 192. Set out markers, glue, and small macaroni circles. Have the children color their pictures. Then let them glue macaroni to the chains falling from Peter. As they work, ask children to retell the Bible story. Point out that 🖊 Jesus helps us serve him and that Peter was set free to continue serving Jesus.

🖊 **The Point**

TODAY I LEARNED . . .

The Point ✏ Jesus helps us serve him.

Today your child learned that Jesus helps us serve him. Children learned that an angel led Peter to freedom. They learned that Jesus can help them serve him in any situation.

Verse to Learn

"You are serving the Lord Christ" (Colossians 3:24b, NCV).

Ask Me . . .

● How was Peter set free from jail?
● Why do we want to serve Jesus?
● What's one way our family can serve Jesus this week?

Family Fun

● For family prayer time, create a prayer chain. Help your child cut a two-by-five-inch paper strip for each family member. Hand each person a paper strip. As each person adds a sentence to a prayer, have him or her tape a link to the chain. When you're finished praying, hang the prayer chain on a door as a reminder that even chains couldn't keep Peter from serving Jesus.

Peter's Set Free (Acts 12:4-17)

LESSON 13